PostCapitalism

PAUL MASON

PostCapitalism

A Guide to Our Future

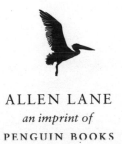

ALLEN LANE
an imprint of
PENGUIN BOOKS

ALLEN LANE

UK | USA | Canada | Ireland | Australia
India | New Zealand | South Africa

Allen Lane is part of the Penguin Random House group of companies
whose addresses can be found at global.penguinrandomhouse.com.

First published 2015
005

Copyright © Paul Mason, 2015

The moral right of the author has been asserted

Set in 10.5/14 pt Sabon LT Std
Typeset by Jouve (UK), Milton Keynes
Printed in Great Britain by Clays Ltd, St Ives plc

A CIP catalogue record for this book is available from the British Library

ISBN: 978–1–846–14738–8

For Calum, Anya, Robbie and James

Contents

Introduction

To find the river Dniestr we drive through cold woodlands, past decomposing flats and railyards where the dominant colour is rust. The freezing water runs clear. It is so quiet that you can hear little pieces of concrete falling off the road bridge above, as it slowly crumbles through neglect.

The Dniestr is the geographic border between free-market capitalism and whatever you want to call the system Vladimir Putin runs. It separates Moldova, a country in Eastern Europe, from a breakaway Russian puppet state called Transnistria, controlled by the mafia and secret police.

On the Moldovan side, elderly people squat on the pavements selling stuff they've grown or made: cheese, pastries, a few turnips. Young people are scarce; one in four adults works abroad. Half the population earns less than $5 a day; one in ten lives in a poverty so extreme it can be measured on the same scale as Africa's.[1] The country was born at the start of the neoliberal era, with the breakup of the Soviet Union in the early 1990s and the entry of market forces – but many of the villagers I talk to would rather live in Putin's police state than in the disgraceful penury of Moldova. This grey world of dirt roads and grim faces was produced by capitalism, not communism. And now capitalism is already past its best.

Moldova, of course, is not a typical European country. But it's in these edge places of the world that we can watch the economic tide receding – and trace the causal links between stagnation, social crisis, armed conflict and the erosion of democracy. The economic failure of the West is eroding belief in values and institutions that we once thought were permanent.

In the financial centres, behind plate glass, things can still look rosy. Since 2008, trillions of dollars of confected money have flowed through the banks, hedge funds, law firms and consultancies to keep the global system functioning.

But the long-term prospects for capitalism are bleak. According to the OECD, growth in the developed world will be 'weak' for the next fifty years. Inequality will rise by 40 per cent. Even in the developing countries, the current dynamism will be exhausted by 2060.[2] The OECD's economists were too polite to say it, so let's spell it out: for the developed world the best of capitalism is behind us, and for the rest it will be over in our lifetime.

What started in 2008 as an economic crisis morphed into a social crisis, leading to mass unrest; and now, as revolutions turn into civil wars, creating military tension between nuclear superpowers, it has become a crisis of the global order.

There are, on the face of it, only two ways it can end. In the first scenario, the global elite clings on, imposing the cost of crisis on to workers, pensioners and the poor over the next ten or twenty years. The global order – as enforced by the IMF, World Bank and World Trade Organisation – survives, but in a weakened form. The cost of saving globalization is borne by the ordinary people of the developed world. But growth stagnates.

In the second scenario, the consensus breaks. Parties of the hard right and left come to power as ordinary people refuse to pay the price of austerity. Instead, states then try to impose the costs of the crisis on each other. Globalization falls apart, the global institutions become powerless and in the process the conflicts that have burned these past twenty years – drug wars, post-Soviet nationalism, jihadism, uncontrolled migration and resistance to it – light a fire at the centre of the system. In this scenario, lip-service to international law evaporates; torture, censorship, arbitrary detention and mass surveillance become the regular tools of statecraft. This is a variant of what happened in the 1930s and there is no guarantee it cannot happen again.

In both scenarios, the serious impacts of climate change, demographic ageing and population growth kick in around the year 2050. If we can't create a sustainable global order and restore economic dynamism, the decades after 2050 will be chaos.

So I want to propose an alternative: first, we save globalization by ditching neoliberalism; then we save the planet – and rescue ourselves from turmoil and inequality – by moving beyond capitalism itself.

Ditching neoliberalism is the easy part. There's a growing consensus among protest movements, radical economists and radical political parties in Europe as to how you do it: suppress high finance, reverse austerity, invest in green energy and promote high-waged work.

But then what?

As the Greek experience demonstrates, any government that defies austerity will instantly clash with the global institutions that protect the 1 per cent. After the radical left party Syriza won the election in January 2015, the European Central Bank, whose job was to promote the stability of Greek banks, pulled the plug on those banks, triggering a €20 billion run on deposits. That forced the left-wing government to choose between bankruptcy and submission. You will find no minutes, no voting records, no explanation for what the ECB did. It was left to the right-wing German newspaper *Stern* to explain: they had 'smashed' Greece.[3] It was done, symbolically, to reinforce the central message of neoliberalism that *there is no alternative*; that all routes away from capitalism end in the kind of disaster that befell the Soviet Union; and that a revolt against capitalism is a revolt against a natural and timeless order.

The current crisis not only spells the end of the neoliberal model, it is a symptom of the longer-term mismatch between market systems and an economy based on information. The aim of this book is to explain why replacing capitalism is no longer a utopian dream, how the basic forms of a postcapitalist economy can be found within the current system, and how they could be expanded rapidly.

Neoliberalism is the doctrine of uncontrolled markets: it says that the best route to prosperity is individuals pursuing their own self-interest, and the market is the only way to express that self-interest. It says the state should be small (except for its riot squad and secret police); that financial speculation is good; that inequality is good; that the natural state of humankind is to be a bunch of ruthless individuals, competing with each other.

Its prestige rests on tangible achievements: in the past twenty-five years, neoliberalism has triggered the biggest surge in development the world has ever seen, and it unleashed an exponential improvement in core information technologies. But in the process, it has revived inequality to a state close to that of 100 years ago and has now triggered a survival-level event.

The civil war in Ukraine, which brought Russian special forces to the banks of the Dniestr; the triumph of ISIS in Syria and Iraq; the rise of fascist parties in Europe; the paralysis of NATO as its populations withhold consent for military intervention – these are not problems separate from the economic crisis. They are signs that the neoliberal order has failed.

Over the past two decades, millions of people have resisted neoliberalism but in general the resistance failed. Beyond all the tactical mistakes, and the repression, the reason is simple: free-market capitalism is a clear and powerful idea, while the forces opposing it looked like they were defending something old, worse and incoherent.

Among the 1 per cent, neoliberalism has the power of a religion: the more you practise it, the better you feel – and the richer you become. Even among the poor, once the system was in full swing, to act in any other way but according to neoliberal strictures became irrational: you borrow, you duck and dive around the edges of the tax system, you stick to the pointless rules imposed at work.

And for decades the opponents of capitalism have revelled in their own incoherence. From the anti-globalization movement of the 1990s through to Occupy and beyond, the movement for social justice has rejected the idea of a coherent programme in favour of 'One No, Many Yes-es'. The incoherence is logical, if you think the only alternative is what the twentieth century left called 'socialism'. Why fight for a big change if it's only a regression – towards state control and economic nationalism, to economies that work only if everyone behaves the same way or submits to a brutal hierarchy? In turn, the absence of a clear alternative explains why most protest movements never win: in their hearts they don't want to. There's even a term for it in the protest movement: 'refusal to win'.[4]

To replace neoliberalism we need something just as powerful and effective; not just a bright idea about how the world could work but a new, holistic model that can run itself and tangibly deliver a better outcome. It has to be based on micro-mechanisms, not diktats or policies; it has to work spontaneously. In this book, I make the case that there is a clear alternative, that it can be global, and that it can deliver a future substantially better than the one capitalism will be offering by the mid-twenty-first century.

It's called postcapitalism.

Capitalism is more than just an economic structure or a set of laws and institutions. It is the *whole* system – social, economic, demographic, cultural, ideological – needed to make a developed society function through markets and private ownership. That includes companies, markets and states. But it also includes criminal gangs, secret power networks, miracle preachers in a Lagos slum, rogue analysts on Wall Street. Capitalism is the Primark factory that collapsed in Bangladesh and it is the rioting teenage girls at the opening of the Primark store in London, overexcited at the prospect of bargain clothes.

By studying capitalism as a whole system, we can identify a number of its fundamental features. Capitalism is an organism: it has a lifecycle – a beginning, a middle and an end. It is a complex system, operating beyond the control of individuals, governments and even superpowers. It creates outcomes that are often contrary to people's intentions, even when they are acting rationally. Capitalism is also a *learning* organism: it adapts constantly, and not just in small increments. At major turning points, it morphs and mutates in response to danger, creating patterns and structures barely recognizable to the generation that came before. And its most basic survival instinct is to drive technological change. If we consider not just info-tech but food production, birth control or global health, the past twenty-five years have probably seen the greatest upsurge in human capability ever. But the technologies we've created are not compatible with capitalism – not in its present form and maybe not in any form. Once capitalism can no longer adapt to technological change, postcapitalism becomes necessary. When behaviours and organizations adapted to exploiting technological change appear spontaneously, postcapitalism becomes possible.

That, in short, is the argument of this book: that capitalism is a complex, adaptive system which has reached the limits of its capacity to adapt.

This, of course, stands miles apart from mainstream economics. In the boom years, economists started to believe the system that had emerged after 1989 was permanent – the perfect expression of human rationality, with all its problems solvable by politicians and central bankers tweaking control dials marked 'fiscal and monetary policy'.

When they considered the possibility that the new technology and the old forms of society were mismatched, economists assumed society would simply remould itself around technology. Their optimism was justified because such adaptations have happened in the past. But today the adaptation process is stalled.

Information is different from every previous technology. As I will show, its spontaneous tendency is to dissolve markets, destroy ownership and break down the relationship between work and wages. And that is the deep background to the crisis we are living through.

If I am right we have to admit that for most of the past century the left has misunderstood what the end of capitalism would look like. The old left's aim was the forced destruction of market mechanisms. The force would be applied by the working class, either at the ballot box or on the barricades. The lever would be the state. The opportunity would come through frequent episodes of economic collapse. Instead, over the past twenty-five years, it is the left's project that has collapsed. The market destroyed the plan; individualism replaced collectivism and solidarity; the massively expanded workforce of the world looks like a 'proletariat', but no longer thinks or behaves purely as one.

If you lived through all this, and hated capitalism, it was traumatic. But in the process, technology has created a new route out, which the remnants of the old left – and all other forces influenced by it – have either to embrace or die.

Capitalism, it turns out, will not be abolished by forced-march techniques. It will be abolished by creating something more dynamic that exists, at first, almost unseen within the old system, but which breaks through, reshaping the economy around new values, behaviours and norms. As with feudalism 500 years ago, capitalism's demise will be accelerated by external shocks and shaped by the emergence of a new kind of human being. And it has started.

Postcapitalism is possible because of three impacts of the new technology in the past twenty-five years.

First, information technology has reduced the need for work, blurred the edges between work and free time and loosened the relationship between work and wages.

Second, information goods are corroding the market's ability to form prices correctly. That is because markets are based on scarcity while information is abundant. The system's defence mechanism is to form monopolies on a scale not seen in the past 200 years – yet these cannot last.

Third, we're seeing the spontaneous rise of collaborative production: goods, services and organizations are appearing that no longer respond to the dictates of the market and the managerial hierarchy. The biggest information product in the world – Wikipedia – is made by 27,000 volunteers, for free, abolishing the encyclopaedia business and depriving the advertising industry of an estimated $3 billion a year in revenue.

Almost unnoticed, in the niches and hollows of the market system, whole swathes of economic life are beginning to move to a different rhythm. Parallel currencies, time banks, cooperatives and self-managed spaces have proliferated, barely noticed by the economics profession, and often as a direct result of the shattering of old structures after the 2008 crisis.

New forms of ownership, new forms of lending, new legal contracts: a whole business subculture has emerged over the past ten years, which the media has dubbed the 'sharing economy'. Buzz-terms such as the 'commons' and 'peer-production' are thrown around, but few have bothered to ask what this means for capitalism itself.

I believe it offers an escape route – but only if these micro-level projects are nurtured, promoted and protected by a massive change in what governments do. This must in turn be driven by a change in our thinking about technology, ownership and work itself. When we create the elements of the new system we should be able to say to ourselves and others: this is no longer my survival mechanism, my bolt-hole from the neoliberal world, this is a new way of living in the process of formation.

In the old socialist project, the state takes over the market, runs it in favour of the poor instead of the rich, then moves key areas of production out of the market and into a planned economy. The one time it was tried, in Russia after 1917, it didn't work. Whether it could have worked is a good question, but a dead one.

Today the terrain of capitalism has changed: it is global, fragmentary, geared to small-scale choices, temporary work and multiple skill-sets. Consumption has become a form of self-expression – and millions of people have a stake in the finance system that they did not have before.

With the new terrain, the old path is lost. But a different path has opened up. Collaborative production, using network technology to produce goods and services that work only when they are free, or shared, defines the route beyond the market system. It will need the state to create the framework, and the postcapitalist sector might coexist with the market sector for decades. But it is happening.

Networks restore 'granularity' to the postcapitalist project; that is, they can be the basis of a non-market system that replicates itself, which does not need to be created afresh every morning on the computer screen of a commissar.

The transition will involve the state, the market and collaborative production beyond the market. But to make it happen, the entire project of the left, from the protest groups to mainstream social-democratic and liberal parties, has to be reconfigured. In fact, once people understand the urgency of this postcapitalist project, it's no longer the property of the left, but of a much wider movement, for which we will probably need new labels.

Who can make this happen? For the old left, it was the industrial working class. Over 200 years ago, the radical journalist John Thelwall warned the men who built the English factories that they had created a new and dangerous form of democracy: 'Every large workshop and manufactory is a sort of political society, which no act of parliament can silence, and no magistrate disperse.'[5]

Today, the whole of society is a factory – and the communication grids vital for everyday work and profit are buzzing with shared knowledge and discontent. Today it is the network – like the work-shop 200 years ago – that 'cannot be silenced or dispersed'.

True, they can shut down Facebook, Twitter, even the entire inter-net and mobile phone network in times of crisis, paralysing the economy in the process. And they can store and monitor every kilo-byte of information we produce. But they cannot reimpose the hierarchical, propaganda-driven and ignorant society of fifty years ago except – as in China, North Korea or Iran – by opting out of key parts of modern life. It would be, as sociologist Manuel Castells puts it, like trying to de-electrify a country.[6]

By creating millions of networked people, financially exploited but with the whole of human intelligence one thumb-swipe away, info-capitalism has created a new agent of change in history: the edu-cated and connected human being.

As a result, in the years since 2008, we've seen the start of a new kind of uprising. Opposition movements have hit the streets determined to avoid the power structures and abuses that hierarchies bring, and to immunize themselves against the mistakes of the twentieth-century left.

The values, voices and morals of the networked generation were so obvious in these revolts that, from the Spanish *indignados* to the Arab Spring, the media at first believed they had been caused by Facebook and Twitter. Then, in 2013–14, revolts broke out in some of the most iconic developing economies: Turkey, Brazil, India, Ukraine and Hong Kong. Millions took to the streets, again with the networked gener-ation in the lead – but now their grievances went to the heart of what is broken in modern capitalism.

In Istanbul, on the barricades around Gezi Park in June 2013, I met doctors, software developers, shipping clerks and accountants – professionals for whom Turkey's 8 per cent GDP growth rate was no compensation for the theft of a modern lifestyle by the ruling Islamists.

In Brazil, just as economists were celebrating the creation of a new middle class, they actually turned out to be low-paid workers. They'd escaped slum life into a world of regular salaries and bank accounts only to find themselves cheated of basic amenities, at the mercy of brutal police and corrupt government. They swarmed on to the streets in millions.

In India, protests sparked by the gang rape and murder of a student in 2012 were a signal that here, too, the educated and networked generation will not tolerate paternalism and backwardness much longer.

Most of these revolts petered out. The Arab Spring was either suppressed, as in Egypt and Bahrain, or swamped by Islamism, as in Libya and Syria. In Europe, repressive policing and a united front of all parties in favour of austerity beat the *indignados* into a sullen silence. But the revolts showed that revolution in a highly complex, information-driven society will look very different from the revolutions of the twentieth century. Without a strong, organized working class to push social issues rapidly to the fore, the revolts often stall. But order is never fully restored.

Instead of moving from thought to action once – as the nineteenth- and twentieth-century radicals did – repression forces radicalized young people to oscillate between the two: you can jail, torture and harass people but you cannot prevent their mental resistance.

In the past, radicalism of the mind would have been pointless without power. How many generations of rebels wasted their lives in garrets writing angry poetry, cursing the injustice of the world and their own paralysis? But in an information economy, the relationship of thought to action changes.

In hi-tech engineering, before a single piece of metal is shaped, objects are designed virtually, tested virtually and even 'manufactured' virtually – the whole process modelled from start to finish – on computers. The mistakes are discovered and rectified at the design stage, in a way that was impossible before 3D simulations came about.

By analogy, the same goes for the design of a postcapitalist. In an information society, no thought, debate or dream is wasted – whether conceived in a tent camp, prison cell or the 'imagineering' session of a startup company.

In the transition to a postcapitalist economy, the work done at the design stage can reduce mistakes in the implementation stage. And the design of the postcapitalist world, as with software, can be modular. Different people can work on it in different places, at different speeds, with relative autonomy from each other. It is not any longer a plan we need – but a modular project design.

However, our need is urgent.

My aim here is not to provide an economic strategy or a guide to organization. It is to map the new contradictions of capitalism so that people, movements and parties can obtain more accurate coordinates for the journey they're trying to make.

The main contradiction today is between the possibility of free, abundant goods and information and a system of monopolies, banks and governments trying to keep things private, scarce and commercial. Everything comes down to the struggle between the network and the hierarchy, between old forms of society moulded around capitalism and new forms of society that prefigure what comes next.

In the face of this change, the power elite of modern capitalism has a lot at stake. While writing this book, my day job as a news reporter has taken me into three iconic conflicts that show how ruthlessly the elite will react.

In Gaza, in August 2014, I spent ten days in a community being systematically destroyed by drone strikes, shelling and sniper fire. Fifteen hundred civilians were killed, one third of them children. In February 2015, I saw the US Congress give twenty-five standing ovations to the man who ordered the attacks.

In Scotland, in September 2014, I found myself in the middle of a sudden and totally unpredicted radical mass movement in favour of independence from Britain. Presented with the opportunity to break with a neoliberal state and start afresh, millions of young people said 'Yes'. They were defeated – but only just – after the CEOs of major corporations threatened to pull their operations out of Scotland, and the Bank of England, for good measure, threatened to sabotage Scotland's desire to go on using Sterling.

Then, in Greece in 2015, I watched euphoria turn to anguish as a population that had voted left for the first time in seventy years saw its democratic wishes trashed by the European Central Bank.

In each case, the struggle for justice collided with the real power that runs the world.

In 2013, surveying the slow progress of austerity in southern

Europe, economists at JP Morgan spelled it out: for neoliberalism to survive, democracy must fade. Greece, Portugal and Spain, they warned, had 'legacy problems of a political nature': 'The constitutions and political settlements in the southern periphery, put in place in the aftermath of the fall of fascism, have a number of features which appear to be unsuited to further integration in the region.'[7] In other words, peoples who insisted on decent welfare systems in return for a peaceful transition out of dictatorship in the 1970s must now give up these things so that banks like JP Morgan survive.

Today there is no Geneva Convention when it comes to the fight between elites and the people they govern: the robo-cop has become the first line of defence against peaceful protest. Tasers, sound lasers and CS gas, combined with intrusive surveillance, infiltration and disinformation, have become standard in the playbook of law enforcement. And the central banks, whose operations most people have no clue about, are prepared to sabotage democracy by triggering bank runs where anti-neoliberal movements threaten to win – as they did with Cyprus in 2013, then Scotland and now Greece.

The elite and their supporters are lined up to defend the same core principles: high finance, low wages, secrecy, militarism, intellectual property and energy based on carbon. The bad news is that they control nearly every government in the world. The good news is that in most countries they enjoy very little consent or popularity among ordinary people.

But in this gap between their popularity and their power lies danger. As I found on the banks of the River Dniestr, a dictatorship that provides cheap gas and a job for your son in the army can look better than a democracy that leaves you to freeze and starve.

In a situation like this, knowledge of history is more powerful than you think.

Neoliberalism, with its belief in the permanence and finality of free markets, tried to rewrite the whole prior history of humanity as 'things that went wrong before us'. But once you begin to think about the history of capitalism, you are forced to ask which events, amid the chaos, are part of a recurrent pattern and which are part of an irreversible change.

So while its aim is to design a framework for the future, parts of this book are about the past. Part I is about the crisis and how we got here. Part II outlines a new, comprehensive theory of postcapitalism. Part III explores what the transition to postcapitalism might look like.

Is this utopian? The utopian socialist communities of the mid-nineteenth century failed because the economy, technology and the levels of human capital were not sufficiently developed. With info-tech, large parts of the utopian socialist project become possible: from cooperatives, to communes, to outbreaks of liberated behaviour that redefine human freedom.

No, it is the elite – cut off in their separate world – who now look as utopian as the millennial sects of the nineteenth century. The democracy of riot squads, corrupt politicians, magnate-controlled newspapers and the surveillance state looks as phony and fragile as East Germany did thirty years ago.

All readings of human history have to allow for the possibility of collapse. Popular culture is obsessed with this: it haunts us in the zombie film, the disaster movie, in the post-Apocalyptic wasteland of *The Road* or *Elysium*. But why should we, as intelligent beings, not form a picture of the ideal life, the perfect society?

Millions of people are beginning to realize they've been sold a dream that they can never live. In its place, we need more than just a bunch of different dreams. We need a coherent project based on reason, evidence and testable designs, one that cuts with the grain of economic history and is sustainable in terms of our planet.

And we need to get on with it.

PART I

For historians each event is unique. Economics, however, maintains that forces in society and nature behave in repetitive ways.

Charles Kindleberger[1]

I

Neoliberalism is Broken

When Lehman Brothers collapsed, on 15 September 2008, my cameraman made me walk several times through the clutter of limos, satellite trucks, bodyguards and sacked bankers outside its New York HQ, so he could film me amid the chaos.

As I watch those rushes nearly seven years later – with the world still reeling from the consequences of that day – the question arises: what does that guy in front of the camera know now that he did not know then?

I knew that a recession had begun: I'd just trekked across America filming the closure of 600 Starbucks branches. I knew there was stress in the global finance system: I'd reported concerns that a major bank was about to go bust six weeks before it happened.[1] I knew the US housing market was destroyed: I'd seen homes in Detroit on sale for $8,000 cash. I knew, in addition to all this, that I did not like capitalism.

But I had no idea that capitalism in its present form was about to self-destruct.

The 2008 crash wiped 13 per cent off global production and 20 per cent off global trade. It took global growth negative – on a scale where anything below +3 per cent is counted as a recession. In the West, it produced a depression phase longer than in 1929–33 and even now, amid a pallid recovery, has got mainstream economists terrified about the prospect of long-term stagnation.

But the post-Lehman depression is not the real problem. The real problem is what comes next. And to understand that we have to look beyond the immediate causes of the 2008 crash to their structural roots.

3

When the global finance system collapsed in 2008, it didn't take long to discover the proximate cause: the debts hidden in mispriced products known as 'structured investment vehicles'; the network of offshore and unregulated companies known – once it had started to implode – as the 'shadow banking system'.[2] Then, as the prosecutions began, we were able to see the scale of the criminality that had become normal in the run-up to the crisis.[3]

Ultimately, though, we were all flying blind. And that's because there is no model of a neoliberal economic crisis. Even if you don't buy the whole ideology – the end of history, the world is flat, friction-free capitalism – the basic idea behind the system is that markets correct themselves. The possibility that neoliberalism could collapse under its own contradictions was then, and remains now, unacceptable to most.

Seven years on, the system has been stabilized. By running government debts close to 100 per cent of GDP, and by printing money worth around a sixth of the world's output, America, Britain, Europe and Japan injected a shot of adrenaline to counteract the seizure. They saved the banks by burying their bad debt; some of it was written off, some assumed as sovereign debt, some buried inside entities made safe simply by central banks staking their credibility on them.

Then, through austerity programmes, they transferred the pain away from people who'd invested money stupidly, punishing instead welfare recipients, public sector workers, pensioners and, above all, future generations. In the worst-hit countries, the pension system has been destroyed, the retirement age is being hiked so that those currently leaving university will retire at seventy, and education is being privatized so that graduates will face a lifetime of high debt. Services are being dismantled and infrastructure projects put on hold.

Yet even now many people fail to grasp the true meaning of the word 'austerity'. Austerity is not seven years of spending cuts, as in the UK, or even the social catastrophe inflicted on Greece. Tidjane Thiam, the CEO of Prudential, spelled out the true meaning of austerity at the Davos forum in 2012. Unions are the 'enemy of young people', he said, and the minimum wage is 'a machine to destroy jobs'. Workers' rights and decent wages stand in the way of capitalism's revival and, says the millionaire finance guy without embarrassment, must go.[4]

This is the real austerity project: to drive down wages and living standards in the West for decades, until they meet those of the middle class in China and India on the way up.

Meanwhile, lacking any alternative model, the conditions for another crisis are being assembled. Real wages have fallen or remained stagnant in Japan, the southern Eurozone, the USA and the UK.[5] The shadow banking system has been reassembled, and is now bigger than it was in 2008.[6] The combined global debt of banks, households, companies and states has risen by $57 trillion since the crisis, and stands at nearly three times global GDP.[7] New rules demanding banks hold more reserves have been watered down and delayed. And the 1 per cent has got richer.

If there is another financial frenzy followed by another collapse, there can be no second bailout. With government debts at a post-war high and welfare systems in some countries crippled, there are no more bullets left in the clip – at least not of the kind fired in 2009–10. The bailout of Cyprus in 2013 was the test bed for what happens if a major bank or a state goes bust again. For savers, everything in the bank over €100,000 was wiped out.

Here's a summary of what I've learned since the day Lehman died: the next generation will be poorer than this one; the old economic model is broken and cannot revive growth without reviving financial fragility. The markets that day were sending us a message about the future of capitalism – but it's a message that, at the time, I only partially understood.

'ANOTHER DRUG WE'RE ON . . .'

In future, we should look for the emoticons, the smileys and digital winks in emails that the finance guys use when they know they're doing wrong.

'It's another drug we're on,' admits the Lehman executive running the infamous Repo 105 tactic in an email. The tactic involved hiding debts away from Lehman's balance sheet by temporarily 'selling' them and then buying them back once the bank's quarterly report had been submitted. Another Lehman exec is asked: is the tactic legal, do other banks do it, and is it disguising holes in our balance sheet? He emails back: 'Yes, no and yes :).'[8]

At the ratings agency Standard & Poor's, where they've knowingly mispriced risk, one guy messages another: 'Let's hope we are all wealthy and retired by the time this house of cards falters,' adding the emoticon ':O)'.[9]

Meanwhile, at Goldman Sachs in London, trader Fabrice Tourre jokes:

> More and more leverage in the system, the entire system is about to crumble any moment ... the only potential survivor the fabulous Fab ... standing in the middle of all these complex, highly levered, exotic trades he created without necessarily understanding all the implications of those monstrosities !!!

As more evidence of criminality and corruption emerges, there is always this knowing informality among bankers as they break the rules. 'Done, for you big boy,' writes one Barclays employee to another as they manipulate LIBOR, the rate at which banks lend to each other, the most important interest rate on the planet.[10]

We should listen carefully to the tone in these emails – the irony, the dishonesty, the repeated use of smileys, slang and manic punctuation. It is evidence of systemic self-deception. At the heart of the finance system, which is itself the heart of the neoliberal world, they knew it didn't work.

John Maynard Keynes once called money 'a link between the present and the future'.[11] He meant that what we do with money today is a signal of how we think things are going to change in years to come. What we did with money in the run-up to 2008 was to massively expand its volume: the global money supply rose from $25 trillion to $70 trillion in the seven years before the crash – incomparably faster than growth in the real economy. When money expands at this rate, it is a sign that we think the future is going to be spectacularly richer than the present. The crisis was simply a feedback signal from the future: we were wrong.

All the global elite could do once the crisis exploded was put more chips on the roulette table. Finding them, to the tune of $12 trillion in quantitative easing, was no problem since they themselves were the cashiers at the casino. But they had to spread their bets more evenly for a while, and become less reckless.[12]

That, effectively, is what the policy of the world has been since 2008. You print so much money that the cost of borrowing it for banks becomes zero, or even negative. When real interest rates turn negative, savers – who can only keep their money safe by buying government bonds – are effectively forced to forgo any income from their savings. That, in turn, stimulates the revival of property, commodity, gold and stock markets by forcing savers to move their money into these more risky areas. The outcome to date has been a shallow recovery – but the strategic problems remain.

Growth in the developed world is slow. America has recovered only by carrying a $17 trillion Federal debt. Trillions of printed dollars, yen, pounds and now Euros are still in circulation. The debts of Western households remain unpaid. Entire ghost towns of speculative property – from Spain to China – continue unsold. The Eurozone – probably the most important and fragile economic construct in the world – remains stagnant, generating a level of political friction between classes and countries that could blow it apart.

Unless the future delivers spectacular riches, none of this is sustainable. But the kind of economy that's emerging from the crisis cannot produce such wealth. So we're at a strategic moment, both for the neoliberal model and, as I will show in chapter 2, for capitalism itself.

If we rewind the tape to New York in September 2008, you can see what was rational about the optimism that drove the boom. In my footage from that day there's a crowd of people outside the Lehman HQ taking photographs on their Nokias, Motorolas and Sony Ericssons. The handsets are long obsolete, the market dominance of those brand names already gone.

The rapid advance in digital technology that drove the pre-2007 boom has barely paused for breath during the slump. In the years since Lehman collapsed, the iPhone conquered the world and was itself surpassed by the Android smartphone. Tablets and e-books took off. Social networking – barely talked about back then – has become a central part of people's lives. Facebook had 100 million users when Lehman went bust; it has 1.3 billion users at time of writing and is bigger than the entire global internet was in 2008.[13]

And technological progress is not confined to the digital sphere. In those seven years, despite a global financial crisis and a massive earthquake, Toyota has manufactured 5 million hybrid cars – five times the number it had made before the crisis hit. In 2008, there were 15,000 megawatts of solar power capacity in the world; by 2014 there were ten times that.[14]

This, then, has been a depression like no other. We have seen crisis and stagnation combined with the rapid rollout of new technologies in a way that just didn't happen in the 1930s. And in policy terms it has been the 1930s in reverse. Instead of exacerbating the crisis, as they did in the 1930s, the global elite reached for policy tools to cushion the real economy – often in defiance of what their own economic theories told them to do. And in key emerging market countries, rising demand for commodities together with the global monetary stimulus turned the first years after 2008 into a bonanza.

The combined impact of technological progress, policy stimulus and the resilience of the emerging markets has produced a depression much milder in human terms than that of the 1930s. But as a turning point, this is bigger than the 1930s. To understand why, we have to explore the chain of cause and effect.

For both left- and right-wing economists, the immediate cause of the collapse is seen as 'cheap money': the decision by Western states to deregulate banking and loosen credit after the dotcom crash in 2001. It created the opportunity for the structured finance bubble – and the motive for all the crimes: bankers were effectively told by politicians that it was their duty to get rich, through speculative finance, so that their wealth could trickle down to the rest of us.

Once you acknowledge the centrality of cheap money, that leads to a deeper problem: 'global imbalances' – the division of labour that allowed countries such as the USA to live on credit and run high deficits while China, Germany, Japan and the other exporting countries took the flip side of the deal. Certainly these imbalances lay behind the glut of credit in Western economies. But why did they exist? Why did Chinese households save 25 per cent of their wages and lend them via the global finance system to American workers who saved nothing?

In the 2000s, economists debated rival explanations: either over-saving by the parsimonious people of Asia was to blame, or over-borrowing by the profligate people of the West. Either way, the imbalances were a fact of life. Dig for any deeper cause and you get to the hard bedrock of globalization itself, and in mainstream economics globalization cannot be questioned; it's just there.

The 'bad banking plus imbalanced growth' thesis became the explanation for the collapse. Put the banks right, manage the debts down, rebalance the world and things will be all right. That is the assumption that has guided policy since 2008.

Yet the persistence of low growth has now driven even mainstream economists beyond such complacency. Larry Summers, Treasury Secretary under Bill Clinton and an architect of bank deregulation, shook the economics world in 2013 by warning that the West faced 'secular stagnation' – that is, low growth for the foreseeable future. 'Unfortunately,' he admitted, low growth 'has been present for a long time, but has been masked by unsustainable finances'.[15] Veteran US economist Robert Gordon went further, predicting persistent low growth in the USA for the next twenty-five years, as a result of lower productivity, an ageing population, high debts and growing inequality.[16] Remorselessly, capitalism's failure to revive has moved concerns away from the scenario of a ten-year stagnation caused by overhanging debts, towards one where the system never regains its dynamism. Ever.

To understand what is rational about these premonitions of doom, we need critically to examine four things that at first allowed neoliberalism to flourish but which have begun to destroy it. They are:

1. 'Fiat money', which allowed every slowdown to be met with credit loosening, and the whole developed world to live on debt.
2. Financialization, which replaced the stagnant incomes of the developed world workforce with credit.
3. The global imbalances, and the risks remaining in the vast debts and currency reserves of major countries.
4. Information technology, which allowed everything else to happen, but whose future contribution to growth is in doubt.

The destiny of neoliberalism depends on whether these four things persist. The long-range destiny of capitalism depends on what happens if they don't. Let's look at them in detail.

FIAT MONEY

In 1837, the newly declared Republic of Texas issued its first bank-notes. There are still a few preserved, crisp and clean, in the state's museums. Lacking a gold reserve, the new country promised to pay the bearer of these notes 10 per cent interest a year. By 1839, the value of a Texan dollar had fallen to 40 US cents. By 1842 the notes were so unpopular that the Texan government refused to let people pay their taxes with them. Shortly afterwards people began demanding the USA should annex Texas. By 1845, when this finally happened, the Texas dollar had recovered much of its value. The USA then wrote off $10 million of Texan public debt in 1850.

The episode is seen as a textbook case of what happens with 'fiat money' – that is, money not backed by gold. The Latin word *'fiat'* means the same as it does in the biblical phrase *fiat lux* – let there be light; it means 'let there be money' created out of nowhere. In Texas, there was land, cattle and trade – but not enough of them to warrant printing $4 million and incurring a public debt of $10 million. The paper money collapsed and ultimately the Texan Republic disappeared.

In August 1971, the USA itself decided to repeat the experiment – this time using the whole world as its laboratory. Richard Nixon unilaterally scrapped an agreement that pegged all other currencies to the dollar and the dollar to gold. From then on, the global currency system was based on fiat money.

In the late 1960s the future Federal Reserve boss Alan Greenspan had denounced the proposed move away from gold as a plot by 'welfare statists' to finance government spending by confiscating people's money.[17] But then, like the rest of America's elite, he realized that it would first allow the USA, effectively, to confiscate other countries' money – setting the scene for Washington to indulge in three decades of currency manipulation. The result enabled America to accumulate, at the time of writing, a $6 trillion debt with the rest of the world.[18]

This move to a pure paper currency was the precondition for every other phase of the neoliberal project. So it took the American right a long time to figure out they didn't like it. Today, however, right-wing economics has become one long howl of rage against fiat money. Its critics believe it is the ultimate source of boom and bust – and they are partly right.

The move away from gold and fixed exchange rates allowed three fundamental reflexes of the neoliberal era to kick in: the expanded creation of money by banks, the assumption that all crises can be resolved, and the idea that profits generated out of speculation can go on rising for ever. These reflexes have become so ingrained in the thinking of millions that, when they no longer worked, it induced paralysis.

It is news to some people that banks 'create' money, but they always have done: they have always lent out more cash than there was in the safe. In the pre-1971 system, though, there were legal limits to such money creation. In the USA, for savings that could be withdrawn at any time, banks had to hold $20 in cash against every $100 of deposits. Even if one in every five people rushed to the bank to take all their money out, there would still be enough.[19]

At every stage in its design, the neoliberal project removed those limits. The first Basel Accord, in 1988, set the reserves needed against $100 of loans to $8. By the time of Basel II in 2004, both deposits and loans had become too complex to balance with a single percentage figure. So they changed the rules: you had to 'weight' your capital according to its quality – and that quality was to be decided by a ratings agency. You had to reveal the financial engineering used to calculate your risks. And you had to take account of 'market risk': in other words, what is going on outside the walls of the bank.

Basel II was an open invitation to game the system – and that's what the bankers and their lawyers did. The ratings agencies misvalued the assets; the law firms designed complex vehicles to get around the transparency rules. As for the market risk, even as America veered into recession in late 2007, the Federal Reserve's Open Market Committee – the room in which they're supposed to know everything – stank of complacency. Tim Geithner, then boss of the New York Fed, predicted: 'Consumer spending slows a bit, and businesses react by scaling back growth in hiring and investment, and this produces several quarters of growth modestly below trend.'[20]

This total failure to measure market risk correctly was not blind optimism; it was supported by experience. When faced with a downturn, the Fed would always slash interest rates, enabling banks to lend even more money against fewer assets. This formed the second basic reflex of neoliberalism: the assumption that all crises were solvable.

From 1987 until 2000, under Greenspan's leadership, the Fed met every downturn with a rate cut. The effect was not only to make investing a one-way bet – since the Fed would always counteract a stock market crash. It was to reduce, over time, the risk of holding equities.[21] The price of shares, which in theory represents a guess as to the future profitability of a firm, came increasingly to represent a guess as to the future policy of the Federal Reserve. The ratio of share prices to earnings (annual profits) for the top 500 companies in the USA, which had meandered between 10x and 25x since the year 1870, now spiked to 35x and 45x earnings.[22]

If money is a 'link to the future', then by 2000 it was signalling a future rosier than at any time in history. The trigger for the dotcom crash of 2001 was Greenspan's decision to raise interest rates in order to choke off what he called 'irrational exuberance'. But following 9/11 and the Enron bankruptcy in 2001, and with the onset of a brief recession, rates were slashed again. And now it was overtly political: irrational exuberance was OK once your country was simultaneously at war with Iraq and Afghanistan, and once confidence in the corporate system had been rocked by scandal after scandal.

This time, the Fed's move was backed with an explicit promise: the government would print money rather than allow prolonged recession and deflation. 'The U. S. government has a technology, called a printing press,' said Fed board member Ben Bernanke in 2002. 'Under a paper-money system, a determined government can always generate higher spending and hence positive inflation.'[23]

When financial conditions are positive and predictable, the profits of banks themselves are always going to be high. Banking became an ever-changing tactical game focused on skimming money off your competitors, your customers and your business clients. This created the third basic reflex of neoliberalism: the widespread illusion that you can generate money out of money alone.

Though they had reduced the percentage of capital banks were required to keep on hand, the US authorities had maintained the strict partition between Main Street lending banks and investment banks imposed in the 1930s by the Glass-Steagall Act. But by the late 1990s, in a rush of mergers and acquisitions, the investment bank sector was going global, making a mockery of the rules. It was Treasury Secretary Larry Summers who, in 1999, through the repeal of Glass-Steagall, opened the banking system to the attentions of those adept at exotic, opaque and offshore forms of finance.

Fiat money, then, contributed to the crisis by creating wave after wave of false signals from the future: the Fed will always save us, shares are not risky and banks can make high profits out of low-risk business.

Nothing demonstrates the continuity between pre- and post-crisis policy better than quantitative easing (QE). In 2009, having wavered before the enormity of the task, Bernanke – together with his UK counterpart Mervyn King, governor of the Bank of England – started the presses rolling. In November 2008 China had already begun printing money in the more direct form of 'soft' bank loans from the state-owned banks to businesses (i.e. loans that nobody expected to be repaid). Now the Fed would print $4 trillion over the next four years – buying up the stressed debts of state-backed mortgage lenders, then government bonds, then mortgage debt, to the tune of $80 billion a month. The combined impact was to flush money into the economy, via rising share prices and revived house prices, which meant that it was first flushed into the pockets of those who were already rich.

Japan had pioneered the money-printing solution after its own housing bubble collapsed in 1990. As its economy floundered, premier Shinzo Abe was forced to restart the printing presses in 2012. Europe – forbidden to print money by rules designed to stop the Euro being debased – waited until 2015, as deflation and stagnation took hold, before pledging to print €1.6 trillion.

I calculate the combined amount of money printed globally, including that pledged by the ECB, at around $12 trillion – one sixth of global GDP.[24]

It worked, in that it prevented a depression. But it was the disease being used as a cure for the disease: cheap money being used to fix a crisis caused by cheap money.

What happens next depends on what you think money actually is.

The opponents of fiat money predict disaster. In fact, books denouncing paper money have become as common as those denouncing banks. With a limited amount of real economic goods but an unlimited amount of money, goes the argument, all paper money systems eventually go the way of nineteenth-century Texas. The 2008 crisis was just the tremor in advance of the earthquake.

As to solutions, they come mainly in millenarian form. There will be, writes former JP Morgan manager Detlev Shlichter, a 'transfer in wealth of historic proportions' from those holding paper assets – whether in bank accounts or pension funds – to those holding real ones, above all gold. Out of the ruins, he predicts, will come a system where all loans have to be backed by cash in the bank, known as '100 per cent reserve banking', together with a new Gold Standard. This will require a massive one-off hike in the price of gold, as the value of all the gold in the world has to rise to make it equal to the world's wealth. (A similar rationale stands behind the Bitcoin movement, which is an attempt to create a digital currency, not backed by any state and with a limited number of digital coins.)

This proposed new world of 'real' money would come at a massive economic cost. If bank reserves have to match loans made, there can be no expansion of the economy through credit, and there can be little space for derivatives markets, where complexity – in normal times – aids resilience to problems such as drought, crop failure, the recall of faulty motor cars etc. In a world where banks hold reserves equivalent to 100 per cent of their deposits, there would have to be repeated stop-go business cycles and high unemployment. And simple maths shows us that we would go into a deflation spiral: 'in an economy with an unchanged money supply but rising productivity ... prices will on trend decline', says Schlichter.[25]

That's the preferred option of the right-wing money fundamentalists. Their big fear is that, in order to keep fiat money alive, the state will nationalize the banks, write off the debts, seize control of the finance system and kill for ever the spirit of free enterprise.

As we'll see, it may come to that. But their reasoning contains a fundamental flaw: they don't understand what money actually is.

In the popular version of economics, money is just a convenient means of exchange, invented because in early societies swapping a handful of potatoes for a raccoon skin was too random. In fact, as the anthropologist David Graeber has shown, there is no evidence that early human societies used barter, or that money emerged from it.[26] They used something much more powerful. They used trust.

Money is created by states and always has been; it is not something that exists independently of governments. Money is always the 'promise to pay' by a government. Its value is not reliant on the intrinsic worth of a metal; it is a measure of people's trust in the permanence of the state.

Fiat money in Texas would have worked if people thought the state would exist for ever. But nobody, not even the Alamo-era settlers, did. As soon as they realized Texas was going to join the USA, the value of the Texan buck revived.

Once you get your head around this, the true nature of neoliberalism's problem becomes clear. The problem is not 'Damn, we printed too much money against the real stuff in the economy!' It is, though few will admit it, 'Damn, nobody believes in our state any more.' The entire system is dependent on the credibility of the state that issues the notes. And in the modern global economy that credibility rests not just on single states but on a multilayered system of debts, payment mechanisms, informal currency pegs, formal currency unions like the Euro, and huge reserves of foreign exchange accumulated by states as insurance in case the system collapses.

The real problem with fiat money comes if, or when, this multilateral system falls apart. But that lies in the future. For now, what we know is that fiat money – when combined with free-market economics – is a machine for producing boom-and-bust cycles. Left to run unsupervised, it could – before we've even considered the other destabilizing factors – push the world economy towards long-term stagnation.

FINANCIALIZATION

Go to any of the British towns devastated by industrial decline and you'll see the same streetscape: payday loan stores, pawnbrokers and shops selling household goods on credit at hyper-inflated interest rates. Next to the pawnbrokers you'll probably find that other gold mine of the poverty-stricken town: the employment agency. Look in the window and you'll see ads for jobs at the minimum wage – but which require more than minimum skill. Press operatives, carers on night shift, distribution centre workers: jobs that used to pay decent wages now pay as little as legally possible. Somewhere else, out of the limelight, you will come across people picking up the pieces: food banks run by churches and charities; Citizens' Advice Bureaux whose main business has become advising those swamped by debt.

Just one generation earlier these streets were home to thriving real businesses. I remember the main street of my home town, Leigh, in northwest England, in the 1970s, thronged on Saturday mornings with prosperous working-class families. There was full employment, high wages and high productivity. There were numerous street-corner banks. It was a world of work, saving and great social solidarity.

Smashing that solidarity, forcing wages down, destroying the social fabric of these towns was done – originally – to clear the ground for the free-market system. For the first decade, the result was simply crime, unemployment, urban decay and a massive deterioration in public health.

But then came financialization.

The urban landscape of today – outlets providing expensive money, cheap labour and free food – is the visual symbol of what neoliberalism has achieved. Stagnant wages were replaced by borrowing: our lives were financialized.

'Financialization' is a long word; if I could use one with fewer syllables I would, because it is at the heart of the neoliberal project and it needs to be better understood. Economists use the term to describe four specific changes that began in the 1980s:

1. Companies turned away from banks and went to the open financial markets to fund expansion.
2. Banks turned to consumers as a new source of profit, and to a set of high-risk, complex activities that we call investment banking.
3. Consumers became direct participants in the financial markets: credit cards, overdrafts, mortgages, student loans and motor car loans became part of everyday life. A growing proportion of

profit in the economy is now being made not by employing workers, or providing goods and services that they buy with their wages, but by lending to them.

4. All simple forms of finance now generate a market in complex finance higher up the chain: every house buyer or car driver is generating a knowable financial return somewhere in the system. Your mobile phone contract, gym membership, household energy – all your regular payments – are packaged into financial instruments, generating steady interest for an investor, long before you decide to buy them. And then somebody you have never met places a bet on whether you will make the payments.

The system may not be specifically designed to keep wages low and productive investment weak – neoliberal politicians constantly claim to be promoting high-value work and productivity – but judged by the results, financialization and low wages are like precarious work and food banks: they go together.

The real wages of production workers in the USA have, according to the government, stagnated since 1973. Over the same period, the amount of debt in the US economy has doubled, to 300 per cent of GDP. Meanwhile, the share of US GDP produced by finance, insurance and real-estate industries has risen from 15 to 24 per cent – making it bigger than manufacturing and close to the size of the service sector.[27]

Financialization also changed the relationship between companies and banks. From the 1980s onwards, the short-term quarterly profit figure became the stick finance used to beat to death the old corporate business models: companies making too little profit were forced to move jobs offshore, to merge, to attempt monopolistic do-or-die strategies, to fragment their operations into various outsourced departments – and to relentlessly slash wages.

The fiction at the heart of neoliberalism is that everybody can enjoy the consumer lifestyle without wages rising. You can borrow, but you can never go bust: if you borrow to buy a home, its value will always rise. And there will always be inflation – so if you borrow to buy a car, the value of the remaining debt is eroded by the time you need a new vehicle, leaving you plenty of scope to borrow more.

Widespread access to the finance system suited everybody: liberal politicians in the USA could point to the growing number of poor, black and Hispanic families with mortgages; bankers and finance companies got rich from selling loans to people who could not afford them. Plus it created the vast service industry that's grown up around the wealthy – the florists, yoga teachers, yacht builders and so on, who provide a kind of fake-tanned Downton Abbey for the rich of the twenty-first century. And it suited the ordinary Joe, too: after all, who is going to turn down cheap money?

But financialization created inherent problems; problems that triggered the crisis, but were not resolved by it.

While paper money is unlimited, wages are real. You can go on creating money for ever but if a declining share of it flows to workers, and yet a growing part of profits is generated out of their mortgages and credit cards, you are eventually going to hit a wall. At some point, the expansion of financial profit through providing loans to stressed consumers will break, and snap back. That is exactly what happened when the US subprime mortgage bubble collapsed.

From 2001 to 2006, US mortgage lending grew from $2.2 trillion a year to just below $3 trillion: significant but not outrageous. But subprime lending – i.e. lending to poor people at high real interest rates – grew from $160 billion to $600 billion. And 'adjustable mortgages' – which start cheap and become more expensive as time goes on – came from nowhere to make up 48 per cent of all loans issued in the last three years of the boom. This market for risky, complex, doomed-to-fail borrowing did not exist until investment banks created it.[28]

That illustrates another inherent problem with financialization: it breaks the link between lending and saving.[29] Banks on Main Street always hold less money than they lend. We've seen how deregulation encouraged them to hold less in reserve and to play the system. But this new process – whereby every stream of interest gets wrapped up into a more complex product, distributed between investors – means ordinary banks are forced into the short-term money market just to run their normal operations.

This drove a fatal shift in the psychology of banking. The long-term nature of their lending (on twenty-five-year mortgages or never-cleared credit cards) got pulled further and further away from the short-term nature of their borrowing. Thus, over and above all the scams and mispricing, financialization creates within banking a structural tendency towards the kind of instant crisis of liquidity – i.e. ready cash – that destroyed Lehman Brothers.

In financialized societies, a banking crisis does not usually see the masses rush to take their money out – for the simple reason that they do not have much money in there to start with. It is banks that have money in the bank – i.e. in other banks – and, as we found in 2008, much of it is in the form of worthless paper.

The problems described here can be solved only if we stop financialization. Allow it to continue and over time more and more of the money in the finance system becomes fictional, and more of its institutions become reliant on short-term borrowing.

But no politician or regulator was prepared to dismantle the system. Instead they have put it back together, primed it with $12 trillion of money created out of thin air, and set it going again. This ensures the same conditions that caused the boom-bust cycle will – should any significant growth occur – create another one.

The historian Ferdinand Braudel suggested that the decline of all economic superpowers begins with a spectacular turn to finance. Surveying the fall of the Netherlands as a trading empire in the seventeenth century, he wrote: 'Every capitalist development of this order seems, by reaching the stage of financial capitalism, to have in some sense announced its maturity: it [is] a sign of autumn.'[30]

Proponents of the 'financial autumn' theory point to the same pattern in the Genoese Republic – the main financial centre of the late Middle Ages – then the Netherlands, and then London towards the end of the British Empire. But in each of these examples, the pattern was for the dominant power to become lender to the world. Under neoliberalism, this has been reversed. The USA – and the West in general – have become the borrowers, not the lenders. This is a break in the long-term pattern.

So, too, is wage stagnation. The big financial empires of the past 500 years were making profits from unequal trade, slavery and usury, which were then used to finance decent lifestyles at home. The USA, under neoliberalism, boosted profits by impoverishing its own citizens.

The truth is, as finance has seeped into our daily lives, we are no longer slaves only to the machine, to the 9-to-5 routine, we've become slaves to interest payments. We no longer just generate profits for our bosses through our work, but also profits for financial middlemen through our borrowing. A single mum on benefits, forced into the world of payday loans and buying household goods on credit, can be generating a much higher profit rate for capital than an auto industry worker with a steady job.

Once every human being can generate a financial profit just by consuming – and the poorest can generate the most – a profound change begins in capitalism's attitude to work. We'll explore this later, in Part II. For now, to summarize: financialization is a permanent feature of neoliberalism. Like fiat money, it leads to breakdown – but the system can't do without it.

THE IMBALANCED WORLD

The inevitable result of neoliberalism was the rise of so-called 'global imbalances' – in trade, saving and investment. For countries that smashed organized labour, offshored large parts of their productive industries and fuelled consumption with rising credit, the outcome was always going to be trade deficits, high government debts and instability in the financial sector. The gurus of neoliberalism urged everybody to follow the Anglo-Saxon model, but in reality the system relied on some key countries choosing not to.

Asia's trade surplus with the rest of the world, Germany's surplus with Europe, the oil exporters' relentless accumulation of other people's debts – none of these were anomalies. They are what allowed the USA, Britain and southern Europe to borrow beyond their means.

In other words, we must understand from the outset that neoliberalism can exist only because certain key countries do not practise it. Germany, China and Japan pursue what their critics call 'neo-mercantilism': manipulating their trade, investment and currency positions to accumulate a large pile of other countries' cash. These surplus countries used to be seen as economic laggards, but in the post-crisis world they are among the few economies left standing. Germany's ability to dictate the terms of humiliation to Greece, in the living memory of people who'd seen the swastika fly from the Acropolis, shows the power of being a producer, exporter and lender once neoliberalism breaks down.

The main measure of global imbalance is the current account – the difference between imports and exports of goods, services and investments. The world's current account imbalance grew steadily through the 1990s then took off rapidly after 2000, rising from 1 per cent of world GDP to 3 per cent in 2006. The main deficit countries were America and most of Europe; the countries in surplus were China, the rest of Asia, Germany and Japan, and the oil producers.[31]

Why do we care? Because the imbalances produced the flammable material for the 2008 crisis by loading the finance systems of America, Britain and Europe with unsustainable debts. It forced countries like Greece, which had no power to export their way out of crisis, into a death spiral of austerity. And it left most neoliberalized countries with unpayable mountains of government debt.

In the wake of the 2008 crisis, the current account imbalance has fallen back – from 3 per cent of global GDP to 1.5 per cent. The IMF's most recent projection sees no danger of a second spike but the conditions for this are stark: that China does not return to its old rate of growth, nor America to its old rate of borrowing and spending. As economists Florence Pisani and Anton Brender put it: 'The only force that could finally rein in the continuous deepening of the global imbalances was the collapse of globalised finance.'[32]

Post-2008, the shrinking current account deficit has persuaded some economists that the risk posed by the imbalances is over.[33] But in the meantime another key measure of imbalance in the world has grown: the stock of money held by the surplus countries in other currencies – known as foreign exchange reserves.

While China has seen growth fall back to 7 per cent and its trade surplus with the West reduced, its foreign exchange reserve pile has actually doubled since 2008 – and by mid-2014 stood at $4 trillion.[34] Global foreign exchange reserves had likewise grown from under $8 trillion to approaching $12 trillion by late 2014.[35]

The imbalances always posed two distinct dangers. First, that they would flood Western economies with so much credit that the finance system collapsed. This happened. Second, more strategically, that all the pent-up risk and instability in the world gets pooled into an arrangement between states, over debt and exchange rates, which then collapses. This danger still exists.

If the USA cannot go on financing its debts, then at some point the dollar will collapse – indeed the mere perception that this might happen would be enough to collapse it. Nevertheless, the mutual dependence of China and the USA and, at a smaller scale, of Germany with the rest of the Eurozone ensures the trigger is never pulled.

All that's happened since 2008, via the build-up of foreign exchange reserves, has to be seen as the surplus countries taking out ever larger insurance policies against an American collapse.

If the world were made up only of economic forces, this outcome would be OK: low or stagnant growth in the deficit countries, a gradual rise in the value of the Chinese RMB against the dollar, a gradual erosion of the US debt by inflation – and a smaller trade deficit for the USA because fracking reduces its dependency on foreign oil.

But the world is made up of classes, religions and nations. The 2014 Euro elections saw parties pledged to rip up the global system win 25 per cent or more – in Denmark, France, Greece and Britain. In 2015, as I write, the far left victory in Greece has thrown the cohesion of the Eurozone into doubt. Plus, the diplomatic crisis over Ukraine has seen the first serious trade and financial sanctions imposed on Russia by the West since globalization began. The Middle East is on fire, from Islamabad to Istanbul, while military rivalries between China and Japan are more intense than at any time since 1945 and underpinned by an intense currency war.

All that would be needed to blow the whole thing apart is for one or more country to 'head for the exit', using protectionism, currency manipulation or debt default. Since the most important nation, the USA, now has a Republican Party rhetorically committed to all three of these things, the chances of this are high.

The imbalances were fundamental to the very nature of globalization and were thrown into reverse only by financial collapse.

Let's spell out what this means: the current form of globalization has a design fault. When it produces high growth it can do so only by fuelling unsustainable distortions, which are corrected by financial crisis. To reduce the distortions – the imbalances – you have to suppress the normal form of neoliberal growth.

THE INFO-TECH REVOLUTION

The one positive factor to set against all the negatives outlined so far is the tech revolution, which was produced by neoliberalism and has stormed ahead in defiance of the economic crisis. 'The information society,' writes the philosopher Luciano Floridi, 'has been brought about by the fastest growing technology in history. No previous generation has ever been exposed to such an extraordinary acceleration of technical power over reality, with corresponding social changes and ethical responsibilities.'[36]

It was the increase in computing power that enabled a complex global finance system. It underpinned the growth of the money supply as digital systems replaced the need for cash. It enabled the physical redistribution of production and supply to the emerging markets, where labour was cheap. It de-skilled the engineering worker, made the labour of semi-skilled workers redundant and accelerated the growth of low-skilled service work.

But though info-tech has become, as Floridi writes, 'the characteristic technology of our time', its emergence takes the form of a disappearing act. Mainframes are born then disappear to be replaced by servers, which also disappear from corporate HQs and now sit in vast air-conditioned sheds elsewhere. The silicon chip gets smaller; the add-on devices that once cluttered our workspaces – modems, hard drives, floppy disks – become smaller, scarcer, and then disappear. Proprietary software gets built by corporate IT departments and is then replaced by off-the-peg versions at one-tenth of the price. And soon, too, the IT departments disappear, to be replaced by call centres in Mumbai. The PC becomes the laptop. The laptop shrinks and gets more powerful but is superseded by the smartphone and the tablet.

At first, this new technology was mapped on to the old structures of capitalism. In the 1990s, the folklore in IT was that the most expensive software – the enterprise resource package – 'moulds like putty, sets like concrete'. By the time you had computerized your production line, innovation elsewhere meant you had to rip it out and start again.

But after around 2004, with the rise of the internet and mobile data, technology began to enable new business models: we called it Web 2.0. It also started to produce tangible new behaviours among large numbers of people. It became normal to pay with plastic; normal to put your whole private life online for ever; normal to go online to get a payday loan at 1,000 per cent interest.

At first, the exhilarating rush of new technology was taken as justifying all the pain we'd gone through to get free markets. The British miners had to be smashed so that we could have Facebook; telecoms had to be privatized so that we could all have 3G mobile phones. That was the implicit rationale.

Above all, however, it was the change in human terms that was critical. The most vital component of neoliberalism – the individualized worker and consumer, creating themselves anew as 'human capital' every morning and competing ferociously with each other – would have been impossible without network technology. Sociologist Michel Foucault's prediction of what it would make us – 'entrepreneurs of the self' – looks all the more visionary because it was made when the only thing resembling the internet was a green-screen network, owned by the French state, called Minitel.[37]

The promise was that new technology would produce an information economy and a knowledge society. These have emerged but not in the form envisaged. In the old dystopias – as with the rogue computer Hal, in *2001: A Space Odyssey* – it is the technology that rebels. In reality, the network has allowed humans to rebel.

It enabled them first of all to produce and consume knowledge independently of the channels formed in the era of industrial capitalism. That's why we noticed the disruptions first in the news industry, in music and the sudden loss of the state's monopoly over political propaganda and ideology.

Next, it began to undermine traditional concepts of property and privacy. Wikileaks and the controversy over the mass surveillance data collected by the NSA are just the latest phase of a war over who can own and store information. But the biggest impact of all is only now being understood.

The 'network effect' was first theorized by Bell Telephone boss Theodore Vail 100 years ago. Vail realized that networks create something extra, for free. In addition to utility for the user of a telephone and revenue for the owner, he noticed a third thing: the more people join the network, the more useful it becomes to everybody.

The problem comes when you try to measure and capture that third thing. Robert Metcalfe, the inventor of the Ethernet switch, claimed in 1980 that a network's value is 'the number of users squared'. So while the cost of building a network rises in a straight line, its value rises in an exponential curve.[38] By implication the art of doing business in a knowledge economy is to capture everything between the straight line and the rising curve.

But how do we measure value? In terms of money saved, revenue earned or profits accrued? In 2013, the OECD's economists agreed that it could not be captured by traditional market metrics. 'While the Internet's impact on market transactions and value added has been undoubtedly far-reaching,' they wrote, 'its effect on non-market interactions . . . is even more profound.'[39]

Economists have tended to ignore non-market interactions: they are, by definition, non-economic – as insignificant as a smile passed between two customers in the Starbucks queue. As to the network effect, they assumed its benefits would be quantified into lower prices and distributed between producers and consumers. But in the space of less than thirty years, network technologies have opened whole areas of economic life to the possibility of collaboration and production beyond the market.

On 15 September 2008, the Nokias and Motorolas pointed at Lehman Brothers HQ, and the free wifi signal in the Starbucks opposite, were in their own way just as significant as the bank that had collapsed. They were conveying the ultimate market signal from the future to the present: *that an information economy may not be compatible with a market economy* – or at least not one dominated and regulated by market forces primarily.

That, I will argue, is the root cause of the collapse, fibrillation and zombie state of neoliberalism. All the money created, all the velocity and momentum of finance built up during the last twenty-five years have to be set against the possibility that capitalism – a system based on markets, property ownership and exchange – cannot capture the 'value' generated by the new technology. In other words, it is increasingly evident that information goods conflict fundamentally with market mechanisms.

THE ZOMBIE SYSTEM

Let's imagine an escape route for capitalism. During the next decade, central banks withdraw from QE in an orderly way. They refrain from using the printed money to write off their own government debts; the private market for government bonds, suppressed for a decade, revives. Plus, governments agree to suppress financial mania for all time: they pledge to raise interest rates in response to all future bubbles; they remove for ever the implicit guarantee of bank bailouts. All other markets – for credit, for shares, for derivatives – would then correct, to reflect the increased risk of financial capitalism. Capital would be reallocated to productive investment and away from speculative finance.

Ultimately, the world would have to return to exchange rates pegged against a new global currency managed by the IMF, with the Chinese RMB becoming a fully tradable reserve currency like the dollar. That would address the systemic threat posed by fiat money – the lack of credibility arising from the danger that globalization will break up. But the price would be a permanent end to the global imbalances: the currencies of surplus countries would rise, and China, India and the rest would have to give up their cheap labour advantage.

At the same time, financialization would have to be reversed. You would need a shift of political power away from banks and the politicians who support them, towards a policy favouring the onshoring of industry and services back to the West in order to create high-wage employment across the developed world. As a result, financial complexity would shrink, wages would grow, and the financial sector's share of GDP would be reduced, as would our reliance on credit.

The most far-sighted among the global elite know this is the only answer: stabilization of fiat money, a retreat from financialization, and an end to the imbalances. But there are enormous social and political obstacles.

In the first place, the rich are opposed to increased wages and regulated finance; they want the opposite. Secondly, there would be winners and losers at a national level: the German ruling elite benefit from the debt-colonization of Greece and Spain; the Chinese ruling elite benefit from being the gatekeeper to a cheap labour economy of 1.4 billion people. They have a vested interest in blocking the escape route.

But here's the biggest problem: for this scenario to work, huge, unpayable sovereign debts would have to be written down, together with a large proportion of the world's household and corporate debts.

There is, however, no global system to achieve this. Write America's debts down and Chinese savers lose; the result would be to break the essential deal between Asia and the West: you borrow, we lend. Write off the Greek debt to the EU and it is German taxpayers who lose tens of billions, again, breaching an essential deal.

The outcome of this best-case scenario, even if the transition could be managed peacefully, would be a complete breakdown of globalization.

And, of course, it cannot be managed peacefully.

Russia has, since 2014, become a power dedicated to disrupting the Western economies, not cooperating with them. China – for all the soft power it has begun to project – cannot do what America did at the end of the Second World War: absorb the world's debts, set explicit rules and create a new global currency system.

Meanwhile, in the West, there is no sign of any strategy resembling the one outlined above. There is talk of it – from the lionizing of the French economist Thomas Piketty to the Bundesbank's calls in 2014 for higher wages in Europe. But in practice, the mainstream parties remain wedded to neoliberalism.

And without the escape route, the prospect looks more and more like long-term stagnation.

In 2014, the OECD released its projections for the world economy in the years between now and 2060.[40] World growth will slow to 2.7 per cent, said the Paris-based think tank, because the catch-up

effects boosting growth in the developing world – growing population, education, urbanization – will peter out. Even before that,
near-stagnation in advanced economies indicates average global
growth of just 3 per cent over the next fifty years, significantly below
the pre-crisis average.

Meanwhile, because semi-skilled jobs will become automated, leaving only high- and low-paid ones, global inequality will rise by 40 per
cent. By 2060, countries such as Sweden will have the levels of inequality currently seen in the USA: think Gary, Indiana in the suburbs of
Stockholm. There is also the very real risk that climate change will
begin to destroy capital, coastal land and agriculture, shaving up to
2.5 per cent off world GDP, and 6 per cent in south-east Asia.

But the bleakest part of the OECD report lies not in what it projects but what it assumes: a rapid rise in productivity due to
information technology. Three-quarters of all the growth to 2060 is
expected to come from increased productivity. However, that assumption is, as the report states euphemistically, 'high compared with
recent history'.

In fact, as I will explore in chapter 5, there is no certainty at all that
the information revolution of the past twenty years will turn into the
kind of growth and productivity that can be measured in market
terms. In that case there is substantial risk that the meagre 3 per cent
annual growth projected by the OECD over the next fifty years will
be closer to 0.75.

Then there's the migration problem. To make the OECD's central
growth scenario work, Europe and the USA have to absorb 50 million migrants each between now and 2060, with the rest of the
developed world assimilating another 30 million. Without them, the
workforce and the tax base of the West shrinks so badly that states go
bust. The risk – as signalled by a 25 per cent vote for the Front
National in France and armed right-wingers haranguing migrant kids
on California's border with Mexico – is that the populations of the
developed world will not accept it.

Allow yourself to imagine the world of 2060 as the OECD predicts it: Los Angeles and Detroit look like Manila today – abject
slums alongside guarded skyscrapers; Stockholm and Copenhagen
look like the destroyed cities of the American rust belt; the

middle-income job has disappeared. Capitalism will be in its fourth decade of stagnation.

Even to achieve this glittering future, says the OECD, we have to make labour 'more flexible' and the economy more globalized. We will have to privatize higher education – for the cost of expanding it to meet the demand for graduates would bankrupt many states – and assimilate tens of millions of migrants into the developed world.

And as we struggle with all this, it is likely that the current means of financing the state will evaporate. The OECD points out that the polarization of populations into high-and-low-income groups will render income taxes ineffective. We will need – as Thomas Piketty suggests – to tax wealth instead. The problem here is that assets – whether they be a star racehorse, a secret bank account or the copyright on the Nike swoosh – tend to be held in jurisdictions dedicated to avoiding wealth taxes, even if anybody had the will to raise them, which they currently don't.

If things do not change, says the OECD, it is realistic to expect stagnation in the West, a slowing pace of growth in emerging markets and the likely bankruptcy of many states.

So what's more likely is that at some point one or more countries will quit globalization, via protectionism, debt write-offs and currency manipulation. Or that a de-globalization crisis originating in diplomatic and military conflict spills over into the world economy and produces the same results.

The lesson from the OECD's report is that we need a complete system redesign. The most highly educated generation in the history of the human race, and the best connected, will not accept a future of high inequality and stagnant growth.

Instead of a chaotic race to de-globalize the world, and decades of stagnation combined with rising inequality, we need a new economic model. To design it will involve more than an effort of utopian thinking. Keynes's genius in the mid-1930s was to understand what the crisis had revealed about the *existing* system: that a workable new model would have to be built around the permanent inefficiencies of the old one, which mainstream economics could not see.

This time the problem is even bigger.

The central premise of this book is that, alongside the long-term stagnation problem arising from the financial crisis and demographics, information technology has robbed market forces of their ability to create dynamism. Instead, it is creating the conditions for a post-capitalist economy. It may not be possible to 'rescue' capitalism, as Keynes did with radical policy solutions, because its technological foundations have changed.

So before we demand a 'Green New Deal', or state-owned banks, or free college education, or long-term zero interest rates, we have to understand how they might fit into the kind of economy that is emerging. And we are very badly equipped to do this. An order has been disrupted but conventional economics has no idea of the magnitude of the disruption.

To go forward we need a mental image smaller than 'the financial autumn of a failing empire', but bigger than a theory of boom-bust cycles. We need a theory that explains why, in the evolution of capitalism over the past two centuries, big moments of metamorphosis have occurred, and how exactly technological change recharges the batteries of capitalist growth.

We need, in short, a theory that fits the current crisis into a picture of capitalism's overall destiny. The search for it will take us beyond conventional economics, and way beyond conventional Marxism. It begins in a Russian prison cell in 1938.

2

Long Waves, Short Memories

The wave-form is beautiful. The sound of the ocean beating against the sand is evidence that order exists in nature.

When you consider the physics of a wave-form, it becomes even more beautiful. It is matter displaying the tendency to invert: the energy that makes the wave rise is the same energy that makes it fall.

When you consider the mathematical properties of the wave-form, it becomes more fascinating still. Fifteen hundred years ago, an Indian mathematician discovered that if you plot every possible ratio between two sides of a triangle it produces a wave-like pattern. Medieval scholars called it a 'sine'. Today we call the smooth, repetitive waves found in nature sine waves. An electrical current moves in the form of a sine wave; so does sound; so does light.

And there are waves within waves. To a surfer, waves seem to come in sets, growing in size, so that the sixth or seventh is the big one that you want to catch. In fact, this is just the result of a longer, flatter wave moving 'through' the short ones.

This relationship – of long waves to short ones – is a source of order in acoustics. For musicians the harmonics created by short waves within longer waves are what gives each instrument its particular sound; music is in tune when long and short waves are in strict mathematical proportion.

Waves are ubiquitous in nature. In fact, at the subatomic level, the wave-like movement of a particle is the only way we can know it exists. But waves also exist within big, complex and unnatural systems – such as markets. For those who analyse stock markets, the wave-form has become like a religious icon: they use tools to filter out the 'noise' of daily fluctuations to produce a predictive curve. 'Peaks' and 'troughs' have become everyday economic terms.

But in economics the wave-form can be dangerous. It can imply order and regularity where there is none. A sound wave simply decays to silence; but waves generated from random data become distorted and disrupted after a time. And the economy is a world of complex, random events, not simple waves.

It was the wave-chart experts of the last boom who failed to predict the slump. In surfing terms, they were looking at waves instead of sets; sets instead of tides; tides instead of the tsunami that was about to hit them. We think of a tsunami as a big wave: a wall of water. In fact a tsunami is a *long* wave: it swells and it keeps on coming.

For the man who discovered their existence in economics, long waves proved fatal.

DEATH BY FIRING SQUAD

The prisoner shuffles; he can't walk. He is partially blind, has chronic heart disease and clinical depression. 'There is no way that I can force myself to think systematically,' he writes. 'To think scientifically at all without actively working on materials and books, and with head-aches, is very difficult.'[1]

Nikolai Kondratieff had spent eight years as a political prisoner in Suzdal, east of Moscow, reading only the books and newspapers per-mitted by Stalin's secret police. He had shivered in winter and sweltered in summer but his ordeal would soon be over. On 17 September 1938, the day his original sentence expired, Kondratieff was tried a second time, convicted of anti-Soviet activity and executed in his cell, by firing squad.

Thus perished one of the giants of twentieth-century economics. In his time, Kondratieff ranked alongside globally influential thinkers such as Keynes, Schumpeter, Hayek and Gini. His 'crimes' were fabri-cated. An underground 'Peasant Labour Party', of which he was supposed to be leader, did not exist.

Kondratieff's real crime, in the eyes of his persecutors, was to think the unthinkable about capitalism: that instead of collapsing under crisis, capitalism generally adapts and mutates. In two pioneering works of data-mining he showed that, beyond short-term business cycles, there is evidence of a longer, fifty-year pattern whose turning points coincide with major structural changes within capitalism and major conflicts. Thus, these moments of extreme crisis and survival were not evidence of chaos but of order. Kondratieff was the first person to show the existence of long waves in economic history.

Though it was later popularized as a 'wave-theory', Kondratieff's most valuable insight was to understand why the global economy goes through sudden change, why capitalism hits structural crisis, and how it morphs and mutates in response. He showed us why business ecosystems that have lasted for decades can suddenly implode. He used the term 'long cycle' rather than 'wave' because cycles in scientific thought create a sub-language that is highly useful: we speak of phases, states and their sudden alternation.

Kondratieff studied industrial capitalism. Though others claim to have found long waves in prices going back to the Middle Ages, his data series begins with the industrial revolution in the 1770s.

In Kondratieff's theory, each long cycle has an upswing lasting about twenty-five years, fuelled by the deployment of new technologies and high capital investment; then a downswing of about the same length, usually ending with a depression. In the 'up' phase, recessions are rare; in the 'down' phase they are frequent. In the up phase, capital flows to productive industries; in the down phase it gets trapped in the finance system.

There's more, but that's the basic theory. In this chapter I will argue that it is essentially right, but that the present crisis represents a disruption of the pattern – and that signals this is something bigger than the end of a fifty-year cycle.

The man himself was supremely cautious about the implications of his theory. He never claimed he could predict events – though he did predict the Depression of the 1930s, ten years before it happened. He arranged for his findings to be published alongside a brutal critique and peer-review.[2]

But Stalin's police had, in a way, understood more about Kondratieff's theory than he did himself. They understood that – if pursued to its conclusion – it would bring Marxism face to face with a dangerous proposition: that there is no 'final' crisis of capitalism. There can be chaos, panic and revolution but, on the basis of Kondratieff's evidence, capitalism's tendency is not to collapse, but rather, to mutate. Huge swathes of capital can be destroyed, business models can be scrapped, empires can be liquidated in global wars, but the system survives – albeit in a different form.

To the orthodox Marxism of the 1920s, Kondratieff's explanation of what caused these transformations was equally dangerous. The events that seem to cause the big turning points – wars, revolutions, discovery of new gold deposits and new colonies – were, he said, mere effects generated by the demands of the economy itself. Humanity, even as it tries to shape economic history, is relatively powerless over the long term.

For a time in the 1930s, long-wave theory became influential in the West. The Austrian economist Joseph Schumpeter produced his own theory of business cycles, popularizing the term 'Kondratieff Wave'. But once capitalism stabilized after 1945, long-wave theory seemed redundant. Economists believed state intervention could flatten out even the minor ups and downs of capitalism. As for a fifty-year cycle, the guru of Keynesian economics, Paul Samuelson, dismissed it as 'science fiction'.[3]

And when the New Left tried to revive Marxism as a critical social science in the 1960s, they had little time for Kondratieff and his waves; they were looking for a theory of capitalist breakdown, not survival.

Only a few diehards, mainly investors, remained obsessed with Kondratieff. In the 1980s, Wall Street analysts turned his careful provisional findings into a bunch of crude, predictive mumbo-jumbo. In place of his complex data, they drew simple lines, showing a wave with a stylized shape: a surge, a plateau, a crisis and a collapse. They called it the 'K-Wave'.

If Kondratieff was right, these investors said, the economic recovery that began in the late 1940s was the start of a fifty-year cycle, which meant that sometime around the end of the 1990s there should be a depression. They built complex investment strategies to hedge against the catastrophe. And then they waited . . .

WHAT KONDRATIEFF REALLY SAID

In 2008, what the investors were waiting for finally happened – though, for reasons we'll come to, ten years later than expected.

Now, people in the mainstream are once again interested in long cycles. As it dawned on them that the Lehman crisis was systemic, analysts began to look for patterns produced by the interplay of tech innovation and growth. In 2010, economists at Standard Chartered announced that we were in the middle of a global 'supercycle'.[4] Carlota Perez, an Anglo-Venezuelan economist and follower of Schumpeter, harnessed wave-theory to promise a new 'golden age' for capitalism if it could only shrug off financial panic and return to the state-funded innovation process that produced the post-war boom.[5]

But to use Kondratieff's insight properly we have to understand what he really said. His original research, in the 1920s, was based on data for five advanced economies between 1790 and 1920. He did not track GDP directly but interest rates, wages, commodity prices, coal and iron production and foreign trade. Using the most advanced statistical techniques of his time – and two assistants whose job-title was 'computer' – he established a trend line out of the raw data. He divided the data against population size and smoothed it out using a nine-year 'moving average' to filter out random fluctuations and shorter cycles.

The result was a collection of charts that look like shallow sine waves. They show the first long cycle, beginning with the emergence of the factory system in Britain in the 1780s and ending around 1849. Then, a much clearer second wave starts in 1849, coinciding with the global deployment of railways, steam ships and the telegraph, before entering its downswing phase, with the so-called 'Long Depression' after 1873, and ending sometime in the 1890s.

By the early 1920s, Kondratieff believed there was a third cycle under way. It had reached its peak and begun its downswing, probably sometime between 1914 and 1920. But this downswing was nowhere near finished. As a result, he predicted, the political crisis that consumed Europe between 1917 and 1921 would not lead to immediate economic collapse. A shaky recovery was possible,

Kondratieff argued, before a depression yet to come. This was completely borne out by events.

Unlike today's Wall Street analysts, Kondratieff was not ultimately interested in the shapes of the waves themselves. He saw the sine waves he'd plotted on to graph paper as evidence of something deeper happening in reality: a succession of alternating 'phases' which, for our purposes, are the most useful tools to understand the fifty-year cycles.[6]

Let's consider in more depth these phases as Kondratieff describes them. The first, up, phase typically begins with a frenetic decade of expansion, accompanied by wars and revolutions, in which new technologies that were invented in the previous downturn are suddenly standardized and rolled out. Next, a slowdown begins, caused by the reduction of capital investment, the rise of savings and the hoarding of capital by banks and industry; it is made worse by the destructive impact of wars and the growth of non-productive military expenditure. However, this slowdown is still part of the up phase: recessions remain short and shallow, while growth periods are frequent and strong.

Finally, a down phase starts, in which commodity prices and interest rates on capital both fall. There is more capital accumulated than can be invested in productive industries, so it tends to get stored inside the finance sector, depressing interest rates because the ample supply of credit depresses the price of borrowing. Recessions get worse and become more frequent. Wages and prices collapse, and finally a depression sets in.

In all this, there is no claim as to the exact timing of events, and no claim that the waves are regular. Kondratieff emphasized that each long wave takes place 'under new concrete-historical conditions, at a new level in the development of the productive forces, and hence is by no means a simple repetition of the preceding cycle'.[7] It is, in short, more new than *déjà vu*.

Now comes Kondratieff's most controversial point. He noticed that the start of each fifty-year cycle was accompanied by trigger events. I will quote him in full, despite the old-fashioned language, because the parallels with the present are striking:

> During roughly the first two decades before the beginning of the rising wave of a long cycle, we observe an invigoration of technical inventions. Before and during the beginning of the rising wave, we observe

the broad application of these inventions to industrial practice, due to the reorganisation of production relations. The beginning of the long cycles usually coincides with an expansion of the orbit of world economic relationships. Finally the beginnings of the last two successive cycles were preceded by major changes in the extraction of precious metals and in monetary circulation.[8]

If we put that into modern English we get the following. The start of a long cycle sees:

- the rollout of new technologies
- the rise of new business models
- new countries dragged into the global market
- a rise in the quantity and availability of money.

The relevance of this list to us is clear: it describes very well what happened to the global economy between the mid-1990s and the Lehman crash. But Kondratieff was convinced such phenomena were not causes, but only triggers. 'We are no way inclined to think that this provides any form of explanation for the causes of long cycles,' he insisted.[9]

Kondratieff was determined to find the cause of long cycles in the economy, not in technology or global politics. And he was right. But in the search for it he relied on theories that had been advanced by Karl Marx to explain the shorter, ten-year business cycles of the nineteenth century: namely, the exhaustion of capital investment and the need for reinvestment.

If, he argued, the 'regular' crises that come along every decade are the result of the need to replace tools and machines, then fifty-year crises are probably caused by 'the wear and tear, replacement and increase in those basic capital goods requiring a long period of time and tremendous investment for their production'.[10] He had in mind, for example, the canal boom of the late eighteenth century and the railway boom of the 1840s.

In Kondratieff's theory, a long wave takes off because large amounts of cheap capital have been accumulated, centralized and mobilized in the financial system, usually accompanied by a rise in the supply of money, which is needed to fund the investment boom. Grandiose investments are begun – canals and factories in the late eighteenth century, railways and urban infrastructures in the mid-nineteenth century. New technology is deployed and new business models created – leading to a struggle for new markets – which stimulates the intensification of wars as rivalries over colonial settlements increase. New social groups associated with the rising industries and technologies clash with the old elites, producing social unrest.

Some of the details are obviously specific to each particular cycle, but what's important in Kondratieff's thesis is the argument about cause and effect. Takeoff is caused by capital accumulating faster than it is invested during the previous depression phase. One effect of this is the search for an expanded supply of money; another is the increased availability of new, cheaper technologies. Once a new growth spurt begins, the effect is a spate of wars and revolutions.

Kondratieff's insistence on economic causes and political/technological effects would come under attack from three directions. First, from Marxists, who insisted that the major turning points in capitalism could only be caused by external shocks. Secondly, from Schumpeter, his contemporary, who argued that long waves are driven by technology, not the rhythms of capital investment. A third set of critics said that in any case Kondratieff's data was at fault and that evidence of waves was overstated.

But Kondratieff was right – and his arguments about causation brilliantly describe what has happened to the economy since 1945. If we can fill in the gaps in Kondratieff's theory we come close to understanding not only how capitalism adapts and morphs in response to crisis, but why this capacity to adapt might reach its limits. I will argue in Part II that we are living through a significant and likely permanent disruption of the patterns industrial capitalism has exhibited for 200 years.

First, though, the critics have to be answered.

THE IMAGINARY CURVE

In 1922, the publication of Kondratieff's first outline of long cycles sparked an immediate controversy. Leon Trotsky, at the time one of the top three leaders of Russian communism, wrote that, if fifty-year cycles existed, 'their character and duration are determined not by the internal interplay of capitalist forces but by those external conditions through whose channel capitalist development flows'.[11]

In the early twentieth century, revolutionary Marxists had become obsessed with the idea that human action – the 'subjective will' – was more important than economics. They felt trapped by economics, which had become the property of moderate socialists who believed revolution was impossible. Kondratieff, Trotsky insisted, had got things the wrong way around:

> The acquisition by capitalism of new countries and continents, the discovery of new natural resources, and, in the wake of these, such major facts of 'superstructural' order as wars and revolutions, determine the character and the replacement of ascending, stagnating or declining epochs of capitalist development.[12]

It may seem strange to those who know Marxism only as a form of economic determinism, but Trotsky was here insisting that political conflict between nations and classes was more important than economic forces. Instead of the long waves, Trotsky argued that Soviet economics should concentrate on explaining the 'entire curve of capitalist development', from birth to takeoff to decline: that is, its whole history. Long waves were interesting, but to those who desired the end of capitalism, the most vital pattern of all was capitalism's complete lifecycle, which must surely be finite.

Marxists had by now evolved their own explanation of the big mutation in business structures after 1890 – which they dubbed 'imperialism' and which, they presumed, was the final or 'highest' stage capitalism could reach. So, confronted with Kondratieff's data, Trotsky too drew a curve – a curve entirely the product of his imagination. It showed the takeoff and decline of an imagined capitalist country over ninety years. The purpose of the chart, Trotsky explained, was to show what a full and painstaking computation of the data might produce. According to him, once you understood the trend-line of a capitalist economy you could understand whether a fifty-year cycle – if it existed at all – was part of the overall upswing, downswing or the end. Trotsky made no apology for the imaginary nature of his curve. The data was not yet good enough to draw a real one, he said, though with work it might be done.

Trotsky's 1922 attack was used then, and has been used since, to refute the idea of long cycles. But it does not. It simply says they are (a) not likely to be regular, caused as they are by external shocks; and (b) need to be fitted into a bigger, single wave-form that is the rise and decline of capitalism itself. Put another way, Trotsky was calling for a better and more historic definition of the 'trend' against which the fifty-year cycles were computed.

This in itself was logical. With all trends, statisticians look for what they call a 'trend break': a clear point where the curve stops rising, flattens out and prepares for a fall. The search for a trend break within capitalism was to obsess left-wing economists throughout the twenti-eth century – and ultimately elude them.

Meanwhile Kondratieff had been busy.

A COLD ROOM IN MOSCOW

In January 1926, Kondratieff published his definitive work, *Long Cycles of the Conjuncture*. On 6 February, the cream of Soviet eco-nomics gathered at Kondratieff's think tank, the Institute for Conjuncture, above Tverskaya Street in Moscow, to rip it to shreds.

The verbatim record of the meeting contains none of the fear and irrationality that Stalin's purges would soon inject into Soviet aca-demic life. The participants speak freely and harshly. They pursue the same three lines of attack that have dominated criticism of Kondrati-eff ever since: that his statistical methods were wrong; that he'd misunderstood the causes of the waves; and that the political conclu-sions were unacceptable.

First, Kondratieff's main opponent, economist Dmitry Oparin, argued that the method he had used to smooth out shorter cycles was false, and had distorted the results. In addition, long-term data on the rise and fall of savings did not support Kondratieff's theory.

Then the seminar turned to the issue of cause-and-effect. The econo-mist V. E. Bogdanov argued that, instead of the rhythm of the long cycles being dictated by capital investment, it must be dictated by innovation. (This makes him the first person to reduce the long-cycle theory to a history of technological innovation, but not the last.)

Bogdanov, however, raised a valid point. It was not logical, he argued, that the cost of building big things such as canals, railways or steel mills should dictate the rhythm of the world economy over fifty years. The objection to a capital-driven cycle led him to propose a tech-driven one, and on this basis he then advanced a more rigorous version of Trotsky's 'external shock' argument.

If long waves did exist, they must, according to Bogdanov, be caused by the 'random intersection of two essentially causal series': the internal dynamics of capitalism and those of the external, non-capitalist environment.[13] For example, the crisis of non-capitalist societies such as China and the Ottoman Empire in the late nineteenth century created new openings for Western capital; the agrarian backwardness of a country like Russia shaped the growth of its capitalist sector, forcing it to seek funds from France and Britain.

Bogdanov had a point. Kondratieff's theory assumed that the rhythms of capitalism exert a one-way gravitational pull on the non-capitalist world. In fact, the two constantly interact, and any synthetic version of Kondratieff's theory would have to take account of that.

Towards the end of the seminar, a long-time Communist Party hack, the agrarian economist Miron Nachimson, weighed in on the political implications of long-wave theory. The obsession with long waves, he said, was ideological. Its purpose was to justify crisis as a normal state of affairs; to say that 'we are dealing with an essentially perpetual movement of capitalism, first upwards and then downwards, and that it is not appropriate to dream of social revolution yet'. Long cycles, Nachimson realized, would pose a big theoretical challenge to Bolshevism, whose premise was capitalism's imminent doom.[14]

The debate gets close to the heart of the problem with Kondratieff's work:

1. He saw the dynamics of capital investment as the primary cause of fifty-year crises. Yet his account of these dynamics was not sophisticated.
2. He assumed the non-capitalist world was the passive bystander to capitalist wave patterns when it was not.

3. At this point, though he saw each wave as a more complicated version of the next, he failed to situate the role of long waves within the ultimate destiny of capitalism.

And there was another, related, problem with Kondratieff's work: the data problem. It has pursued long-cycle theory all the way through from the era of the slide rule to that of the Linux box. We must consider it here because the data problem has acted like a 'no entry' sign to Kondratieff's work for a generation.

THE CHALLENGE OF RANDOM NUMBERS

It's a mark of Kondratieff's ambition that the research group he ran employed one of the great mathematicians of the twentieth century, Eugen Slutsky. And while Kondratieff wrestled with real data, Slutsky was engaged in a project of his own, using random numbers.

Slutsky showed that, by applying a moving average to random data, you can easily generate wave-patterns that look like real economic facts. To prove the point, he produced a wave-pattern from random lottery numbers and superimposed it on to a chart of British growth statistics: when the one was squashed down on to the other, the shapes looked remarkably similar. In statistics, this is known as the 'Yule-Slutsky Effect', and is now understood to mean that the very act of smoothing out data generates spurious results. However, Slutsky believed the opposite. He believed that the emergence of regular wave-patterns from random events was real[15] – not just in economics but in nature:

> It seems probable, that an especially prominent role is played in nature by the process of moving summation with weights of one kind or another, where the magnitude of each consequence is determined by the influence, not of one, but of a number of the preceding causes, as for instance, the size of a crop is determined, not by one day's rainfall, but by many.[16]

In other words, raindrops fall randomly into a square kilometre, but at the end of the season you have a crop yield that you can measure against last year's. The cumulative impact of random events can produce regular, cyclical patterns.

By the time Slutsky wrote this, Kondratieff was becoming dangerous to know. In 1927 conflicts within the Soviet bureaucracy erupted into expulsions and street fighting. Historian Judy Klein points out that it would have been easy for Slutsky to disown Kondratieff, who was under suspicion as an avowed market socialist. Instead, he supported Kondratieff's basic theory.[17]

In fact, Slutsky's experiment added a crucial insight to long-wave theory. He noted that waves generated by filtering random data do not repeat for ever. As he computed them over time, the patterns would suddenly break down, an event he dubbed 'regime change': 'After a more or less considerable number of periods every regime becomes disarranged, the transition to another regime occurring sometimes rather gradually, sometimes more or less abruptly, around certain critical points.'[18]

To anybody interested in the long-range patterns in economics, the challenge posed by Slutsky's observation is clear. First, long waves may not be traceable to a tangible cause – whether it be innovation, external shocks or the rhythms of capital investment. They may just be a regular feature of any complex economic system over time. Secondly, whatever the cause, we should expect regular wave patterns to break down and reset themselves.

Slutsky himself believed this pattern of sudden breakdown could operate at two levels: inside the ten-year business cycle and across the fifty-year long cycles. But his work raises a third possibility. If industrial capitalism has produced a sequence of fifty-year waves over a period of more than 200 years, then maybe at some point this too breaks down, inaugurating a regime change that leads to a whole different pattern.

In the past twenty years there has been a stats-driven backlash against Kondratieff. Various modern studies claim to show that, if better smoothing-out techniques are used, Kondratieff's waves simply disappear, or become patchy. Others correctly point out that the long-term price fluctuations observed within the first three waves disappear once a sophisticated global marketplace emerges after 1945.[19]

However, given the massive amount of extra data and better

methods that we possess, it should be possible to detect Kondratieff waves in the global growth statistics.

In 2010, the Russian researchers Korotayev and Tsirel did just that.[20] They used a technique called 'frequency-analysis' to show convincingly that there are powerful fifty-year pulses in the GDP data. For the post-1945 period, they show that even the raw data contains clear evidence of an up phase after 1945 and a prolonged down phase beginning in 1973.

In fact, using the IMF's definition of recession (six months during which global growth dips below 3 per cent), they calculate that, while there were no recessions for the period 1945–73, there have been six recessions since 1973. They are confident that the Kondratieff wave is present in world GDP figures after 1870, and observable in Western economies before that.

There is more evidence for the existence of long cycles in the work of Cesare Marchetti, an Italian physicist who analysed historical data on energy consumption and infrastructure projects. The result, he concluded in 1986, 'very clearly reveals cyclic or pulsed behaviour' in many areas of economic life, with cycles lasting roughly fifty-five years.[21]

Marchetti rejects the idea that these are waves, or primarily economic – preferring to call them long-term 'pulses' in social behaviour. But, he says, signals that are unclear in economics 'become crystal clear when the "physicals" are analysed'.

Marchetti says that the clearest evidence for long cycles lies in the pattern of investment in physical communication 'grids'. Taking canals, rail, paved roads and airline networks as his examples, he showed how the build-out of each peaked roughly fifty years after the previous technology had done so. On this basis, he predicted that a new type of grid should appear around the year 2000. Though writing a mere fourteen years before the millennium he could not guess what it would be. Today we have the answer: the information network.

There is, then, physical and economic evidence that a fifty-year pattern exists. The wave shapes generated by such a pattern, or pulse, are of secondary importance to the fact of the pattern's existence. To an economist they indicate deeper processes at work – just as for the astrophysicist a black hole can be detected only by the movement of matter around it.

And here's why it's important. Kondratieff gave us a way of understanding *mutations* within capitalism. Left-wing economics had been looking for a process that led only to breakdown. Kondratieff showed how the threat of breakdown usually leads to adaptation and survival.

The problem with Kondratieff remains his account of the economic force that drives the cycle; and how this relates to the ultimate destiny and longevity of the system. It is this we have to fix.

SAVING KONDRATIEFF

I once gave a lecture on Kondratieff to 200 economics students at a British university. They had not a clue who, or what, I was talking about. 'Your mistake,' said an academic to me after the talk, 'was to mix micro- and macro-economics. They are just not used to that.' Another lecturer, whose job it was to teach economic history, had never heard of Kondratieff.

But they'd heard of Josef Schumpeter. In *Business Cycles* (1939), Schumpeter argued that capitalism is shaped by interlocking wave-cycles, ranging from a short-wave three- to five-year cycle produced by the build-up of stocks inside businesses, through to the fifty-year waves Kondratieff had observed.

In a tortuous logical exercise, Schumpeter ruled out the credit cycle, external shocks, changes in taste and what he termed 'growth' as causes of the fifty-year cycle. Instead he argued: 'Innovation is the outstanding fact in the economic history of capitalist society and ... is largely responsible for most of what we would at first sight attribute to other factors.'[22] He then supplied a detailed history of each of Kondratieff's waves as an innovation cycle: the first is triggered by the invention of the factory system in the 1780s, the second driven by railways from 1842, the third by a cluster of innovations we now call the Second Industrial Revolution, in the 1880s and 90s.[23]

Schumpeter took Kondratieff's wave-theory and made it highly attractive to capitalists: in his version the entrepreneur and the innovator drive each new cycle. Conversely, periods of breakdown are the result of innovation becoming exhausted, and capital being hoarded in the finance system. For Schumpeter, crisis is a necessary feature of the capitalist system, in that it promotes the 'creative destruction' of old and inefficient models.

And though Kondratieff was largely forgotten, Schumpeter's work has lived on as a kind of religious insight: a techno-determinist account of boom and bust that mainstream economists can turn to at times of crisis, when their normative beliefs fail.

The most prominent modern follower of Schumpeter, Carlota Perez, has used the tech-driven theory to urge policymakers to give state support to info-tech, biotech and green energy – with the promise of a new 'golden age' to follow sometime in the 2020s, once the next wave takes off.

Perez added some refinements to wave-theory that are useful for understanding the present phase. The most important is her idea of the 'techno-economic paradigm'. It is, she argues, not enough for there to be a cluster of innovations at the start of each wave-cycle, nor for these innovations merely to interact with each other. A 'new common sense, guiding the diffusion of each revolution' has to emerge, a recognizable 'logic of the new' that enables the replacement of one set of technologies and business practices with another.

But by dating the waves from the invention of key technologies, not their rollout, Perez departs both from Kondratieff and Schumpeter. And she proposes a different causal sequence: innovators invent, financiers get excited and speculate, it all ends in tears and the state moves in, regularizing the situation so that a golden age of high growth and productivity can occur.

Perez's supporters say this date sequence is just a repackaging of Schumpeter, with the start-point of each wave dragged twenty-five years earlier. But it is more than that. For her, the primary focus of long-wave theory is 'the irruption and gradual assimilation of each technological revolution', not the upswings and downswings in GDP that were the focus for Kondratieff.[24]

As a result, she is left with all kinds of consistency problems. Why is the fourth wave (1909–71) nearly seventy years long? Because the policy response to the 1930s Depression did not bear fruit until 1945, she answers. Why does the clear sequence 'innovation, bubble, bust' happen twice between 1990 and 2008? Again, she answers, because of policy mistakes.

Perez's version of wave-theory stresses the response of governments at crisis points, but puts very little emphasis on the struggles between classes or the distribution of wealth. In an almost pure inversion of Kondratieff, the economics are driven by technology, and technology is driven by governments.

The attraction of the tech-driven wave-theory is that the evidence for it is tangible: clusters of innovation do take place before the start of long waves, and their synergies can be documented. It is material-ist, in that it sees revolutions and changes in social attitudes as the product of something deeper. New technologies bring to power what Schumpeter called 'new men' – who in turn bring with them their own tastes and norms of consumption.

But Kondratieff was right to reject technology as the driver of big change. It is adequate for describing the start of fifty-year cycles but does not fully explain why the clustering of inventions takes place, nor why a new social paradigm emerges – nor indeed why the wave ends.

If we stick with Kondratieff, and extend his sequence of long cycles to the present, drawing on Marchetti's 'physicals', and much better data than that which was available in the 1920s, we can draw the fol-lowing outline.

Industrial capitalism has gone through four long cycles, leading to a fifth whose takeoff has stalled:

1. 1790–1848: The first long cycle is discernible in the English, French and US data. The factory system, steam-powered machinery and canals are the basis of the new paradigm. The turning point is the depression of the late 1820s. The 1848–51 revolutionary crisis in Europe, mirrored by the Mexican War and Missouri compromise in the USA, forms a clear punctuation point.
2. 1848–mid-1890s: The second long cycle is tangible across the developed world and, by the end of it, the global economy. Railways, the telegraph, ocean-going steamers, stable currencies and machine-produced machinery set the paradigm. The wave peaks in the mid-1870s, with financial crisis in the USA and Europe leading to the Long Depression (1873–96). During the

1880s and 90s, new technologies are developed in response to economic and social crises, coming together at the start of the third cycle.

3. 1890s–1945: In the third cycle heavy industry, electrical engineering, the telephone, scientific management and mass production are the key technologies. The break occurs at the end of the First World War; the 1930s Depression, followed by the destruction of capital during the Second World War terminate the downswing.

4. Late-1940s–2008: In the fourth long cycle transistors, synthetic materials, mass consumer goods, factory automation, nuclear power and automatic calculation create the paradigm – producing the longest economic boom in history. The peak could not be clearer: the oil shock of October 1973, after which a long period of instability takes place, but no major depression.

5. In the late–1990s, overlapping with the end of the previous wave, the basic elements of the fifth long cycle appear. It is driven by network technology, mobile communications, a truly global marketplace and information goods. But it has stalled. And the reason it has stalled has something to do with neoliberalism and something to do with the technology itself.

This is just an outline: a list of start- and end-points, technology clusters and significant crises. To go any further, we need to understand the dynamics of capital accumulation better than Kondratieff did, and in ways the techno-theorists barely touch. We need not only to understand that capitalism mutates but also to understand what within the economy drives the mutations, and what might limit them.

Kondratieff gave us a way to understand what systems theorists call the 'meso' level in economics: something between an abstract model of the system and its concrete history. He left us a better way to understand its mutations than the theories advanced by twentieth century followers of Marx, who focused on external factors and doom scenarios.

We are not done with Kondratieff yet. But to complete what he tried to do we have to dive into a problem that has obsessed economics for more than a century: what causes crisis.

3

Was Marx Right?

In 2008 something bizarre happened to Karl Marx: 'He's Back!' shouted a headline in the London *Times*. The German publishers of Marx's *Capital* reported a 300 per cent increase in sales after a government minister declared his ideas 'not so bad'. Meanwhile in Japan, a manga version of *Capital* went viral. In France Nicolas Sarkozy was photographed leafing through the French edition of Marx's masterpiece.

The catalyst for Marx-mania was, of course, the financial crisis. Capitalism was collapsing. Marx had predicted it so he should be deemed right, or reappraised, or at least allowed some posthumous *schadenfreude*.

But there's a problem. Marxism is both a theory of history and a theory of crisis. As a theory of history it is superb: armed with an understanding of class, power and technology, we can predict the actions of powerful men before they know what they're going to do themselves. But as a theory of crisis, Marxism is flawed. If we are going to utilize Marx in the present situation, we need to understand his limitations – and the theoretical mess his followers got into as they tried to overcome those limitations.

These are not dead questions. The more Marx's bearded face pops up in the panicked pages of mainstream newspapers, and the deeper the social catastrophe inflicted on the youth of tomorrow, the greater the chance becomes that they will try to repeat the failed experiments of Marx's followers: Bolshevism and the forced-march abolition of the market. The premise of this book – that there is a different route beyond capitalism, and different means to achieve it – demands we deal with the Marxist theory of crisis here.

So what's the problem?

Marx understood that capitalism is an unstable, fragile and complex system. He recognized that class gives different agents in the market unequal power. But Marxism underestimated capitalism's capacity to adapt.

The man himself had witnessed only one global adaptation: the upswing of the second long wave in the two decades following the 1848 revolution. Tragically, by the time his followers were in the middle of the third long wave, Marxist economics had stopped evolving as an effective theory of systems.

In the end, three general features of complex adaptive systems were to challenge Marxism. First, such systems tend to be 'open' – that is, they thrive on contact with the world outside. Second, they respond to challenges by innovating and transforming in unpredictable ways, with each innovation producing an intricate new set of opportunities for growth and expansion within the system. Third, they generate 'emergent' phenomena, which can only be studied at a higher level than the workings of the system itself. For example, the behaviour of an ant colony might be a product of the ant's genetic code, but it has to be studied as behaviour, not genetics.

Marxism was, in a way, the most systematic study ever attempted of emergent phenomena, but was constantly confused as to their nature. Only in the 1970s, when the idea of 'relative autonomy' arrived in Marxist economics, did the discipline begin to understand that not all layers of reality are a simple expression of the layers beneath them.

In this chapter, I will show how for the past 100 years capitalism's adaptive nature has confused not only Marxism but the wider left. Yet the original insight of Marx's *Capital*, which describes how market mechanisms lead to breakdown, remains not only valid but essential for understanding the big adaptations.

Marx's theory of crisis, when properly understood, provides a better explanation than Kondratieff for what drives the major mutations – and why they might stop occurring. But the Marx we are concerned with here is a twenty-first-century imagination trapped in a nineteenth-century brain.

WHAT MARX SAID . . .

For the first eighty years of industrial capitalism, economists were pessimistic about its future. The classic economists – Smith, Say, Mill, Malthus and Ricardo – were haunted by doubts as to whether it would survive at all. The theme of their work was the limits to capital: the barriers to its expansion, the decline of profit, the fragility of stable growth.

At the centre of their disputes was the idea that human labour is the source of value and determines the average price of things. This is known as the 'labour theory of value', and in chapter 6 I will explain in detail how it helps us map the transition from capitalism to a non-market economy.

Marx spent his life trying to rectify flaws in the labour-theory, in order to explain the crises and breakdowns early capitalism had been plagued with. According to Marx, a fully fledged market economy creates inherent instability. For the first time in history, there is the possibility of crisis amid abundance. Things are made that cannot be bought or used – a situation that would have seemed crazy under feudalism or in the ancient world.

Marx also recognized a tension in economics between what is real and what we assume is real. The market is a machine for reconciling the two. The real value of things is dictated by the quantity of work, machinery and raw materials used to make them – all measured in terms of labour value – but this can't be calculated in advance. Nor can we see it, because the laws of economics work 'behind the backs' of everybody involved.

This tension drives both the small corrections – as when the market stall has too much fruit at closing time – and the big ones, as when the US government is required to bail out Lehman Brothers. It means that when you study a crisis you have to look for what is wrong at a level deeper than the facts presented on the front page of the *Wall Street Journal*.

Marx argued that in fully fledged capitalism profits have a tendency to converge on the average. So managers – even as their minds tell them they are savagely competing with each other – actually create a discernible average rate of profit in each sector and in the whole economy, against which they set prices and judge performance. Then, via the finance system, they create an aggregate pool of profits into which investors can dip at fairly constant rates of return for any given level of risk. Though the finance sector was small when Marx wrote *Capital*, he grasped very clearly the way finance – in the form of interest – becomes the main mechanism for allocating capital rationally in response to average sectoral risks and rewards.

He also realized that the ultimate source of profit is work; specifically, the extra value coerced out of employees by the unequal power relationships in the workplace. But there is an inbuilt tendency to replace labour with machinery, driven by the need to increase productivity. Since labour is the ultimate source of profit this will tend, as mechanization spreads across the whole economy, to erode the rate of profit. In a company, sector or whole economy where increasing proportions of capital are invested in machinery, raw materials and other non-labour inputs, you are reducing the scope for labour to generate profit. Marx called this 'the most fundamental law of capitalism'.

However, the system reacts to this threat spontaneously: it creates institutions and behaviours that counteract the tendency of the profit rate to fall. Investors switch to new markets where profits are higher; labour costs are driven down by cheapening consumer goods and food; managers search for new sources of cheap labour in foreign countries; or they produce machinery that costs less in labour-terms to make; or they move out of machine-intensive industries into labour-intensive ones; or they pursue market share (profit size) instead of margins (profit rate).

Marx identified the rise of finance as a more strategic counter-tendency: a proportion of investors begin to accept interest – rather than the outright entrepreneurial profit that comes from setting up a company and operating it – as the normal reward for owning large amounts of money. Entrepreneurs will still take one-sided risks, as private capital and hedge funds do today, but large parts of the system are geared to survive on low-risk, low-reward investments via the finance system – which Marx says allows capitalism to go on operating when profits are depressed.

We must be crystal clear on this: *for Marx, these counter-tendencies operate constantly.* A crisis happens only when they become exhausted or break down.[1] That is, when you run out of cheap labour, or new markets fail to appear, or the finance system can no longer safely hold all the capital that risk-averse investors are trying to store there.

In summary, Marx argued that crisis is the pressure valve for the system as a whole. It is a normal feature of capitalism and a product of its technological dynamism.

It can be seen, even from this basic outline, that Marx is modelling capitalism as a complex system. Even when it looks stable, capitalism is not in equilibrium: there is a spontaneous breakdown process counterbalanced by numerous spontaneous stabilizers. Crisis theory explains when and why these stabilizers stop working.

Across the three volumes of *Capital*, Marx describes several forms of crisis. The first is an overproduction crisis, when too many commodities are chasing too little demand, leaving the profits generated in the production process unable to be realized by selling the goods. Marx also expected crises to emerge from the inefficient flow of capital between sectors: he lived through numerous crises where heavy industry had grown out of step with the consumer goods producing sector, leading to a recession until they rebalance. Then there is crisis triggered by the failure of the counteracting tendencies listed above, leading to a tangible collapse in the profit rate, an investment freeze, layoffs and falling GDP.

Finally, in volume III of *Capital*, Marx describes how financial crisis happens: credit becomes massively overextended, and then speculation and crime drive it to unsustainable limits where the bust inevitably overcorrects the boom – pushing the economy into a multi-year depression. In one evocative sentence Marx anticipated the world of Enron, Bernie Madoff and the wealthy 1 per cent. The main function of credit, he wrote, is to develop exploitation 'to the purest and most colossal form of gambling and swindling, and to reduce more and more the number of the few who exploit the social wealth'.[2] In 2008 it was the parallels between the collapse of finance and the famous passage quoted above that provoked the articles claiming Marx was right. Today, as the financial crisis recedes but real incomes stagnate across the Western world, people are once more saying 'Marx was right' – this time on the problem of overproduction, where profits and growth rebound but the workers' wages do not.

However, Marx's theory of crisis is incomplete. It contains logical flaws that took its supporters a long time to resolve, above all at the point where he tries to connect his abstract model to concrete reality. Furthermore, it is a product of its time: Marx could not take into account the major phenomena of the twentieth century – state capitalism, monopolies, complex financial markets and globalization.

In order for Marx to be right – that is, as anything more than a prophet who said 'crisis is normal' – we have to make the theory both internally coherent and consistent with the evidence. We have to fine-tune it so that it includes the features common to complex adaptive systems which it has struggled with: openness, unpredictable response to danger, and long cycles (which lie somewhere between a normal crisis and the final collapse). But even when thus corrected, a theory of cyclical crisis is not enough when faced with the survival-level changes we are exploring in this book.

In a famous line written in 1859, Marx predicted that 'At a certain stage of their development, the material productive forces of society come into conflict with the existing relations of production . . . From forms of development of the productive forces these relations turn into their fetters. Then begins an epoch of social revolution.'[3] But he never explained how the sporadic crises would – or could – create the conditions for the new system. It was left to his followers to fill that gap.

After Marx died, his supporters assumed that overproduction crises could not be alleviated for long by finding or inventing new markets. 'There is a limit to the extension of the markets,' wrote the German socialist leader Karl Kautsky in 1892. 'Today there are hardly any other markets to be opened.'[4] They expected short-term crises to gather momentum and snowball into total collapse. By 1898, the Polish socialist Rosa Luxemburg was predicting that, once the system ran out of new markets to exploit, there would be 'an explosion, a collapse, at which point we will play the role of the *syndic* [administrator] who liquidates a bankrupt company'.[5]

Instead, as we know, the start of its third long cycle saw capitalism mutate. Its adaptive nature enabled it to create markets internally, even when the scramble for colonies reached a dead end. And it proved able to suppress aspects of the market for the sake of its own survival.

The doom premonitions of the Marxist left in the 1890s were proved false. They would first have to live through a massive upswing of capitalism, then through chaos and collapse in the years 1914–21. The impact would disorientate left-wing economics for the best part of a century.

CAPITALISM SUPPRESSES THE MARKET

By 1900 the world economy was in the grip of major change. Technologies, business models, trade patterns and consumption habits had been evolving rapidly side by side. Now they were fused into a new kind of capitalism.

What strikes us today is the audacity and speed of it all: steel replaces iron; electricity replaces gas; the telephone supersedes the telegraph; motion pictures and tabloid newspapers are launched; industrial output surges; spectacular steel-framed buildings appear in the capital cities of the world, and motor cars drive past them.

At the time, however, business leaders took all this for granted. What concerned them was the relationship between large-scale companies and market forces. If possible, they concluded, market forces should be abolished.

'Competition is industrial war,' wrote James Logan, the boss of the US Envelope Company, in 1901. 'Ignorant, unrestricted competition carried to its logical conclusion means death to some of the combatants and injury for all.'[6] At the time, his company enjoyed near-total domination of the US market. At the same time Theodore Vail, the kingpin at Bell Telephone, warned that 'all costs of aggressive, uncontrolled competition are eventually borne, directly or indirectly, by the public'.[7] To relieve the public of such burdens, Vail himself would acquire every single telephone exchange in America.

Competition, argued the business magnates, brought chaos to production and depressed prices to the point where new technology could not be rolled out at a profit. The solutions were to be found at three levels: monopoly, price fixing and protected markets. The means to these ends were (i) mergers, fostered by aggressive new investment banks; (ii) the creation of cartels and 'concerns' to set prices; (iii) government-imposed restrictions on imported goods.

The United States Steel Corporation was formed in 1901 out of 138 different companies, immediately controlling 60 per cent of the market. Meanwhile, Standard Oil had 90 per cent of the USA's refining capacity, and used its power so ruthlessly that it forced railway companies to transport oil at a loss. Bell Telephone enjoyed a total telecoms monopoly until the mid-1890s, and regained it in 1909 when JP Morgan teamed up with Vail to buy up the competition.

In Germany, where price-fixing cartels were politically encouraged and legally registered, their number more than doubled between 1901 and 1911.[8] Just one of these cartels, the Rhine-Westphalia Coal Syndicate, involved sixty-seven companies, had the power to set 1400 different prices and controlled 95 per cent of the region's energy market.[9]

To be absolutely clear, because it's difficult to comprehend today, this was a system where supply and demand did not set prices: millionaires did.

By 1915, two industrial giants dominated the German electrical sector; the chemical, mining and shipping industries likewise each had just two dominant players. In Japan the whole economy was dominated by six *zaibatsu*, conglomerates that had begun as trading companies but evolved into industrial empires, vertically integrated around mining, steel, shipping and weapons with a powerful banking operation at the centre. By 1909, for example, Mitsui produced at least 60 per cent of Japan's electrical engineering output.[10]

To create these massive companies, finance was organized in a new way. In the USA, Britain and France, the stock market and investment banks drove the process. In 1890 there were ten industrial companies quoted on Wall Street; by 1897 more than 200.[11] In Japan and Germany, where industrial capitalism had been created 'from above' under authoritarian governments, finance was mobilized not so much through the stock market but via the banks, and even the state itself. Russia – the latecomer – would adopt a hybrid model, with much of its industry foreign-owned.

The Anglo-Saxon model and the German-Japanese model, therefore, looked very different, and that would provoke a 100-year-long debate over which was best.* But within each lay a variant of the same basic idea: finance took a controlling stake in industry, carving out monopoly positions where possible, suppressing market forces – and the state was directly allied to the whole project.

The market had, in short, become organized. Now it had to be protected. Alongside the scramble for colonies, the great powers threw up numerous tariffs on external trade, explicitly designed to promote the interests of their companies. By 1913, for example, most industrial countries were protecting their domestic industries with double-digit import taxes on manufactured goods.[12] The monopolies, in return, placed key personnel inside governments. The ideology of the state as a 'nightwatchman', standing aloof from economic life, was dead.

The emergence of this new system was not crisis-free. In America, a mini-depression in 1893–7 accelerated the merger process; then in 1907 a financial crash corrected the over-valuation of stocks issued during the merger boom. Both Japan and Germany saw the process of concentration accelerated by short spasms of boom and bust in the 1890s.

But if we take the whole period from around 1895 through to the First World War, progress outweighed crisis: the US economy doubled in size in the decade to 1910, while Canada's trebled.[13] Even in Europe, where the boost from labour migration was not as great, Italy's economy grew by one third in these ten years and Germany's by a quarter.

This was the upswing of the third Kondratieff Wave. You can 'read' the results in the cityscapes of New York, Shanghai, Paris and Barcelona: the most enduring and beautiful public buildings – libraries, pubs, offices, even bath houses – are usually from the period

---

* It is complicated by the fact that the US model evolved after 1911, away from outright monopolies towards a system of regulated competition between big industrial firms, with the real monopoly power concentrated on Wall Street and the newly created Fed. This generated a lot of anti-monopoly bluster from the American right, clouding the fact that throughout the whole period under consideration, monopolies were the norm in the USA.

between 1890 and 1914. The story they tell is clear: during the time we call the *belle époque* or the Progressive Era – a time of rapid growth, liberalization and cultural uplift – the world prospered not through the market but by the controlled suppression of it. Back then, this caused scant confusion for conservatives. The people it confused were the Marxists.

CAPITALISM MUTATES

The task of updating Marxist economics fell to a 33-year-old Austrian doctor called Rudolf Hilferding. Hilferding was a classic intellectual of the *belle époque*: while studying paediatric medicine in Vienna in the late 1890s he threw himself into the economics scene, which had a stellar cast. Eugen Böhm-Bawerk, the economics professor who had written a famous critique of Marx, hosted seminars at which Hilferding would tough it out with, among others, Schumpeter, Ludwig von Mises – the founder of neoliberalism – and a Hungarian student, Jeno Varga, who would make his own spectacular impact later.

In 1906 Hilferding quit medicine and moved to Berlin to teach economics at the training centre of the German socialist party, which formed the intellectual powerhouse of the global left. In 1910 Hilferding gave the fusion of bank and industrial capital a name: 'Through this relationship ... capital assumes the form of finance capital, its supreme and most abstract expression.'[14]

His book, *Finance Capital*, would become the reference point for all left-wing debates on the future of capitalism for a century. Hilferding was the first Marxist to understand the scale of capitalism's mutation. What is more, in the new structure many of the permanent features looked exactly like those Marx had listed as counter-tendencies to the falling profit rate: the export of capital, the export, via migration, of surplus workers to white-colonial settlements abroad, the pooling of profits via the stock market, the move away from entrepreneurship into rentier-style investing.

The finance system, which in the previous century had functioned as a puny redistribution centre for business profit and an unreliable source of capital, now dominated and controlled the business world.

The counter-tendencies to crisis had become synthesized into a new, more stable system.

Hilferding argued that this new structure could suppress cyclical crisis. Big firms and big banks could survive for long periods on low or zero profits. And investors would rather accept prolonged stagnation than see a sudden crisis destroy firms like Siemens, Bell or Mitsui. As a result, crisis periods under finance capitalism would be long and stagnant rather than sharp and traumatic. Banks would suppress speculation because they understood its destructive power. Cartels would suppress the operation of market forces – and therefore crisis – for major firms, dumping the losses on less powerful sectors of the economy. Small firms would bear the brunt of any recessions, hastening their acquisition by monopolies.

For Hilferding, the forces of instability had not disappeared, but had been driven into a single sphere: the imbalance between the production and consumption-oriented sectors of the economy. He explicitly ruled out 'under-consumption' as a cause of crisis, pointing out that capitalism could always create new markets where old ones were exhausted, and thus go on expanding output. But the possibility remained that sectors would expand at different rates. Hence the need for state intervention to prevent such an imbalance.

Hilferding's book was a massively influential reality-check for the left. It dispensed with the thesis of the 'snowballing crisis' as the trigger for social change; it introduced concepts and terms that Marxism would share with mainstream economics. And it said – earlier than Schumpeter – that the main driver of innovation was now the big company using applied science, not the entrepreneur tinkering in his workshop.[15]

But Hilferding's book steered left-wing economics into a dead end. Though he described finance capital as only the 'latest stage' of the system, the implication was that it would be the last. A system in which finance capital dominates, he wrote, is the 'supreme and most abstract' form of capitalism and it can go no further:

> The socializing function of finance capital facilitates enormously the task of overcoming capitalism. Once finance capital has brought the most important branches of production under its control, it is enough

for society, through its conscious executive organ – the state conquered by the working class – to seize finance capital in order to gain immediate control of these branches of production.

Hilferding was a moderate socialist and would become more moderate as time went on. He believed capitalism would gradually evolve into socialism. His ideas, however, influenced reformists and revolutionaries alike. Both wings of the labour movement became wedded to the belief that socialism could be introduced by taking control of the state and the organized market. Finance capital was, as Lenin later put it, 'moribund capitalism, capitalism in *transition* to socialism . . . *already* dying capitalism'.[16] All that the socialists differed on was the kind of action needed to make it die.

What's important is that Hilferding not only tied socialism to a project of state-led transition, but also that he effectively ruled out any further mutation of capitalism beyond the model established in the 1900s. And his basic theory remained influential well into our lifetime. As late as the 1970s you could argue that, though capitalism had survived longer than expected, it was still essentially a state-directed, heavily monopolized and national system. Left-wing workers could rationally believe that a world of state-owned airlines, steel mills and auto companies was stage two of the progression: free markets -> monopoly -> socialism.

This was the idea that died after 1989, with the collapse of the Soviet bloc, the rise of globalization and the creation of the fragmentary, marketized and privatized economy we see today. The progression Hilferding imagined, which had implicitly guided socialism for eighty years, has been broken and indeed reversed.

While it lasted, though, the doctrine of an inevitable linear transition – from Standard Oil to socialism – was all-powerful.

THE LEFT'S NEED FOR CATASTROPHE

By 1910, when Hilferding's book came out, social-democracy was influential in every advanced country. Its acknowledged nerve-centre was Berlin, and the work of its German-speaking leaders would be translated and discussed in the factories of Chicago, the gold mines of New South Wales and clandestine cells aboard Russian battleships. But even as workers digested Hilferding's message, something rang false. Mass strikes were in progress, from the New York garment workers to the streetcar drivers of Tokyo and all points between. There was a war brewing in the Balkans. For a system that had supposedly become crisis-free, politically and socially there was turmoil.

Rosa Luxemburg, who had now replaced Hilferding at the Berlin socialist training school, began work on a massive book that would refute his stability thesis. Luxemburg had promoted mass strikes and attacked militarism – indeed, attacked Lenin for his elitist conception of revolutionary politics. Now she attacked Hilferding.

Luxemburg's 1913 book, *The Accumulation of Capital*, was written with twin purposes: to explain the economic motivation for the colonial rivalry between the big powers, and to show that capitalism was doomed. In the process she produced the first modern theory of under-consumption.

By reworking Marx's calculations she proved, to herself at least, that capitalism is in a permanent state of overproduction. It is forever beset by the problem of too little spending power among the workers. So it is forced to open up colonies, not just as sources of raw material but as markets. The military costs incurred while conquering and defending colonies have the added benefit of soaking up excess capital. It is, said Luxemburg, akin to waste or luxury consumption: it drains off excess capital.

Since colonial expansion was the only pressure valve in a system prone to crisis, Luxemburg predicted that once the entire globe had been colonized, and capitalism introduced across the colonial world, the system must collapse. Capitalism, she concluded, is 'the first mode of economy which is unable to exist by itself, which needs other economic systems as a medium and soil. Although it strives to become universal . . . it must break down because it is immanently incapable of becoming a universal form of production.'[17]

Her book was immediately torn to shreds – by Lenin and by most of the socialist professors she had worked with. They argued, correctly, that any mismatch between production and consumption was temporary, and would be solved by capital investment moving from heavy industry to consumer goods. In any case, new colonial markets were not the only escape valve from crisis.

But Luxemburg's book went on to become hugely significant. It introduced the idea of 'final crisis' into left-wing economics. It expressed the intuition felt by many activists that monopoly, finance and colonialism were, even amid the peace and prosperity of the 1900s, storing up an almighty final catastrophe. By the 1920s, under-consumption became the left's main theory of crisis and – once things calmed down – provided its common ground with Keynesian economics for the next fifty years.

Luxemburg remains relevant because she identified something critical to the debate on postcapitalism today: the importance of an 'outside world' for systems that successfully adapt.

If we ignore her obsession with colonies and military spending, and instead simply say that 'capitalism is an open system', then we are nearer to acknowledging its adaptive nature than those who had followed Marx in trying to model it as a closed one.

What irked the socialist professors about Luxemburg was precisely this insight: that, throughout its entire history and as part of its essence, capitalism must interact with an outside world that is not capitalist. Once the immediate outside world is transformed – indigenous societies annihilated, peasants cleared from the land – it has to find new places to repeat the process.

But Luxemburg was wrong to limit this to the possession of colonies. New markets can also be created at home, not just by boosting the workers' spending power, but by transforming non-market activities into market ones. And it is curious that Luxemburg missed this, for just such a transformation was going on all around her.

Even as she worked on her book, the first cars were coming off the Ford production line at Highland Park, Detroit. The Victor Gramophone Company was selling 250,000 machines a year in the USA. When she started writing in 1911, Berlin had just one dedicated movie theatre; by 1915 there would be 168.[18] The spectacular upswing of the third long wave (1896–1945) was unfolding, above all, as the expansion of a new consumer market among the lower-middle class and skilled workers. Leisure, the ultimate non-market activity in the nineteenth century, was becoming commercialized.

Luxemburg had ignored the fact that new markets are formed in a complex way, interactively, and that they can be created not only in colonies but within national economies, local sectors, people's homes and indeed inside their brains.

The real question posed by Luxemburg's insight is not 'what happens when the whole world is industrialised', but what happens if capitalism runs out of ways to interact with an outside world? On top of that, what happens if it can't create new markets within the existing economy? As we'll see, this is exactly the problem information technology poses for capitalism today.

THE GREAT DISORIENTATION

In January 1919 Rosa Luxemburg was murdered by a right-wing militia, her body thrown into a canal, following a failed insurrection in Berlin. Rudolf Hilferding died – either by suicide or torture – in a Gestapo cell in Paris in 1941. Between these two events, the economics of anti-capitalism were to become seriously disorientated.

Luxemburg had always opposed Bolshevism, predicting that if Lenin's party took power in Russia it would end up ruling autocratically. But by the mid-1920s, with supreme irony, her theory had become the state doctrine of the Soviet Union. To understand why, and how the consequences still haunt the left, we have to understand what people lived through in the early 1920s – which was chaos.

The years 1919–20 saw the sharpest boom-bust cycle in history. Rampant inflation was followed by sudden hikes in interest rates, which produced a stock market crash reverberating from Washington to Tokyo. Mass unemployment and giant factories lying idle kept output levels well below those of 1914.

Amid this came events most socialists hadn't dared dream of. The 1917 Revolution in Russia was just over a year old when workers' republics sprang up in Bavaria and Hungary. Germany headed off a socialist revolution only through far-reaching reforms at the outset of the Weimar Republic, including the promise to 'socialize' the economy. The year 1919 saw the seizure of factories in Italy, strike action bordering on insurgency in both France and Scotland, general strikes in Seattle and Shanghai. All across the Western world, mainstream politicians had to face the possibility of revolution.

By now the left had more than just Luxemburg's book to go on. During the war, both Lenin and the Bolshevik theorist Nikolai Bukharin had produced works inspired by Hilferding, each drawing the conclusion that finance-dominated capitalism was proof of the system's imminent doom. Lenin called this new, declining model 'imperialism', and defined it as 'capitalism in transition'. The scale of organization – by vertically integrated corporations, cartels and the state – meant that the economy was actually becoming socialized under capitalism: 'Private property relations,' Lenin wrote in *Imperialism* (1916), 'constitute a shell which no longer fits its contents, a shell which must inevitably decay if its removal is artificially delayed, a shell which may remain in a state of decay for a fairly long period . . . but which will inevitably be removed.'[19]

Bukharin's pamphlet, written in an all-night library in New York in 1915, went further. He asserted that, because nation states had become aligned with the interests of their dominant industrial companies, the only form of competition left was war.[20]

If these pamphlets were venerated on the left for decades it was because, though written by amateur economists, they told a story coherent with the data. Monopoly led to colonial conquest; that in turn led to total war – and war led to revolution. Financial dominance led to organized capitalism, which was ripe for takeover by the working class to run on socialized lines.

Both Lenin and Bukharin spent considerable time demolishing the idea that any new kind of capitalism could emerge, in which transnational cooperation could exist. It was the moderate German socialist Kautsky who'd had this brainwave on the eve of the First World War: he envisaged the creation of a single world market dominated by transnational corporations. But by the time his article 'Ultra-imperialism' was published, the war had begun and the whole issue might have seemed academic.[21]

But the Bolsheviks understood that Kautsky's ultra-imperialism thesis was a major challenge to them. Their attack on it spelled out in clear terms that capitalism had reached its limits, that seizure of power at the first opportunity was necessary, and that all talk of the working class needing 'more time' to become better educated and more politically mature was wrong.

There was, in the Bolsheviks' eyes, a clear dialectical progression – from free market to monopoly, from colonization to global war. Once this had taken place, their philosophical scheme could brook no further evolution: capitalism could not progress except to its own destruction.

By now, the whole far left had effectively accepted one of Luxemburg's key proposals: crisis theory should describe the finality of capitalism – not its cyclical movement.

Between 1917 and 1923 both wings of socialism got to test out the idea that workers could use state power to socialize capitalism.

In January 1919, Hilferding joined the German government's socialization commission in Berlin, which for four months attempted to nationalize and plan the economy. But the project collapsed at the design stage, after obstruction by moderate socialists and liberals in government. In Austria – a new country formed from the ruins of the Austro-Hungarian Empire – socialization was more successful. The Socialist-Christian coalition government pushed through a law allowing the nationalization of failing firms, but a socialist plan to take over the banking system was rejected. In the end, Austria was left with three significant state enterprises: a shoe factory, a pharmaceuticals plant and the arsenal of the Austro-Hungarian Empire, which the government tried to convert into a diversified manufacturing company. The fate of this project is best summed up by the man who tried to run it: 'The problem before the newly founded corporation was to employ its men and machines in producing goods for which a market had yet to be created.'[22]

In Hungary, during the brief Soviet republic of 1919, Jeno Varga, a one-time acolyte of Hilferding in the Vienna seminars, became finance minister. He decreed that all businesses with more than twenty workers should be nationalized. All large shops were closed to prevent the middle classes buying luxury goods and using them as investments. Land was nationalized. Soon the Hungarian workers' republic faced another problem. Factories needed managing, but the workers could not manage. Varga outlined the problem frankly:

The members of the works committees endeavoured to evade productive labour. In the capacity of controllers, they all sat round the office table . . . they sought to win the favour of the workers, through concessions in discipline, in the amount of work exacted, and in wages, to the detriment of the general interest.'[23]

The works committees, in other words, acted in the interest of workers and not of the commissars.

In Russia, the Bolsheviks had overcome such problems by introducing military discipline into the factories and abolishing workers' control. Now they had a bigger problem: the economy was collapsing under the strain of industrial chaos, shortages and the refusal of peasants to supply grain to the cities.

In 1920 Bukharin outlined a solution: a detailed plan to move rapidly from this improvised system, known as 'war communism', to a permanent one of central planning across the entire economy. Lenin scrapped this a year later, as starvation and chaos forced the Bolsheviks to switch to a crude form of market socialism.

For decades, the leaders of pre-war social-democracy had insisted it was pointless to outline a plan for what they would do if they gained power. This was something everybody from the Bolsheviks to the moderates who ran the British Labour Party agreed on: their entire mindset had been created in opposition to utopian socialism, with its doomed experiments and dreams. They recognized that technological progress and business reorganization were so rapid in the run-up to 1914 that any plan locked in the drawer at the party HQ would be outmoded by the time it was needed. They knew they had to control or nationalize the finance system; they knew there would be a conflict between the needs of farmers and urban consumers, as you can't satisfy both at once. But they showed very little forethought about the problem that would take down both the reformist and revolutionary versions of socialization: namely, the independent action of workers, pursuing their own short-term interests, and its conflict with the need for technocratic management and centralized planning.

From Varga's recalcitrant works committees in Budapest to the Russian workers who insisted on self-control, or the Fiat workers in Milan who even tried to produce cars without the help of managers, this problem – workers control *vs* planning – would hit the socialist leaders as a total surprise.

If these early attempts at socialism failed, it is worth remembering that capitalist attempts at stabilization also failed. The peace deal of 1919 condemned Germany's recovery to stall under the stranglehold of reparations. 'In continental Europe,' wrote a distraught John Maynard Keynes, shortly after storming out of the British delegation at Versailles, 'the earth heaves and no one but is aware of the rumblings. There it is not just a matter of extravagance or "labour troubles"; but of life and death, of starvation and existence, and of the fearful convulsions of a dying civilization.'[24]

With hindsight, we can see 1917–21 as a near-terminal social crisis, but as an economic crisis it was not inevitable; it was the result of poor policy decisions. For Germany it was the outcome of unpayable war reparations; in Britain and the USA it was caused by central banks setting interest rates too high, to choke off the 1919 boom. In Austria and Hungary it was the result of being hung out to dry at Versailles, with huge debts and no more empire to pay for them.

After 1921, the situation began to stabilize. Kondratieff, as we've seen, described 1917–21 as just the first crisis in a long downswing. But stabilization left the Marxists who had embraced the sequence 'monopoly–war–collapse' with nowhere to go. Capitalism, they assumed, remained on life support simply due to the immaturity of the proletariat, the unwillingness among workers to take power – plus tactical mistakes by socialist parties. Lenin allowed for the possibility of growth spurts in this or that sector, but not for the entire system's survival.

But by 1924 Lenin was dead, Trotsky had been sidelined and Stalin was in control; Varga, who'd fled Hungary for Moscow, was his chief economist. Stalin did not need a theory to explain complexity – he needed a theory of certainty. The certainty of capitalism's eventual collapse would justify the attempt to build what all left-wing economists said was impossible: 'socialism in one country' – and an extremely backward country at that. The basis for a theory of catastrophe had been laid in Luxemburg's book but it needed more, and this was supplied by Varga.

'Varga's Law' predicted the constant decline of workers' real incomes. This, he wrote, 'is the economic basis for the general crisis of capitalism ... the absolute impoverishment of the working class comes to the fore'.[25] Varga was explicit: the downward trend of mass consumption was a non-cyclical, general feature of the twentieth century and would, given time, destroy all support for reformist and liberal politics among workers. Instead of growth there would be, in Varga's phrase, 'decumulation'.

It's hard to remember now how powerful such ideas became once they were spread by word of mouth across the kitchen tables of the working class. In the 1920s and 30s, Varga's Law was a phrase routinely used by labour movement activists. It made sense of their own experience: wasn't the whole strategy of British and French governments in the 1920s to enforce wage cuts? And when the collapse occurred, in 1929, didn't the American government make things worse on purpose, in an attempt to drive down wages? Though completely wrong, the prestige of under-consumption theory soared.

Varga himself produced work of some subtlety in the 1930s. As a follower of Luxemburg, he remained aware that conditions in the world beyond the developed economies could impact on crisis dynamics – so he placed a heavy emphasis on the failure of agriculture in the colonial world as a factor suppressing economic revival in the West. As a result, the 'authorized version' of Marxist economics – inevitable and imminent collapse – was plausible. Even the Trotskyists, hounded by Stalin, were convinced of capitalism's doom by the late 1930s, their leader insisting that 'the productive forces stagnate'.[26]

In a global labour movement now dominated by the Moscow variant of Marxism, no possibility other than collapse was allowed.

Marx had tried to describe capitalism in the abstract: to use a minimum number of general concepts and work upwards from that towards an explanation of the complex, surface reality of crisis. So in Marx, the falling profit rate produces counter-tendencies at many levels of abstraction, both in the pure world of aggregated profits and the dirty world of colonies and exploitation. For Marx, while every real crisis has a concrete cause, the aim is to explain the deep process at work behind all crises.

But the first major structural mutation of capitalism could not be contained within this framework. Finance capitalism created a new reality.

In the 1900s, the attempt to understand finance capitalism inevitably pulled Marxist theory towards concrete phenomena: to questions of sector mismatches and low consumption, to the multi-sector economy, to real prices rather than the abstract amounts of labour Marx dealt in.

This focus on the 'real' led Hilferding to conclude the cyclical crisis was over, Luxemburg to move crisis theory to the terrain of collapse, Lenin to assume the irreversibility of economic decline. With Varga, we move from rationality to dogma: the least sophisticated of all the crisis theories becomes the unchallengeable doctrine of a merciless state, every communist party in the world becomes its emissary, and every left-wing intellectual for a generation gets taught utter rubbish.

Throughout the whole debate, the participants were haunted by its political implications in a way no social scientist should be. If Hilferding is right, said Luxemburg, then socialism is not inevitable. It becomes a 'luxury' for the working class. They can just as easily choose to coexist with capitalism, and – given their political consciousness – probably will. So Luxemburg was driven to search for an objective rationale for breakdown.

However, all forms of under-consumption theory have an Achilles heel: what if capitalism *does* find a way of overcoming the low spending power of the masses? By 1928, Bukharin was struck by the intuition that it had done so. Capitalism, he claimed, had stabilized in the 1920s – not temporarily, nor partially – and unleashed a new surge of technical innovation. The cause of this surge, he said, was the emergence of 'state capitalism' – a fusion of monopolies, banks and cartels with the state itself.[27]

With this, crisis theory had come full circle, back to the possibility that organized capitalism could suppress crisis. Bukharin's misfortune was to say it on the eve of the Wall Street Crash, amid a factional dispute with Stalin. He was expelled from the party leadership and, despite an uneasy decade trying to coexist with Stalin and publicly recanting his former views, was executed like Kondratieff in 1938.

THE PROBLEM WITH CRISIS THEORY

It was not until the 1970s that a solid body of academic work began linking the disparate parts of Marx's theory into a usable whole. Despite the achievements of economists from the New Left generation in clarifying and rescuing the real Marx, the fundamental problem remains: to understand the fate of capitalism, and its major mutations, crisis theory is not enough.

There is, as Marx suggested, a process whereby labour is expelled by machinery; the result is a tendency for the profit-rate to fall. There is an equal tendency for falling profits to be offset by adaptation (the counteracting tendencies), and a cyclical crisis is what happens when these adaptations break down.

But Kondratieff shows us how at a certain point – when crises become frequent, deep and chaotic – a more structural adaptation is triggered. Because their economic model could not accommodate structural adaptation, Marxists in the early twentieth century had to describe this in terms of historical 'epochs', or philosophical categories such as parasitism, decay and transition.

In fact, the moment of mutation is fundamentally economic. It is the exhaustion of an entire structure – of business models, skill-sets, markets, currencies, technologies – and its rapid replacement by a new one.

It happens – in systems terminology – at the 'meso' level, between micro- and macro economics. Its scale locates it somewhere between the credit cycle and the doom of the entire system. Once the mutations are understood as likely and regular events, then any model of capitalism that treats them as accidental or optional is going to be wrong.

There is no form of crisis theory that can contain the whole phenomenon of system mutation, but crisis theory can describe what causes it in each specific case.

Modern crisis theory has to be macro-economic, not abstract. It can use abstractions to locate fundamental market mechanisms, as Marx does, but you cannot ignore the state as an economic force, organized labour, monopolies, currencies or central banks. Nor can you ignore the finance system as an accelerator of crisis, and – in the present context – the effects of financialized consumer behaviour, the instabilities injected by fiat money, which allows credit expansion and speculation on a scale nineteenth-century capitalism could not have withstood.

In this sense Hilferding, Luxemburg and the rest were not 'bad Marxists' when they began to move away from abstractions and towards the concrete facts: they were being good materialists. Their mistake was to assert that monopolized state capitalism is the only pathway to a post-capitalist system. We can be certain today that it is not.

Marxist economists have made perceptive contributions to our understanding of what happened in 2008. The French economist Michel Husson and New School professor Ahmed Shaikh have both demonstrated how neoliberalism restored profit rates from the late 1980s onward. But these show a sharp fall in the final years before the 2008 financial crisis.[28] Husson argues, correctly, that neoliberalism 'solves' the problem of profitability – for both individual firms (by suppressing labour costs) and for the system as a whole (by massively expanding financial profits). But alongside higher profits, the overall rate of investment after the 1970s is low.

This conundrum of rising profits alongside falling investment should be the real focus for modern crisis theory. But there is a fairly clear explanation: in the neoliberal system, firms use profits to pay dividends rather than to reinvest. And in conditions of financial stress – obvious after the Asian crisis of 1997 – they use profits to build up cash reserves as a buffer against a credit crunch. They also relentlessly pay down debt, and in the good times buy back shares as a kind of windfall profit distribution to their financial owners. They are minimizing their exposure to being financially exploited, and maximizing their own ability to play in the financial markets.

So while Husson and Shaikh successfully demonstrate a 'falling profit rate' prior to 2008, the crisis is a result of something bigger and more structural. Its cause (as Larry Summers suggested in his work on secular stagnation) is the sudden disappearance of factors that had compensated for inefficiency and low productivity for decades.[29]

The determination to trace crises in general to one abstract cause, ignoring the structural mutation that was actually going on, was the original source of confusion in Marxist theory. This time around we have to avoid it. The account must be concrete: it must include the real structures of capitalism: states, corporations, welfare systems, financial markets.

The crisis that broke out in 2008 was not the result of a breakdown of this or that counteracting factor, or due to a short-term fall in the profit rate. It was the breakdown of an entire system of factors supporting the profit rate, called neoliberalism. Neoliberalism was neither a great boom nor, as some claim, a hidden period of stagnation. It was a failed experiment.

THE PERFECT WAVE

In the next chapter I will explain what led to this experiment. I will describe in detail how the fourth Kondratieff Wave unfolded between 1948 and 2008; what disrupted it and what prolonged it. I will propose that the impact of technology, and the sudden availability of a new outside world, created a break in the long-term pattern.

First we must establish – as a mental tool – a model of a normal wave. Kondratieff was right to warn that each wave, building on the next, creates a new version of the pattern. But only by distilling the essence of the first three waves can we see how the fourth diverged.

What follows is my 'normative' restatement of long-cycle theory, merged with what is rational about the Marxist understanding of crisis:

1. The start of a wave is usually preceded by the build-up of capital in the finance system, which stimulates the search for new markets and triggers the rollout of clusters of new technologies. The initial surge sparks wars and revolutions, leading at some point to the stabilization of the world market around a new set of rules or arrangements.
2. Once the new technologies, business models and market structures begin to work in synergy – and the new 'technological paradigm' is obvious – capital rushes into the productive sector, fuelling a golden age of above-average growth with few

recessions. Since profit is everywhere, the concept of allocating it rationally between players becomes popular, as does the possibility of redistributing wealth downwards. The era feels like one of 'collaborative competition' and social peace.

3. Throughout the whole cycle, the tendency to replace labour with machines operates. But in the upswing, any fall in the profit rate is counterbalanced by the expanded scale of production, so overall profits rise. In each of the up cycles, the economy has no trouble absorbing new workers into the workforce even as productivity increases. By the 1910s, for example, the glass-blower displaced by machinery becomes the projectionist in a cinema, or the worker on a car production line.

4. When the golden age stalls, it is often because euphoria has produced sectoral over-investment, or inflation, or a hubristic war led by the dominant powers. There is usually a traumatic 'break point' – where uncertainty over the future of business models, currency arrangements and global stability becomes general.

5. Now the first adaptation begins: there is an attack on wages and an attempt to de-skill the workforce. Redistribution projects, such as the welfare state or the public provision of urban infrastructure, come under pressure. Business models evolve rapidly in order to grab what profit there is; the state is urged to organize more rapid change. Recessions become more frequent.

6. If the initial attempt to adapt fails (as it did in the 1830s, 1870s and 1920s), capital retreats from the productive sector and into the finance system, so that crises assume a more overtly financial form. Prices fall. Panic is followed by depression. A search begins for more radical new technologies, business models and new supplies of money. Global power structures become unstable.

At this point we need to factor in the concept of 'agents': social groups pursuing their own interests. A problem with the Schumpeter-inspired version of wave-theory is its tendency to obsess about innovators and technologies, and not see classes. When we look closely at social history, each 'failed adaptation' phase happens because of working-class resistance; each successful one is organized by the state.

During the first long wave, roughly between 1790 and 1848 in Britain, you have an industrial economy trapped within an aristocratic state. A prolonged crisis begins in the late 1820s, characterized by the factory owners' determination to survive by de-skilling the workforce and cutting wages, and also by chaos in the banking system. Working-class resistance – the Chartist movement culminating in the General Strike of 1842 – forces the state to stabilize the economy.

But in the 1840s a successful adaptation takes place: the Bank of England gains a monopoly over the issue of banknotes; factory legislation ends the dream of replacing the skilled male workers with women and children. The Corn Laws – a protective tariff favouring the aristocracy – are abolished. Income tax is levied and the British state finally begins to function as a machine for the ruling industrial capitalists, not as a battleground between them and the old aristocracy.

In the second wave – which starts with Britain, Western Europe and North America but pulls in Russia and Japan – the downswing begins in 1873. The system tries to adapt through the creation of monopolies, with agrarian reform, an attack on skilled wages and by pulling in new migrant workers where possible as cheap labour. Countries move on to the Gold Standard, form currency blocs and impose trade tariff measures. But sporadic instability still plagues growth. The 1880s see the first mass workers' movements. Though the movements themselves are often defeated, skilled workers succeed spectacularly in resisting automation, while unskilled workers benefit from the beginnings of a social welfare system. Only in the 1890s, as monopolies become fused with banks or backed by a liquid financial market, does a strategic change take place. A cluster of radically new technologies is deployed and – as in the 1840s – there is a step change in the economic role of the state. The state – whether in Berlin, Tokyo or Washington – becomes indispensable to maintaining optimum conditions for big monopoly companies through tariffs, empire expansion and infrastructure building.

Once more, it is working-class resistance that prevents the system adapting on the cheap, without technological innovation.

For the third wave, if we take 1917–21 as the start of the downswing, the system adapts by tightening state control of industry, and by trying to revive the Gold Standard. In most countries there is an attack on wages during the 1920s but they do not fall fast enough to solve the crisis. Then, once the Depression begins, fear of social unrest pushes each major country to pursue a competitive exit route: destroying the Gold Standard, creating closed trading blocs, using state spending to boost growth and reduce unemployment.

In emphasizing this, I am making what I consider a crucial addition to wave-theory: in each long cycle, the attack on wages and working conditions at the start of the downswing is one of the clearest features of the pattern. It sparks the class warfare of the 1830s, the unionization drives of the 1880s and 90s, the social strife of the 1920s. The outcome is critical: if the working class resists the attack, the system is forced into a more fundamental mutation, allowing a new paradigm to emerge. But in the fourth wave we found out what happens if the workers do not successfully resist.

The role of the state in creating the new paradigm is equally clear. The 1840s see the triumph of the Currency School economists, who impose sound money on British capitalism by insisting the Bank of England has a monopoly on issuing notes. In the 1880s and 90s, there is the rise of state intervention. In the 1930s, it is outright state capitalism and fascism.

The history of long cycles shows that only when capital fails to drive down wages and when new business models are swamped by poor conditions is the state forced to act: to formalize new systems, reward new technologies, provide capital and protection for innovators.

The role of the state in major transformations has been well understood. By contrast, the importance of class has been underplayed. Carlota Perez's work on long cycles deals with workers' resistance as a sub-set of the more general problem of 'resistance to change'. For me workers' resistance plays a crucial role in shaping the next long wave.

If the working class is able to resist wage cuts and attacks on the welfare system, the innovators are forced to search for new technologies and business models that can restore dynamism on the basis of higher wages – through innovation and higher productivity, not exploitation. In general, for the first three long cycles, working-class resistance did force capitalism to reinvent itself on the basis of existing or higher consumption levels (although the flipside was that imperial powers then sought ever more brutal ways to extract profits from the periphery).

In Perez's account of long waves, resistance to the death of the old system is cast as futile. A line is drawn 'between those who look back with nostalgia, trying to hold on to past practices, and those who embrace the new paradigm'.[30]

However, once you factor in class, wages and welfare states, working-class resistance can be technologically progressive; it forces the new paradigm to emerge on a higher plane of productivity and consumption. It forces the 'new men and women' of the next era to promise and find ways of delivering a form of capitalism that is more productive and which can raise real wages.

Long cycles are not produced by just technology plus economics, the third critical driver is class struggle. And it is in this context that Marx's original theory of crisis provides a better understanding than Kondratieff's 'exhausted investment' theory.

WHAT CREATES THE WAVE?

Marx's theory effectively describes where the energy that creates the fifty-year wave comes from. If we strip away the false additions made by his followers, we can understand what was right about Marx, and where it fits with the fifty-year mutations we've described.

The falling profit rate and its counteracting tendencies can be assumed to operate throughout the fifty-year cycle. Breakdowns happen when the counter-tendencies become exhausted. In the immature capitalism of the nineteenth century, they were frequent – but always more frequent in the decline phase. Marx, for example, underestimated the possibility that working-class resistance to wage cuts could be a factor in triggering profit crises. However, the falling profit rate – fundamental as it is – now operates beneath layer upon layer of social practice designed to counteract it.

Kondratieff's account – which said that the fifty-year cycles were driven by the need to renew major infrastructure – was far too simplistic. Better to say each wave generates a specific and concrete solution to falling profit rates during the upswing – a set of business models, skills and technologies – and that the downswing starts when this solution becomes exhausted or disrupted. The most effective forms of the solution during the upswing are the ones Marxist theory describes at a deep level within the production process: increased productivity, cheaper inputs, a rising mass of profits. Once the wave inverts and the solution's downturn begins, it is the more contingent surface factors that tend to kick in. Can new markets be found outside the system? Will investors take a reduced portion of profit in the form of dividends?

The tendency of the rate of profit to fall, interacting constantly with the counter-tendencies, is a much better explanation of what drives the fifty-year cycle than the one Kondratieff gave. And once you meld the two, long-cycle theory becomes a much more powerful tool than the orthodox Marxist left suspected.

Put simply: fifty-year cycles are the long-term rhythm of the profit system.

An arrangement that allows for the rapid replacement of labour by machinery works for a while, generating expanded profits, and then breaks down. This is my alternative to Kondratieff's 'exhaustion of investment' thesis.

As to financial crisis, it is always possible during the up phase of the long cycle (for example in the US panic of 1907) – but virtually certain during the down phase. As capital flows out of the troubled productive sector and into finance, it destabilizes the latter, leading to speculative boom-bust cycles. And across the first three long cycles capital became more financially sophisticated and complex overall.

A final observation concerns the need for capitalism to interact with a world outside to search for new markets for goods and a new labour supply. This is a crucial consideration in systems theory but is underplayed by Marxist crisis theory with its focus on closed and abstract models.

During the nineteenth century there was a ready internal market waiting to be developed within most capitalist countries provided that the agrarian economy could survive the shock of disruption. Likewise, an ample labour supply was on hand. But after 1848, adaptation also involved the search for external markets.

By the start of the twentieth century, the internal supply of labour was constrained – in part by the working-class resistance to child and female labour, in part by the birth-rate. As for new markets, by the 1930s virtually the whole world was cordoned off into closed trading blocs.

With the fourth wave, a substantial part of the world outside is initially closed off. Once the Cold War starts, about 20 per cent of the world's GDP is being produced outside the market.[31] After 1989 the sudden availability of new markets and a new labour force plays an important part in prolonging the wave; so does the West's new freedom of action to shape markets in neutral countries that were formerly off-limits.

In other words, between 1917 and 1989 capitalism's full potential for complex adaptive behaviour was suppressed. After 1989 it experienced a sugar-rush: labour, markets, entrepreneurial freedom and new economies of scale. On this basis, 1989 must – on its own – account for some of the phase-distortion story I am about to tell. But it cannot account for all of it.

The long-wave pattern has been disrupted. The fourth long cycle was prolonged, distorted and ultimately broken by factors that have not occurred before in the history of capitalism: the defeat and moral surrender of organized labour, the rise of information technology and the discovery that once an unchallenged superpower exists, it can create money out of nothing for a long time.

4

The Long, Disrupted Wave

In 1948 the Marshall Plan kicked in, the Cold War began and Bell Laboratories invented the transistor. Each of these events would shape the fourth long cycle that was about to unfold.

The Marshall Plan, a $12 billion US aid package to Europe, ensured the post-war economic boom would take place under American leadership. The Cold War would distort the unfolding wave, first by taking 20 per cent of world production out of the reach of capital and then fuelling a new surge of growth when it ended in 1989. As for the transistor, it would become the core technology of the post-war era, enabling the use of information on an industrial scale.

Those who lived through the post-war boom were amazed, mystified and constantly worried that it would end. Even Harold Macmillan, who told Britons in 1957 that they'd 'never had it so good', added: 'What is beginning to worry some of us is, is it too good to be true?'[1] In Germany, Japan and Italy the popular press – quite separately in each country – dubbed the nation's growth a 'miracle'.

The numbers were startling. The Marshall Plan, combined with domestic rebuilding efforts, allowed most European economies to grow at well above 10 per cent per year until they reached their pre-war highpoint, which for most was achieved by 1951.[2] Regular growth took off spectacularly – and didn't stop. The US economy more than doubled in size between 1948 and 1973.[3] The economies of the UK, West Germany and Italy each grew fourfold in the same period. Japan's economy, meanwhile, grew *tenfold* – and this was against a baseline figure close to pre-war normality, not some catch-up effect due to the scale of nuclear destruction. For the entire period,

Western Europe's average annual growth rate was 4.6 per cent – close to double that of the 1900-1913 upswing.[4]

This was growth driven by productivity on an unprecedented scale. The results are evident in the GDP per-person data. For the sixteen most advanced countries, per-person GDP grew at an average of 3.2 per cent per year between 1950 and 1973. For the entire period between 1870 and 1950 it had averaged 1.3 per cent.[5] Real incomes soared: in the USA, the majority of households saw their real incomes rise by more than 90 per cent between 1947 and 1975;[6] in Japan the average real income increased a staggering 700 per cent.[7]

Across the developed world, the new techno-economic paradigm was clear – even if each country had its own version. Standardized mass production – with wages high enough to drive consumption of what the factories produced – was unleashed across society. There was male full employment and, subject to cultural variations, increased employment of teenagers and women once the reconstruction phase was over. In the developed world, people moved from the land to the factories in large numbers: between 1950 and 1970 the agricultural workforce in Europe declined from 66 million to 40 million; in the USA it collapsed from 16 per cent of the population to just 4 per cent.[8]

The most frenetic period of growth in human history was bound to produce glitches. But there were sophisticated economic management techniques to overcome them: realtime statistics, economic planning bodies at a national level, armies of economists and number crunchers in the HQs of the big corporations.

As the boom unfolded, it produced disorientation on the left. Varga – Stalin's tame economist – actually got it right: in 1946 he warned the Soviet leaders that the state-capitalist methods pioneered during the war could stabilize the West.[9] The dominant Anglo-Saxon powers would, he forecast, probably loan the rest of the world enough money to kickstart consumption again, and the wartime methods of state organization would replace the 'anarchy of capitalist production'.[10] For saying this he was hounded from his post, forced to recant and admit to being 'cosmopolitan'. Stabilization of the Western economies was impossible, Stalin had decreed.

In the West, the far left remained on the doomy side of the

argument: "The revival of economic activity in capitalist countries weakened by the war ... will be characterised by an especially slow tempo which will keep their economies at levels bordering on stagnation and slump,' wrote the Trotskyists in 1946.[11]

When this was proved nonsense, Marxists were not the only ones left confused. Even the theorists of moderate social-democracy were so perplexed that they declared the West's economic system had effectively become non-capitalist. 'The most characteristic features of capitalism have disappeared,' wrote Labour MP Anthony Crosland in 1956, 'the absolute rule of private property, the subjection of all life to market influences, the domination of the profit motive, the neutrality of government, typical laissez-faire division of income and the ideology of individual rights.'[12]

By the mid-1950s, almost the whole left had embraced the theory of 'state monopoly capitalism' – first suggested by Bukharin, then by Varga, and now turned into a full-blown theory by the US left economist Paul Sweezy.[13] He believed that state intervention, welfare measures and permanently high military spending had abolished the tendency to crisis. The falling profit rate could be offset by rising productivity – again, permanently. The Soviet Union, it was clear, would have to get used to coexisting with capitalism; the Western labour movement would have to forget revolution and take the upside of the boom, which was considerable.

For the whole period, the focus of debate was on what had changed at the level of the state, the factory, the supermarket, the boardroom and the laboratory. Very little attention was paid to money. However, the crucial factor that underpinned economic reality in the 1950s and 60s was a stable international currency system, and the effective suppression of financial markets.

THE POWER OF EXPLICIT RULES

On 1 July 1944, a special train delivered a cargo of economists, statesmen and bankers to White River Junction, Vermont, from where they were ferried to a hotel in New Hampshire. 'All trains, regular or scheduled, had to look out for us,' the train's fireman remembered, 'we had the right over everything.'[14] Their destination was Bretton Woods. There they would design a global monetary system that, like the train, had 'the right over everything'.

The Bretton Woods Conference agreed a system of fixed exchange rates designed to restore pre-1914 stability, only this time with explicit rules. All currencies would be pegged against the dollar, and the USA would peg the dollar to gold at $35 an ounce. Countries whose trade balance became seriously out of kilter would have to buy or sell dollars to keep their own currency at the agreed peg.

At the conference, the British economist John Maynard Keynes pushed for the creation of a separate global currency, but the USA rejected the idea. Instead, it secured the dollar's position as the unofficial global currency. There was no global central bank, but the International Monetary Fund and the World Bank were designed to reduce friction in the system, with the IMF acting as a short-term lender of last resort and enforcer of the rules.

The system was overtly stacked in favour of the USA: not only was it the biggest economy in the world, it had an infrastructure undamaged by the war and – for now – the highest productivity. It also got to appoint the boss of the Fund. The system was also stacked in favour of inflation. Because the link to gold was indirect, because there was leeway in the currency peg, and because the rules on balanced trade and structural reform were loose, the system was designed to produce inflation. This was recognized by the free-market right even before the train to Bretton Woods left the station. The journalist Henry Hazlitt, a confidant of free-market guru Ludwig von Mises, railed against the plan in the *New York Times*: 'It would be difficult to think of a more serious threat to world stability and full production than the continual prospect of a uniform world inflation to which the politicians of every country would be so easily tempted.'[15]

But this was a system also stacked against high finance. Strict limits on bank leverage were imposed by law and 'moral suasion' – quiet pressure from central banks on banks that lent too much. In the USA, big banks were required to hold cash or bonds equivalent to 24 per cent of the money they'd lent out.[16] In the UK it was 28 per cent. By 1950, bank loans across fourteen advanced capitalist countries equalled just one fifth of GDP – the lowest since 1870, and much smaller than the scale of bank lending during the pre-1914 upswing.

The result created a form of capitalism that was profoundly national. Banks and pension funds were required by law to hold the debt of their own countries; and they were discouraged from making cross-border financial trades. Add to that an explicit ceiling on interest rates and you have what we now call 'financial repression'.

Here's how financial repression works: you hold interest rates below inflation, so savers are effectively paying for the privilege of having money; you prevent them moving money out of the country in search of a better deal, and force them to buy the debts of their own country at a premium. The effect, as the economists Reinhart and Sbrancia have shown, was to shrink the combined debts of the developed world dramatically.[17]

In 1945, because of war spending, the public debts of the developed countries were close to 90 per cent of GDP. But with an inflation spike straight after the war, and then moderate inflation throughout the post-war boom, real interest rates became negative: in the USA between 1945 and 1973, long-term real interest rates were on average minus 1.6 per cent. Because the banking regulations acted as an effective tax on financial assets, economists calculate they raised the equivalent of a fifth of all government income during the boom, even more in the UK.[18] The result was to shrink advanced country debts to a historic low of 25 per cent of GDP by 1973.

In short, Bretton Woods achieved something unprecedented: it shrank the debts run up during a global war, suppressed speculation, mobilized savings into productive investment and enabled spectacular growth. It pushed all the latent instability of the system into the sphere of relationships between currencies, but US dominance ensured these were, at first, contained. Right-wing outrage over the inflationary aspect of Bretton Woods was overcome by the greatest period of stability and full production ever known.

Keynes had emphasized, at the design stage the importance of explicit rules – going beyond the gentlemen's agreement that lay behind the Gold Standard. In the event, explicit rules backed by a global superpower had a multiplier effect few could have imagined.

If the Depression was in part a product of Britain's decline and America's refusal to become a global superpower, then it was at Bretton Woods that the USA assumed the duties of a superpower with great passion. In fact, the twenty-five post-war years are the only time in modern history when a great power was truly hegemonic. Britain's nineteenth-century dominance was always negotiated and relative. Within the capitalist world of the mid-twentieth century, America's dominance was absolute. This acted like a massive reset button on the world economy, amplifying the upswing. But this was not the only reset button pressed.

THE POST-WAR BOOM AS A CYCLE

A second major change had taken place during wartime, with the state taking control of innovation. By 1945, national bureaucracies had become adept in the use of state ownership and control – and indeed mass communication – to shape private-sector behaviour. Perfectly ordinary managers, under the ultimate pressure of 'you lose, you die', had fine-tuned technocracy. Even in the Axis powers, where the state was dismantled in 1945, this culture of innovation and a large part of the technocratic system survived the war.

The case of General Motors is instructive. In 1940, the US government hired GM's president, Alfred Knudsen, to run its Office of Production Management, which coordinated the whole war economy. He proceeded to place $14 billion-worth of contracts with GM during the war. The corporation converted all of its 200 factories to war production, making – among other things – 38,000 tanks, 206,000 aircraft engines and 119 million shells. It became, in other words, a massive arms company with a single customer. Within this and other giant segments of American industry management effectively operated like a profit-driven state-planning bureau. Nothing like it had been seen before – or since.

At the Federal level, research and development was centralized and industrialized by the Office of Scientific Research and Development. Key to the whole deal was the prohibition of profit directly from research. 'Profit is a function of the production activities of an industrial establishment, not of a research department,' the OSRD decreed.[19] Contracts were placed where skills were high, where the danger of mass-production overload was least and 'spread among as many organizations as possible'. Only when all these criteria were equal could the lowest cost be brought into consideration. Competition and patent ownership issues were put on hold.[20]

These were remarkable things to achieve within capitalism: to treat research as public property, to suppress competition and to plan not just production but the direction of research. And though the USA perfected it, all major combatant states attempted it. The result was to stimulate an unprecedented culture of cross-fertilization in strategic disciplines. The new approach inserted maths and science into the heart of the industrial process; economics and data management into political decision-making.

It was the OSRD that took Claude Shannon, the founder of information theory, out of Princeton and put him into Bell Labs to design algorithms for anti-aircraft guns.[21] There, he would meet Alan Turing and discuss the possibility of 'thinking machines'. Turing, too, had been scooped out of academia by the British government to run the Enigma codebreaking operation at Bletchley Park.

This culture of innovation survived the transition to peacetime, even as individual corporations tried to monopolize the results and scrapped over patent rights. And it was not limited to technical innovation.

In 1942, GM gave management theorist Peter Drucker open access to study its operations. Drucker went on to write *The Concept of the Corporation*, arguably the first modern management book, which advocated the breakup of command structures and the decentralization of control. Though GM rejected his advice, thousands of other firms did not: the post-war Japanese auto industry adopted them in full. Management theory became a generalized discipline, not secret knowledge, with a whole cohort of consulting firms dedicated to spreading successful techniques rather than hoarding them.

In this sense, the wartime economy gave birth to one of the most fundamental reflexes within the capitalism of the long boom: to solve problems through audacious technological leaps, pulling in experts from across disciplines, spreading the best practice in a sector, and changing the business process as the product itself changed.

The role of the state in all this contrasts with the meagre role of finance. In all normative models of long cycles, it is finance that fuels innovation and helps capital flow into new, more productive areas. But finance had been effectively flattened during the 1930s.

What emerged from the war was a very different capitalism. All it needed was a raft of new technologies – and these were plentiful: the jet engine, the integrated circuit, nuclear energy and synthetic materials. After 1945, the world suddenly smelled of nylon, plastic and vinyl, and buzzed with electrified processes.

But one key technology was invisible: information. Though the 'information economy' lay decades in the future, the post-war economies saw information used on an industrial scale. It flowed as science, as management theory, as data, as mass communications and even – in a few hallowed places – out of a computer and into a tray of folding paper.

A transistor is simply a switch with no moving parts. Information theory plus transistors gives you the ability to automate physical processes. So factories throughout the West were re-tooled with semi-automated machinery: pneumatic presses, drills, cutters, lathes, sewing machines and production lines. What they lacked was sophisticated feedback mechanisms: electronic sensors and automated logic systems were so crude that the latter used compressed air to do what we now do with iPhone apps. But human beings were plentiful – and for many manual work became the act of controlling a semi-automated process.

The Cambridge economist Andrew Glyn believed the extraordinary success of the post-war boom could only be explained by 'a unique economic regime'.[22] He described this regime as a mixture of economic, social and geopolitical factors, which operated benignly throughout the upswing until they began to clash and grind in the late 1960s.

State direction produced a culture of science-led innovation. Innovation stimulated high productivity. Productivity allowed high wages, so consumption kept pace with production for twenty-five years. An explicit global rules system amplified the upside. Fractional reserve banking stimulated a 'benign' inflation which, combined with financial repression, forced capital into productive sectors and kept speculative finance marginal. The use of fertilizers and mechanization in the developed world boosted land productivity, keeping the cost of inputs cheap. Energy inputs were, at the time, also cheap.

As a result, the period 1948–73 unfolded as a Kondratieff upswing on steroids.

WHAT CAUSED THE WAVE TO BREAK?

There is no dividing line in economic history clearer than 17 October 1973. With their armies at war with Israel, the majority of the oil-exporting Arab countries imposed an oil embargo on the USA and slashed output. The oil price quadrupled. The resulting shock pushed key economies into recession. America's economy shrank by 6.5 per cent between January 1974 and March 1975,[23] Britain's by 3.4 per cent. Even Japan – which had averaged growth rates close to 10 per cent in the post-war period – went briefly negative.[24] The crisis was unique because in the worst-hit countries falling growth coincided with high inflation. By 1975, inflation in Britain reached 20 per cent, and 11 per cent in the USA. The word 'stagflation' hit the headlines.

Yet even at the time it was obvious that the oil shock was merely the trigger. The upswing had already been stuttering. In each developed country, growth in the late 1960s seemed beset by national or local problems: inflation, labour troubles, productivity concerns and flurries of financial scandal. But 1973 was the watershed, the point where the energy driving the fourth wave upwards caused it to peak and then invert. What made it happen is a question that has defined modern economics.

For right-wing economists, the answer lay in the exhaustion of Keynesian policy. For the left, however, the explanations have varied over time: in the late 1960s, high wages were seen as responsible; in the following decade, economists of the New Left tried to apply the Marxist overproduction theory.

In fact, 1973 can best be understood as a classic phase change on the Kondratieff pattern. It occurs about twenty-five years into the economic cycle. It is global in scope. It heralds a long period of recurrent

crisis. And once we understand what caused the upturn – high productivity, explicit global rules and financial repression – we can
understand how it became exhausted.

The post-war arrangements had effectively locked away instability
into two zones of control: relations between currencies and relations
between classes. Under the Bretton Woods rules, you were not supposed to devalue your currency to make your exports cheap and
boost employment. Instead, if your economy was uncompetitive, you
could either protect yourself from international competition through
trade barriers, or impose 'internal devaluation' – cutting wages, controlling prices, reducing the amount spent on welfare payments. In
practice, protectionism was discouraged by the Bretton Woods rules
and wage cutting was never seriously attempted until the mid-1970s –
which left devaluation. In 1949, Britain devalued Sterling by 30 per
cent against the dollar and twenty-three other countries followed suit.
A total of 400 official devaluations took place before 1973.

So, from the outset, Bretton Woods was a system where states were
repeatedly trying to offset their economic failings by manipulating
their exchange rates against the dollar. This was seen in Washington
as a form of unfair competition, and the USA fought back. By the
1960s, it was devaluing its own currency in real terms, as measured
by price differences, against those of its competitors. This subcutane-
ous economic warfare became overt during the inflation crises of the
late 1960s.

Inside the factories, the long boom had been a productivity story
and a wages story. In the advanced countries productivity grew at
4.5 per cent per year, while private consumption grew at 4.2 per cent.
The rising output of automated machinery more than paid for the rising wages of those operating them. All this was the result of new
investment. But the upswing ended once investment could no longer
increase productivity at the previous rate.

There are clear signs of a productivity slowdown in the pre-1973
data, and of a fall in the ratio of output to capital invested.[25] Productivity, as a counter-tendency to the downward pressure on profits, ran
out of steam. But as conditions tightened, the sheer strength of
working-class bargaining power in countries with full employment
and no will to break the post-war social contract made wage cuts a

non-starter. Rather, managers were forced to increase wages and non-wage benefits, while reducing working hours.

As a result, a 'profit squeeze' kicked in. Comparing profit rates for America, Europe and Japan in 1973 to their respective peak years during the boom, Andrew Glyn found that in each case they had fallen by one-third. With falling profits, rising wages and alarming levels of shop-floor militancy, there were two pressure valves: to let inflation rip, eroding the value of real wages without having to provoke more disputes; and to go along with social wage rises – easing the pressure on individual businesses by, for example, boosting family allowance and other payments from the state to workers. As a result, social spending by the state – on benefits, subsidies and other income-boosting measures – soared to dysfunctional levels, especially in Europe: from 8 per cent of GDP in the late 1950s to 16 per cent by 1975.[26] Over roughly the same period in the USA, Federal spending on welfare, pensions and health doubled to 10 per cent of GDP by the late 1970s.

All it needed to tip this fragile system into crisis was a shock. And in August 1971, Richard Nixon delivered one, unilaterally breaking the commitment to exchange dollars for gold, and thereby destroying Bretton Woods.

Nixon's reasons for doing so are well documented.[27] As America's competitors caught up in productivity terms, capital flowed out of the US into Europe while its trade balance declined. By the late 1960s, with every country engaged in expansionary policies – with high state spending and low interest rates – America had become the big loser from Bretton Woods. It needed to pay for the Vietnam War and the welfare reforms of the late 1960s, but could not. It needed to devalue but could not, because to make that happen, other countries had to raise their own currencies against the dollar, and they refused. So Nixon acted.

The world moved from exchange rates fixed against the dollar and gold to totally free-floating currencies. From then on, the global banking system was effectively creating money out of nothing.

With this change, each stricken country was temporarily free to solve the underlying problems of productivity and profitability in ways the old system had made impossible: with higher state spending and lower interest rates. The years 1971–3 were lived in a kind of nervous euphoria.

The inevitable stock market crash hit Wall Street and London in January 1973, triggering the collapse of several investment banks. The oil shock of October 1973 was the final straw.

CARRY ON KEYNES

By 1973, every aspect of the unique regime that had sustained the long boom was broken. But the crisis looked accidental: low input prices destroyed by OPEC; global rules ripped up by Richard Nixon; profits eroded by that figure of loathing, the 'greedy worker'.

The iconic British *Carry On* movie franchise chose this moment to switch from ludicrous historical parodies to an attempt at razor-sharp social commentary. *Carry On At Your Convenience* (1971), set in a toilet factory, satirizes a world in which workers control production, where managers are incompetent, and where sexual freedom is transforming life even on the small-town factory floor. The subtext of *Carry On At Your Convenience* is that the present system is ludicrous: we can't go on, but we don't seem to have an alternative. This, it turned out, was the subtext of the policy response as well.

After 1973, governments tried to fix the system by applying the old, Keynesian rules harder. They used price and wage control policies in an attempt to suppress inflation and appease worker unrest. They used state spending – and borrowing on an increased scale to maintain demand in the face of the slump. But though growth recovered after 1975, it could never reach its old levels.

During the late 1970s, the Keynesian system destroyed itself. This destruction was not just the work of policymakers but of all the players in the Keynesian game: the workers, the bureaucrats, the technocrats, the politicians.

Working-class militancy had already moved out of the factory and into the arena of bargaining nationally with the government. In the mid-1970s, in almost every country the attention of trade union leaders was focused on national wage agreements, price controls, social reform programmes, together with strategies that would maintain their grip over specific sectors – such as the British dockers' attempt to resist container technology. The ultimate aim of labour movements in the developed world became to put in power leftist social-democratic governments that would permanently guarantee Keynesian policies.

But by this time the business class and key politicians of the right had walked away from the Keynesian world altogether.

THE ATTACK ON LABOUR

It has become commonplace to think that the triumph of globalization and neoliberalism was inevitable. But it was not. Their emergence was just as much the result of government action as corporatism and fascism had been in the 1930s.

Neoliberalism was designed and implemented by visionary politicians: Pinochet in Chile; Thatcher and her ultra-conservative circle in Britain; Reagan and the Cold Warriors who brought him to power. They'd faced massive resistance from organized labour and they'd had enough. In response, these pioneers of neoliberalism drew a conclusion that has shaped our age: that a modern economy cannot coexist with an organized working class. Consequently, they resolved to smash labour's collective bargaining power, traditions and social cohesion completely.

Unions had come under attack before – but always from paternalist politicians who had proffered the lesser of two evils: in place of militancy, they'd encouraged a 'good' workforce, defined by moderate socialism, unions run by agents of the state. And they helped build stable, socially conservative communities that could be the breeding ground for soldiers and servants. The general programme of conservatism, and even fascism, had been to promote a different kind of solidarity that served to reinforce the interests of capital. But it was still solidarity.

The neoliberals sought something different: atomization. Because today's generation sees only the outcome of neoliberalism, it is easy to miss the fact that this goal – the destruction of labour's bargaining power – was the essence of the entire project: it was a means to all the other ends. Neoliberalism's guiding principle is not free markets, nor fiscal discipline, nor sound money, nor privatization and offshoring – not even globalization. All these things were byproducts or weapons of its main endeavour: to remove organized labour from the equation.

Not all the industrialized countries followed the same path, nor at the same pace. Japan had blazed the trail for flexible working in the 1970s by introducing small-team work into production lines, through individual wage bargaining and shouted propaganda sessions in the factory. Of all the advanced economies, Japan was the only one to successfully rationalize industrial business models after 1973. There was of course resistance, dealt with in a brutal fashion – by taking out the ringleaders and beating them physically every day until resistance stopped. 'It is as though the "company world" were immune from the law of the state,' wrote the Japanese leftist Muto Ichiyo, who witnessed some of these beatings. 'And it is natural that in this company world, workers, petrified with horror, their free thinking frozen, keep their mouths shut.'[28]

Germany, by contrast, resisted labour reforms until the early 2000s, preferring instead to create a peripheral migrant workforce in low-grade service and construction jobs alongside the paternalistic world of the production line. For this it was branded the 'sick man of the euro' by *The Economist* magazine, which as late as 1999 lamented its 'bloated welfare system and excessive labour costs'.[29] These were eradicated in the Harz II labour reforms (2003), which have now left Germany a highly unequal society, with many of its communities gripped by poverty.[30]

Many developed countries took advantage of the recession of the early 1980s to impose mass unemployment. They adopted policies overtly designed to make the recession deeper: they hiked interest rates, sending old industrial businesses to the wall. They privatized or closed large swathes of coal, steel, auto and heavy engineering production owned by the state. They banned the wildcat and solidarity actions that had plagued managers in the boom years. But they did not, yet, try to dismantle welfare systems; these were needed to maintain social order in communities whose hearts had been ripped out.

The attack on organized labour was punctuated by signal moments.

In 1981, the US air traffic control union leaders were arrested, paraded in chains, and the entire workforce sacked for taking strike action. Thatcher used paramilitary policing to destroy the miners' strike in 1984–5. But the anti-labour offensive's true success was on a moral and cultural level. From 1980 onward, in the developed world, strikes diminished and so did union density. In the USA, union membership fell from an already low 20 per cent of the workforce in 1980 to 12 per cent by 2003, the survivors heavily clustered in the public sector.[31] In Japan it went from 31 per cent to 20 per cent, and in the UK the fall was even more spectacular, from 50 per cent to 30 per cent.[32]

With the unions sidelined, the transformation of work could begin in earnest, creating the atomized and precarious workforce of today. Those of us who lived through the defeat of organized labour in the 1980s experienced it as traumatic, but told ourselves that our grandfathers had lived through just the same. But if we step back and look at it through the kaleidoscope of long-wave theory, it is in fact unique.

The 1980s saw the first 'adaptation phase' in the history of long waves where worker resistance collapsed. In the normal pattern, outlined in chapter 3, resistance forces the capitalists to adapt more radically, creating a new model based on higher productivity and higher real wages. After 1979, the workers' failure to resist allows key capitalist countries to find a solution to the crisis through lower wages and low-value models of production. This is the fundamental fact, the key to understanding everything that happens next.

The defeat of organized labour did not enable – as the neoliberals thought – a 'new kind of capitalism' but rather the extension of the fourth long wave on the basis of stagnant wage growth and atomization. Instead of being forced to innovate their way out of the crisis using technology, as during the late stage of all three previous cycles, the 1 per cent simply imposed penury and atomization on the working class.

Across the Western world the wage share of GDP fell markedly. The economist Engelbert Stockhammer, surveying the damage for the International Labour Organization, showed that this fall in the wage share had been driven entirely by the impact of globalization, financialization and reductions in welfare provision. He wrote: 'This constitutes a major historical change as wage shares had been stable or increasing in the post-war era.'[33]

That, as it turns out, is an understatement. It was to trigger the reshaping of the world.

THE DISRUPTED WAVE IN PICTURES

When change is massive and obvious but takes place over decades, two-dimensional charts are sometimes the clearest way to see the big picture. The graphs that follow indicate very clearly what does and does not fit the classic pattern predicted by Kondratieff. They can also give us a clue as to why.

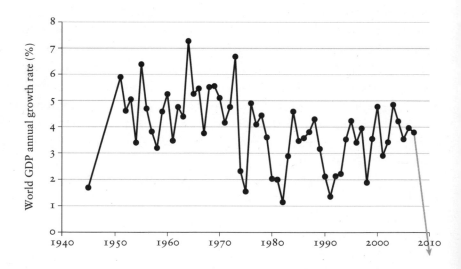

1. *World GDP growth*

The chart above shows the overall shape of the fourth long wave at a single glance. There's a clear phase change in the early 1970s. Using the IMF definition of a global recession – when the growth rate dips below 3 per cent – there were no recessions for the first twenty-five years of the wave and six after 1973, the last one a humdinger.[34]

2. *Interest rates*[35]

Kondratieff measured his waves using interest rates, and for the post-1945 period there is no clearer metric than this one: the average interest rates banks charge to companies and individuals in the USA. Interest rates rose gradually during the long boom, spiked in the early 1980s – when high interest rates were used to wipe out swathes of the old industries – and have gradually declined, flatlining at the end of the graph because of quantitative easing. Kondratieff's colleagues, who'd seen this exact pattern in all the previous cycles, would have concluded: 'Comrade, that's a long wave.'

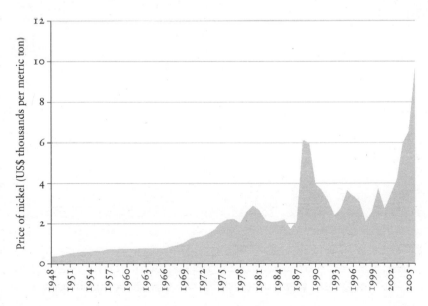

3. Commodity prices: nickel

However, Kondratieff also tracked the prices of basic commodities, such as coal and iron. This graph tracks the price of a modern equivalent, nickel – a key component of stainless steel – over fifty-seven years. I think it would have knocked Kondratieff off his chair. It's only one commodity but with just a few exceptions, it is fairly representative of what has happened to raw material prices since 1945: there is always a spike to the right of the graph, caused by the rapid development of industry and mass consumption in the global south, above all in China.

A 2007 report by the US Geological Survey shows how, after 1989, all industrial metal prices were driven upwards by China's entry into the global marketplace.[36] China's nickel usage goes from 30 kt in 1991 to 60 kt in 2001 to 780 kt in 2012. By contrast, over the same period most other major producers' consumption of nickel and other metals rises fairly slowly, with Germany going from 80 kt to 110 kt.*

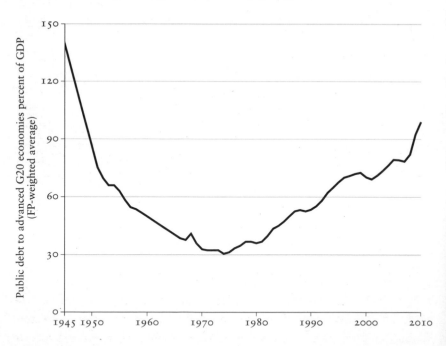

* It's normal for economists to compare prices to inflation; if you do, the price of this and many other metals is fairly constant over the post-1989 period, and even declines. However, in long-cycle analysis we want to *see* inflation and deflation, not factor it out.

4. *Government debt to GDP in twenty advanced economies*[37]

Kondratieff didn't measure government debt, but in a modern nation it is a good indicator of the economy's overall health. The chart above shows the debt of states compared to their annual GDP. Financial repression combined with inflation wiped out their war debts over twenty-five years of sustained growth. Then, in the face of crisis from 1973 onwards, the advanced world was forced to raise its debts relentlessly. This debt piles up close to 100 per cent of GDP, despite three decades of welfare cuts and privatization receipts.

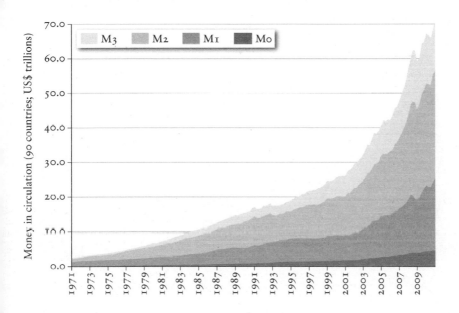

5. *Money in circulation*

This is Exhibit A in the story of fiat money, money not backed by gold. The graph starts from the moment Nixon abolished Bretton Woods in 1971, and shows the volume of money in circulation in ninety countries, in different forms, ranging from cash, which barely changes, to credit and financial instruments, which grow steadily in the neoliberal era and take off massively after 2000.[38]

Nixon had detached money and credit from the underlying reality and, although it took decades to create a financial system that could exploit this freedom to the full, from the late 1990s the rate of increase becomes steep.

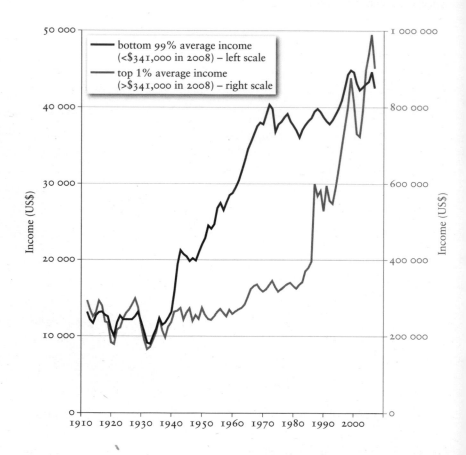

6. Inequality

The dark line shows the real income of the 99 per cent over the fourth long wave. It had already doubled during the Second World War, as people moved from farms to factories, and doubled again between the war and the oil shock. Then it grows very slowly for the whole period after 1989. But for the 1 per cent it is the opposite: the downswing of the cycle is immensely lucrative. Having plateaued during the boom and the crisis years, their incomes (grey line) rocket once free-market economics are unleashed in the late 1980s. There is no more graphic example of who wins and who loses[39] within developed countries once the cycle turns downwards.

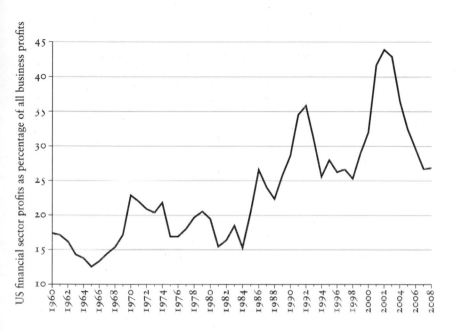

7. *Financialization*[40]

This graph shows US finance sector profits as a total of all business profits. During the long boom, financial sector profits in the USA are small. The change picks up pace in the mid-1980s, and in the years before Lehman Brothers collapses we see banks, hedge funds and insurance companies making over 40 per cent of all corporate profit. This is clear evidence for the idea that more of the profits raked in by financialized capitalism are generated by our borrowing and consumption, and less from employing us. On the eve of the crisis, financial profits made up four out of every ten dollars of corporate profit.

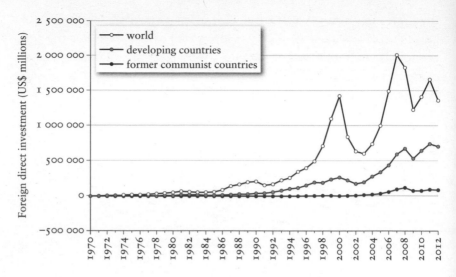

8. Global investment flows

This graph shows in one striking image the reality of globalization. The top line is the total amount of foreign direct investment (FDI) in the world, between 1970 and 2012 (in millions of US dollars at current prices and exchange rates). The middle line shows the amount flowing into developing countries; the bottom line into former communist countries. The gap between the top and middle lines represents the amount of foreign investment flowing between advanced countries.[41]

Globalization begins the moment the Keynesian paradigm is abandoned. There is a surge of cross-border investments between the advanced countries, mirrored by a steady flow of investment into what we called the 'Third World'. Capital flows into Russia and its satellites are significant given the size of their economies, but not significant in terms of the bigger picture.

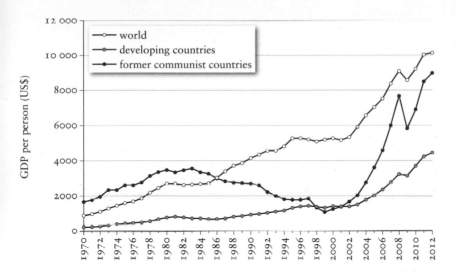

9. GDP per person[42]

GDP per person is a way of illustrating human progress: how much growth is shared among how many people? The top line shows global GDP per person rising by 162 per cent across the whole world between 1989 and 2012. The former communist countries achieve about the same – albeit via twelve years of catastrophic decline and then a growth surge spurred by Euro entry for the satellites and oil money for Russia itself. But the most spectacular thing is what happens to the bottom line – the developing world. It grows by 404 per cent after 1989.

It is this that prompted the British economist Douglas McWilliams, in his Gresham lectures, to nominate the last twenty-five years as the 'greatest economic event in human history'. World GDP rose by 33 per cent in the 100 years after the discovery of the Americas, and GDP per person by 5 per cent. In the fifty years after 1820, with the Industrial Revolution underway in Europe and the Americas only, world GDP grew by 60 per cent, and GDP per person by 30 per cent. But between 1989 and 2012 world GDP grew from $20 trillion to $71 trillion – 272 per cent – and, as we've seen, GDP per person increased by 162 per cent. On both measures, the period after 1989 outpaces the long post-war boom.[43]

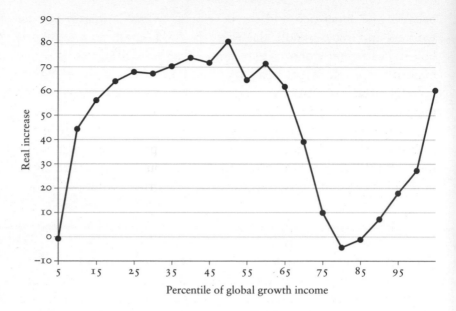

Percentile of global growth income

10. Globalization's winners

During the post-war boom, capitalism suppressed the development of the global south. The means by which it did so are clear and well documented.[44] Unequal trade relationships forced much of Latin America, all of Africa and most of Asia to adopt development models that led to super-profits for Western companies and poverty at home. Countries that tried to reject these models, such as Chile or Guyana, had their governments overthrown by CIA coups or, as with Grenada, by invasion. Many found their economies destroyed by debt and by the 'structural adjustment programmes' the IMF dictated in return for debt write-offs. With little domestic industry, their growth models relied on the export of raw materials, and the incomes of the poor stagnated.

Globalization changed all that. Between 1988 and 2008 – as the chart shows – the real incomes of two-thirds of the world's people grew significantly. That's what the hump on the left-hand side of the graph proves.

Now move to the right-hand side of the graph: the top 1 per cent also see their incomes rise, by 60 per cent. But for everybody in between the super-rich and the developing world – that is for the workers and lower-middle classes of the West – there is a U-shaped hole indicating little or no real increase. That hole tells the story of the majority of people in America, Japan and Europe – they gained almost nothing from capitalism in the past twenty years. In fact, some of them lost out. That dip below zero is likely to include black America, poor white Britain and much of the workforce of southern Europe.

Branko Milanovic, the economist who prepared these figures for the World Bank, called this 'probably the profoundest global reshuffle of people's economic positions since the industrial revolution'.[45]

11. Doubling the world's workforce

The Harvard economist Richard Freeman calculated that between 1980 and 2000, the world's workforce doubled in absolute numbers, halving the ratio of capital to labour.[46] Population growth and foreign investment boosted the workforce of the developing world, urbanization created a 250-million-strong working class in China, while the former Comecon countries' workforces were suddenly available to the global market.

The next two graphs show the limits to what can be achieved simply by employing large numbers of low-wage, poor-country workers.

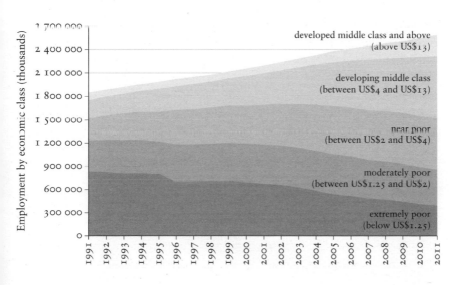

First, above, here's what has happened to the incomes of the work-force in the developing world since globalization began.

Strikingly, the graph shows the group earning between $4 and $13 a day growing the most rapidly: from 600 million to 1.4 billion.[47] (Though the demographers call them the 'developing middle class', the $13-a-day mark corresponds roughly to the poverty line in the USA.) These people are mainly workers. They have access to banking and insurance, are likely to own a TV, and usually live in small family groups, not the multigenerational families of the slum, or the solitude of the dormitory. Three-quarters of them work in service industries. The growth of service sector jobs in the developing world reflects both the natural evolution of the job mix under modern capitalism and a second round of offshoring, focused on call centres, IT depart-ments and back-office functions. In short, the graph shows the limits of what offshoring can achieve. That growing wedge of $13-a-day workers is nudging into the income bracket of the poorest American workers.

This means that the days of easy wins for firms offshoring their production are drawing to a close. For the last twenty-five years, large parts of industry in the global south have used 'extensive', rather than intensive, methods to boost production. Meaning, if you want to make double the number of trainers, you build an extra factory rather

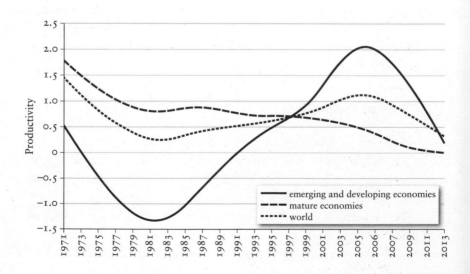

than work on more efficient production methods. But that option is closed down once you have to start paying your most skilled workers the same as a poor person in America. In fact, the impact of rising wages in the developing world is apparent once we look at the second graph, opposite. This stark calculation shows that the initial boost to productivity from the offshoring of hundreds of millions of jobs is over.

Look at the three lines. Dashed, for the developed world, declines to zero. Its workers are making almost no contribution to productivity in the world. Solid, for the developing world, shows a massive contribution in the first years of globalization, petering out to almost nothing in the last few years. It's evident from this that much of the productivity boost from globalizing the workforce is over, and that the slowdown in growth in the emerging markets – from China to Brazil – is about to turn into a strategic problem. It is clear from these graphs that the normal wave pattern has been utterly disrupted.

HOW IS THE PATTERN BROKEN?

When the upswing runs out of steam, in the 1960s, it does so for a reason that would not have surprised Kondratieff: the exhaustion of the regime that promoted high productivity alongside wage growth. This led to the famous stop-go crises of the 1960s, when the global system forced governments to rein in growth, and then a breakdown of the global economic order, high inflation and a war in Vietnam so hubristic that the American psyche has still not recovered from the shock of losing it.

Here is the critical difference: in all three previous cycles, workers had resisted the cheap and nasty solution to the crisis – wage cuts, de-skilling and a reduction in the social wage. In the fourth wave, for reasons we will explore in chapter 7, their resistance failed. It was this failure that enabled the entire global economy to be rebalanced in favour of capital.

For about twenty years, this rebalancing worked – and worked so well that it convinced many rational people that a new age had dawned. What the Kondratieff theory had indicated should lead to downturn and depression led instead to two exhilarating decades in which an upswing in profits coexisted with social breakdown, military conflict, the return of abject poverty and criminality to communities in the West – and spectacular riches for the 1 per cent.

But this is not a social order, it is a disorder; it is what you get when you combine the move from production to finance (which Kondratieff would have expected) with a defeated and atomized workforce, and a super-rich elite living off financial profits.

We have listed the factors that allowed neoliberalism to happen: fiat money, financialization, the doubling of the workforce, the global imbalances, including the deflationary effect of cheap labour, plus the cheapening of everything else as a result of information technology. Each seemed like a 'Get Out of Jail Free' card, allowing the ordinary karma of economics to be suspended. But as we have seen – and as most of us have experienced in some way – there has been a huge price to pay.

What emerges from this shattered dream? The new technical and economic system will have to be built from the materials to hand. We know it will involve networks, knowledge work, the application of science and a large amount of green technology investment.

The question is: can it be capitalism?

PART II

We are now engaged in a grand scheme to augment, amplify, enhance and extend the relationships and communications between all beings and all objects.

Kevin Kelly, 1997[1]

5

The Prophets of Postcapitalism

The jet engine was one of the core technologies of the post-1945 long wave. Invented during the Second World War, the turbofan – to give it its proper name – is a mature technology and should not be producing surprises. Yet it is.

It works by sucking compressed air in at the front and firing a flame through it so that the air expands. This drives a set of fans at the back, which transform the heat into energy. But turbofans are highly inefficient. The first jet engines converted 20 per cent of the heat into thrust. By the year 2001 they had achieved 35 per cent efficiency, with one industry veteran cautiously predicting 55 per cent 'during the second quarter of the 21st century'.[1]

Why should we care? Because by 2030, manufacturers expect the number of airliners in operation to double. That means 60,000 new turbofans.[2] They will boost the airline industry's contribution to global warming from 3.5 per cent in 2005 to something like 5 per cent at mid-century.[3] So the efficiency of a turbofan is not a geek issue, it's a global survival issue.

Over the first fifty years of its life, designers managed to improve the turbofan's efficiency by 0.5 per cent per year. Today, however, they are making innovative leaps: 65 per cent efficiency is within reach and radically new kinds of engine are on the cusp of being deployed. What's driving the change is a mixture of carbon emission rules and the price of fuel. What's allowing it to happen is the core technology of the fifth long wave: information.

In the living memory of the people who make them, fan blades were hammered from solid metal. From the 1960s they were cast – that is, moulded from liquid metal. But cast metal contains imperfections, making the blades prone to failure.

Enter one of the most spectacular engineering solutions you have probably never heard of. In 1980, engineers at US aviation manufacturer Pratt & Whitney grew a fan blade out of a single metal crystal formed in a vacuum.[4] The result was a metal with an atomic structure that had never before existed. A single crystal blade can tolerate higher speeds. With superalloy metals, the blade can cope with air hotter than its own melting point. So the official roadmap[5] for aircraft engines now sees gears being added in 2015, a weird-shaped open fan system by 2020 and, sometime after 2035, a self-cooled engine that should take thermal efficiency close to 100 per cent.

Information technology is driving every aspect of this evolution. Modern jet engines are controlled by a computer that can analyse performance, predict failure and manage maintenance. The most advanced engines beam their data from the plane in flight back to the manufacturer's HQ in realtime.

Now consider what information technology has done to the design process. There are aircraft still flying that were designed on paper, stress-tested using slide rules, constructed from full-sized templates drawn on silk. New aircraft are designed and tested virtually, on a supercomputer. 'When we designed the tail fin of the Tornado fighter we did twelve stress cases on it,' one veteran engineer told me. 'With its replacement the Typhoon, we did 186 million.'

Computers have revolutionized the building process as well. Engineers now build every element of the aircraft 'virtually', using 3D digital mockups on supercomputers. In these models, every brass screw has the physical qualities of a brass screw, every sheet of carbon fibre bends and flexes as if real. Every stage of the manufacturing process is modelled before a single physical object is made.

The global market for turbofans is worth $21 billion a year, so what follows is a $21 billion question: how much of the value of a turbofan lies in the physical components used to make it, how much in the labour, and how much in the information it embodies?

You won't find an answer in the accounts: in modern accounting standards, intellectual property is valued by guesswork. A study for the SAS Institute in 2013 found that, in an attempt to put a value on data, neither the cost of gathering it, nor its market value, nor the future income it might generate could be adequately calculated. Only through a form of accounting that included non-economic benefits and risks could companies actually explain to their shareholders what their data was really worth.[6]

The report showed that while 'intangible assets' were growing on US and UK company balance sheets at nearly three times the rate of tangible assets, the actual size of the digital sector in the GDP figures had remained static. So something is broken in the logic we use to value the most important thing in the modern economy.

However, by any measure, it is clear that the mix of inputs has altered. An airliner looks like old technology. But from the atomic structure of the fan blades, to the compressed design cycle, to the stream of data it is firing back to its fleet HQ, it is 'alive' with information.

This phenomenon, merging the virtual world with the real, can be seen across many sectors: auto engines whose physical performance is dictated by a silicon chip; digital pianos that can pick from thousands of samples of real pianos, depending on how hard you stroke the keys. Today we watch movies that consist of pixels instead of grains of celluloid and contain whole scenes in which nothing real ever stood before a camera. On car production lines each component is bar-coded: what the humans do, alongside the whizz and purr of robots, is ordered and checked by a computer algorithm. The relationship between physical work and information has changed.

The great technological advance of the early twenty-first century consists not of new objects but of old ones made intelligent. The knowledge content of products is becoming more valuable than the physical elements used to produce them.

In the 1990s, as the impact of info-tech began to be understood, people from several disciplines had the same thought at once: capitalism is becoming qualitatively different.

Buzz phrases appeared: the knowledge economy, the information society, cognitive capitalism. The assumption was that info-capitalism and the free-market model worked in tandem; one produced and reinforced the other. To some the change looked big enough to conclude it was as important as the move from merchant capitalism to industrial capitalism in the eighteenth century. But just as economists got busy explaining how this 'third kind of capitalism' works, they ran into a problem: it doesn't.

There is a growing body of evidence that information technology, far from creating a new and stable form of capitalism, is dissolving it: corroding market mechanisms, eroding property rights and destroying the old relationship between wages, work and profit. The first people to say this were an awkward squad of philosophers, management gurus and lawyers.

In this chapter, I am going to survey and critique their main ideas. Then I am going to propose something even more radical: that information technology is leading us towards a postcapitalist economy.

DRUCKER: ASKING THE RIGHT QUESTIONS

In 1993, the management guru Peter Drucker wrote: 'That knowledge has become *the* resource, rather than *a* resource, is what makes our society "post-capitalist". It changes, and fundamentally, the structure of society. It creates new social dynamics. It creates new economic dynamics. It creates new politics.'[7] At the age of ninety, the last surviving pupil of Josef Schumpeter had jumped the gun a little, but the insight was correct.

Drucker's case rests on the assertion that the old factors of production – land, labour and capital – have become secondary to information. In his book *Post-Capitalist Society*, Drucker argued that certain norms essential to capitalism were being replaced. Writing before anybody had seen an internet browser, Drucker observed the information-rich capitalism of the 1980s and imagined in broad outline the network economy that would emerge in the next twenty years.

And that's what visionaries are for. While many around him saw 'info-tech plus neoliberalism' as capitalism perfected, Drucker allowed himself to imagine info-capitalism as a transition to something else. He noted that, despite the rhetoric about information, there was no theory of how information actually behaves in economic terms. In the absence of such a theory, he posed a series of questions about what a postcapitalist economy might entail.

First, he asked, how do we improve the productivity of knowledge? If previous eras of capitalism had been based on the increased productivity of machines and labour, then the next must be based on the increased productivity of knowledge. Drucker guessed that the solution must be to connect, creatively, the different knowledge disciplines: 'The capacity to connect may be inborn and part of that mystery we call genius. But to a large extent to connect and thus raise the yield of existing knowledge, whether for an individual, for a team or for an entire organisation, is learnable.'[8]

The challenge was to train knowledge workers to make the kind of connections that the brain of an Einstein would make spontaneously. Drucker's solution was straight out of the playbook of management theory: a methodology, a project plan, better training.

Humanity came up with a better solution: the network. This was not the result of any centralized plan or management group, but the spontaneous interaction of people using information pathways and forms of organization that did not exist until twenty-five years ago. Nevertheless, Drucker's focus on 'connection' and the modular use of information as the key to productivity was inspired.

His second question was equally profound: who is the social archetype of postcapitalism? If feudal society was epitomized by the medieval knight, and capitalism by the bourgeoisie, then who is in the historical scheme of things the bearer of postcapitalist social relations? It's the same question that preoccupied Karl Marx, but Drucker's answer would dismay most traditional leftists, who think it's the proletariat. It would be, Drucker proposed, 'the universal educated person'.

Drucker imagined this new kind of person emerging as a fusion of the managerial and intellectual classes of Western society, combining the manager's ability to apply knowledge with the intellectual's ability to deal with pure concepts. Such an individual would be the opposite of the polymath – those rare people who are simultaneously expert in Mandarin Chinese and nuclear physics. This new type of person would, on the contrary, be someone able to pick up and run with the products of expert research in narrow fields and apply them generally: applying chaos theory to economics, genetics to archaeology, or data-mining to social history.

Drucker made a plea for the emergence of such people as the 'leadership group' of the new society: 'a unifying force . . . which can focus particular, separate traditions onto a common and shared commitment to values, onto a common concept of excellence, and onto mutual respect'.[9]

Since he wrote that, such a group has emerged: the T-shirted techno-bourgeoisie of the early twenty-first century, their information stored in the Cloud and their ultra-liberal attitudes to sexuality, ecology and philanthropy seen as the new normal. If all we are talking about in the next fifty years is a fifth long wave of capitalism based on information, then we already have the new men and new women that the theory of long waves would lead us to expect. The problem is, they show no interest at all in overthrowing the old capitalism, and scant interest in politics at all.

However, if we are talking about postcapitalism, then this universal educated person would have to exist in large numbers and have some interest opposed to that of the big hierarchical firms that dominated the twentieth century. They would have to fight, as the bourgeoisie did, for the new economic model and to embody its values in their behaviour. They would have to be, as in the materialist approach to history, the bearer of the new social relations inside the old.

Now look around you.

On the London Underground, I'm in a carriage where everybody under the age of thirty-five has white wires connecting their ears to a device on which they're listening to something they've downloaded via a network. Even those obviously going to business or management jobs have a studiedly informal air and mode of dress. Some – even here where there is no wifi – are working through emails on their smartphones. Or maybe they're playing games, for the physical actions and intense levels of concentration required are the same. They are glued to digital information and the first thing they'll do on emerging at street level is to plug back into the global network via 3G.

Everybody else in the carriage fits into a demographic from the twentieth century: the elderly middle-class couple in their hats and tweeds; the stubbly manual worker reading his newspaper; the guy in the suit typing on his laptop, too busy for headphones, but who's taken the time to polish his shoes (i.e. me).

The first group consists of what sociologists call 'networked individuals', adept at drawing down knowledge from a relatively open and global system. They behave in a networked way – from work to consumption to relationships and culture. Thirty years on from Stewart Brand's famous claim that 'information wants to be free', they instinctively believe that under normal circumstances it *should* be free. They will pay for their drugs at a dance club but still find it an imposition to pay for downloaded music.

This group is already so large and well defined that in some cities – London, Tokyo, Sydney – it is the twentieth-century types that are the minority: still consulting analogue maps instead of GPS, still confused by the coffee options available at Starbucks, appalled and fascinated by the mercurial lifestyles that the other group sees as normal.

The networked individuals of the early twenty-first century – the 'white wire people' – conform exactly to the kind of person Drucker expected to emerge: the universal educated person. They're no longer confined to a niche techno demographic. Any barista, or admin worker, or legal temp can become, if they want to, a universal educated person – as long as they have a basic education and a smartphone. In fact, with the rise of the mobile internet, the most recent studies show that even Chinese factory workers have become – in the face of stringent work discipline and long hours – avidly networked people in their non-work time.[10]

Once you understand how information behaves as an economic resource, and who the new social archetype is, you are part of the way to understanding how the transition to postcapitalism *could* occur. But this still leaves the question: why *should* it occur? Drucker's answers are speculative but they provide the first glimpse of the framework on which a rigorous theory of postcapitalism would have to be based.

Drucker divides the history of industrial capitalism into four phases: a mechanical revolution lasting most of the nineteenth century; a productivity revolution with the advent of scientific management in the 1890s; a management revolution after 1945, driven by the application of knowledge to business processes; and finally an information revolution, based on 'the application of knowledge to knowledge'.

Drucker, a pupil of Schumpeter, was consciously using the

Kondratieff long cycles here (although merging the first two together), but seen from the viewpoint of the individual firm. This leads to Drucker's most profound observation: that none of these turning points can be grasped without understanding the economics of work. From Virgil to Marx, he argued, nobody had bothered to study what the farmer or factory worker did on a day-to-day basis. Only in the late nineteenth century did capitalists notice what their workers were actually doing, and try to change it.

'There is still no history of work,' Drucker complained, and twenty-five years later the history of work remains under-explored. Labour market economics continues focused on unemployment and pay rates, and occupies a lowly status in academia. But once we understand what information is doing to work, to the boundaries between work and free time, and to wages, the scale of the change we're living through will be apparent.

In the end, Drucker left us with a series of questions. They were the right questions, but twenty-five years on we still have no synthetic theory of info-capitalism, let alone postcapitalism. However, mainstream economics has – accidentally – come close to discovering one.

INFO-GOODS CHANGE EVERYTHING

In 1990 the American economist Paul Romer blew apart one of the key assumptions of modern economics and in the process thrust the question of info-capitalism into the mainstream.

In their search for a model that could predict a country's rate of growth, economists had listed various factors: savings, productivity, population growth. They knew that technological change influenced all these factors but they assumed, for the purposes of the model, that it was 'exogenous' – external to their model and therefore irrelevant to the equation they were trying to write. Then, in a paper titled *Endogenous Technological Change*, Romer reset the whole argument.[11] He demonstrated that, since innovation is driven by market forces, it cannot be treated as accidental or external to economic growth but must be an intrinsic ('endogenous') part of it. Innovation itself has to be situated within growth theory: its impact is predictable, not random.

But as well as completing a neat piece of algebra about capitalism in general, Romer had come up with a proposition specific to info-capitalism, with revolutionary implications. He defined technological change in a deliberately facile way, as an 'improvement in the instructions for mixing together raw materials'. That is, he separated out things and ideas – for that is what 'instructions' are. Information, for Romer, is like a blueprint or recipe for making something either in the physical world or in the digital world. This led to what he called a new fundamental premise: 'that instructions for working with raw materials are inherently different from other economic goods'.[12]

An information product is different from every physical commodity so far produced. And an economy primarily based on information products will behave differently from one based on making things and providing services. Romer spelled out why: 'Once the cost of creating a new set of instructions has been incurred, the instructions can be used over and over again at no additional cost. Developing new and better instructions is equivalent to incurring a fixed cost.'[13]

In one paragraph Romer had summed up the revolutionary potential of the tiny gesture I just made to extract that quote out of a PDF and put it into this book: copy and paste. Once you can copy/paste a paragraph, you can do it with a music track, a movie, the design of a turbofan engine and the digital mockup of the factory that will make it.

Once you can copy and paste something, it can be reproduced for free. It has, in economics-speak, a 'zero marginal cost'.

Info-capitalists have a solution to this: make it legally impossible to copy certain kinds of information. For example, while I'm allowed to quote Romer for free in this book, downloading the PDF of his famous 1990 paper cost me $16.80 on the JSTOR academic website. If I tried to copy and paste the design of a turbofan engine I could end up in jail.

But intellectual property rights are notoriously messy: I can legally copy a CD that I own into my iTunes folder, but it's illegal to rip a DVD. The laws of what you can and can't copy are unclear. They are enforced socially as much as by law, and like the patents of the pre-digital era, they decay over time.

If you are trying to 'own' a piece of information – whether you're a rock band or a turbofan manufacturer – your problem lies in the fact that it does not degrade with use, and that one person consuming it does not prevent another person consuming it. Economists call this 'non-rivalry'. A simpler word for it would be 'shareable'.

With purely physical goods, consumption by one person generally blocks their use by another: it's my cigarette not yours, my hire car, my cappuccino, my half-hour of psychotherapy. Not yours. But with an mp3 track, the information *is* the commodity. It can technically exist in many physical forms, and at a scale so small that it allows me to carry around every piece of music I have ever bought in my life on a 2-inch flash drive, a.k.a. an iPod.

Once a commodity is 'non-rival', the only way you can defend your ownership of it is by what economists call 'exclusion'. So you can either put a bug into the software that makes it impossible to copy – as with a DVD – or you can make copying illegal. But the fact remains, whatever you do to protect the information – bug it, encrypt it, arrest the pirate-DVD seller in the car park – the information itself remains copiable and shareable, and at negligible cost.

This has major implications for the way the market operates.

Mainstream economists assume that markets promote perfect competition and that imperfections – such as monopolies, patents, trade unions, price-fixing cartels – are always temporary. They also assume that people in the marketplace have perfect information. Romer showed that, once the economy is composed of shareable information goods, imperfect competition becomes the norm.

The equilibrium state of an info-tech economy is one where monopolies dominate and people have unequal access to the information they need to make rational buying decisions. Info-tech, in short, destroys the normal price mechanism, whereby competition drives prices down towards the cost of production. A track on iTunes costs next to zero to store on Apple's server, and next to zero to transmit to my computer. Whatever it cost the record company to produce (in terms of artist fees and marketing costs) it costs me 99p simply because it's unlawful to copy it for free.

The interplay between supply and demand does not come into the price of an iTunes track: the supply of the Beatles 'Love Me Do' on iTunes is infinite. And, unlike with that of physical records, the price doesn't change as demand fluctuates either. Apple's absolute legal right to charge 99p is what sets the price.

To run a multibillion dollar business based on information, Apple does not only rely on copyright law, it has built an entire walled garden of expensive technologies that work together – the Mac, iTunes, the iPod, the iCloud, the iPhone and the iPad – to make it easier for us to obey the law than break it. As a result iTunes dominates global digital music sales, with around 75 per cent of the market.[14]

With info-capitalism, a monopoly is not just some clever tactic to maximize profit. It is the only way an industry can run. The small number of companies that dominate each sector is striking. In traditional sectors you have usually four to six big players in every market: the big four accountancy firms; four or five big supermarket groups; four big turbofan makers. But the signature brands of info-tech need total dominance: Google needs to be the only search company; Facebook has to be the only place you construct your online identity; Twitter where you post your thoughts; iTunes the go-to online music store. In two key markets – online search and mobile operating systems – there is a two-firm death match, with Google currently winning both of them.

Until we had shareable information goods, the basic law of economics was that everything is scarce. Supply and demand assumes scarcity. Now certain goods are not scarce, they are abundant – so supply and demand become irrelevant. The supply of an iTunes track is ultimately one file on a server in Cupertino, technically shareable by everyone. Only intellectual property law and a small piece of code in the iTunes track prevent everybody on earth from owning every piece of music ever made. Apple's mission statement, properly expressed, is to prevent the abundance of music.

So Romer's new theory was simultaneously bad news for mainstream economics and reassuring news for the emerging giants of info-capitalism. It tied together in a single explanation many of the anomalies conventional economics had struggled to explain. And it gave a tacit justification for the market position of tech monopolies. The journalist David Warsh summed up its impact:

> The fundamental categories of economic analysis ceased to be, as they had been for two hundred years, land, labour and capital. This most

elementary classification was supplanted by people, ideas and things . . . the familiar principle of scarcity had been augmented by the important principle of abundance.[15]

On the publication of Romer's paper in 1990, then, did the world of economics start singing 'Hallelujah'? It did not. Romer was greeted with hostility and indifference. Critics of mainstream economics, Joseph Stiglitz at their head, had been saying for years that its general assumptions – of perfect information and efficient markets – were wrong. Now Romer, working inside the mainstream and using its methods, had knocked down the mainstream's defence against these critics. For Romer's research had shown that, once you move to an information economy, the market mechanism for setting prices will drive the marginal cost of certain goods, over time, towards zero – eroding profits in the process.

In short, information technology is corroding the normal operation of the price mechanism. This has revolutionary implications for everything, as the rest of this book explores.

If they'd understood capitalism as a finite system, Romer and his supporters might have explored the massive implications of this extraordinary statement – but they did not. They assumed the economy was, as in the textbooks, composed of price makers and price takers: rational individuals trying to pursue their self-interest through the market.

Those who did see the bigger picture were not to be found in the world of professional economics but among the tech visionaries. By the late 1990s they had begun to understand what Romer did not: that info-tech makes possible a non-market economy and creates a demographic prepared to pursue their self-interest through non-market actions.

THE RISE OF OPEN SOURCE

There is a chance you are reading this on a tablet: a Kindle, Nexus or iPad. They rarely crash and you would not even dream of programming them but they are computers nonetheless. The chip in an iPad

Air has one billion transistors etched into a single piece of silicon – that's equivalent to the processing power of 5,000 desktop computers thirty years ago.[16]

The base-layer of software needed for an iPad to work is the operating system: iOS. Because computing is today so easy, we barely comprehend the challenge that operating systems presented to the pioneers in the 1970s. In the early years of software, a struggle began over operating systems, which spiralled into a struggle over who should, or can, own information.

For the first thirty years, computers were big and rare, and computing took place in businesses and universities. When desktop PCs were invented in the mid 1970s, they were little more than an assembly of electronic boards and a screen. And corporations did not build them, hobbyists did.

The Altair 8800 was a breakthrough machine, sold via magazine ads to a subculture of geeky people who wanted to learn programming. You needed a programming language to make the computer do what you wanted, and two Seattle-based guys came up with one: Altair BASIC, distributed on a reel of paper with holes punched through it, price $200. But soon they noticed that sales of the language were lagging behind sales of the computer. Users were copying and distributing the punched paper reels for free. In an angry 'Open Letter' the software's author urged them to kick pirates out of computer club meetings and to pay up: 'Most of you steal your software. [You believe] hardware must be paid for but software is something to share. Who cares if the people who worked on it get paid.'[17]

The author was Bill Gates, and he soon came up with a solution: to own the operating system as well as the programming language. Gates designed Windows, which became the standard operating system on PCs. Soon Windows built a near monopoly of the corporate desktop and Gates became a billionaire. His 'Open Letter' would go down as the second most important document in the history of digital economics.

Now here is an excerpt from what I think is the most important document:

If anything deserves a reward, it is social contribution. Creativity can be a social contribution, but only in so far as society is free to use the results. Extracting money from users of a program by restricting their use of it is destructive because the restrictions reduce the amount and the ways that the program can be used. This reduces the amount of wealth that humanity derives from the program.[18]

That was Richard Stallman in *The GNU Manifesto*, which launched the free software movement in 1985. Stallman had been irked not just by Microsoft but by the attempt by makers of much more powerful business computers to 'own' a rival operating system called Unix. His plan was to write a free version of Unix, called GNU, distribute it for free, and invite enthusiasts to collaborate on improving it – with the proviso that nobody could own or make money out of it. These principles have become known as 'Open Source'.

By 1991 GNU had incorporated Linux – a version of Unix for PCs developed by hundreds of programmers working collaboratively, for free, and licensed under the original legal contract that Stallman had designed.

Fast-forward to 2014 and maybe 10 per cent of all corporate computers are running Linux. The ten fastest supercomputers in the world all run Linux. More importantly, the standard tools for running a website – from the operating system to the web server to the database and the programming language – are Open Source.

Firefox, an Open Source browser, has currently around 24 per cent of the global browser market.[19] A staggering 70 per cent of all smartphones run on Android, which is also technically Open Source.[20] This is in part due to an overt strategy by Samsung and Google to use Open Source software to undermine Apple's monopoly and maintain their own market position, but it does not alter the fact that the dominant smartphone on the planet runs on software nobody can own.

The success of Open Source software is startling. It demonstrates that new forms of property ownership and management become not just possible but imperative in an information-rich economy. It shows there are things about information goods that even monopolies can't monopolize.

According to standard economics a person like Richard Stallman should not exist: he is not following his self-interest but suppressing it in favour of a collective interest that is not just economic but moral.

According to market theory, it is those motivated by the pursuit of private property who should be the more efficient innovators. According to mainstream economics, large corporations such as Google should be doing what Bill Gates did: making a land-grab for everything and trying to destroy Open Source software. Now Google is a hard-assed capitalist firm, but in pursuit of its own interests it is forced to fight for some standards to be open and some software to be free. Google is not postcapitalist – but as long as it keeps Android Open Source it is being forced to act in a way that prefigures non-capitalist forms of ownership and exchange, even if, as the EU is investigating, they use this position to carve out dominance.

The birth of free software and the pursuit of collaborative software projects in the 1980s were just the opening shots of a war that is still raging, and whose battlefront is fluid. The Open Source movement also gave impetus to a movement for freedom of information, to Wikipedia, Wikileaks and a branch of the legal profession dedicated to writing contracts that could defend openness and shareability.

It was within this milieu, in the late 1990s, that the first systematic thinking took place about a question obvious to Drucker, but not to Romer: could an economy based on information networks create a *new mode of production* beyond capitalism?

SKATING TO THE EDGE OF CHAOS

There is a sound, now forgotten, that will remain hardwired into the memory of the generation born before 1980: a high-pitched whine, which fluctuates and then dissolves into a series of crackles, punctuated by two buzzy bass notes. It's the sound of a dial-up modem logging on.

When I first heard it sometime in the 1980s, I was trying to get on to Compuserve. Compuserve was a private network, offering email, file transfers and a massive community of bulletin boards. It was a world of words only – in black and white. Even then it was brimming with anger, subversion and pornography.

In 1994 I left Compuserve and joined Easynet, one of the first internet service providers: same technology, different ballgame. Now, the manual proclaimed, I had access to 'the whole road system, not just one service station'. It gave you access to the World Wide Web, a system for finding everything available on the linked-up computers of the world.

There was not much there. My workplace computer was linked only to the other computers in the building of the publishing company Reed Elsevier. When we tried to write our first web page the IT department refused to allow us to store it on 'their' server, which was for doing the payroll. There was no email on my workplace Mac and no web access. Computers were for processing data and were linked together for specific tasks only.

What a visionary, then, was the US journalist Kevin Kelly, to write this in 1997:

> The grand irony of our times is that the era of computers is over. All the major consequences of stand-alone computers have already taken place. Computers have speeded up our lives a bit, and that's it. In contrast, all the most promising technologies making their debut now are chiefly due to communication between computers that is, to connections rather than to computations.[21]

Kelly's article in *Wired* triggered a moment of recognition for my generation. Everything up to now – the 5-inch floppy discs for the university mainframe, the green screens of the early Amstrads, the crackle and buzz of the modem – had been the prologue. Suddenly a network economy was taking shape. Kelly wrote: 'I prefer the term network economy, because information isn't enough to explain the discontinuities we see. We have been awash in a steadily increasing tide of information for the past century . . . but only recently has a total reconfiguration of information itself shifted the whole economy.'[22]

Kelly himself was no advocate of postcapitalism. Indeed, his book *New Rules for the New Economy* was a breathless survival manual for old businesses as they tried to engage with the interconnected world. But his contribution was important. It was the moment we began to understand that the 'intelligent machine' was not the computer but the network, and that the network would speed up the rate of change and make it unpredictable. In a statement that defines our era, Kelly said: 'We are now engaged in a grand scheme to augment, amplify, enhance, and extend the relationships and communications between all beings and all objects.'[23]

The milestones between then and now are the launch of eBay (1997), which led to the dotcom boom. The first wifi-enabled laptop (a Mac) in 1999. The rollout of the broadband internet, which was always on and ten times faster than dial-up (2000). The expansion of 3G telecoms after 2001, which made the mobile internet possible. The launch of Wikipedia in 2001. The sudden arrival of cheap, standardized digital tools, which was dubbed Web 2.0, in 2004.

At this point, programs and data began to sit within the network rather than on individual computers; the archetypal activities became search, self-publishing and interaction, including through multibillion dollar online games.

Now came the launch of social networks with MySpace (2003), Facebook (2004) and Twitter (2006); and the launch of the iPhone (2007), the first true smartphone. The iPad and the Kindle in the same year sparked the rapid rise of e-book publishing, whose value has grown from under $1.5 billion in 2009 to $15 billion worldwide (2015). Desktop PC sales were overtaken by notebook sales in 2008. Samsung's first Android phone was launched in 2009.[24]

Meanwhile, in high-end computing, the first computer to achieve one quadrillion calculations per second was an IBM, in 2008. By 2014, Tianhe 2 in China, running Linux, could do 33 quadrillion. In terms of data storage, 2002 was the year in which the volume of digital information in the world overtook the amount of analog information. Between 2006 and 2012 humanity's annual information output grew tenfold.[25]

It's hard to tell exactly where you are in a tech revolution but my hunch is the simultaneous arrival of tablets, streaming video and music and the takeoff of social media between 2009 and 2014 will be seen as the key moment of synergy. The rollout of billions of machine-to-machine connections, known as the 'Internet of Things', in the next ten years will then populate the global information network with more intelligent devices than there are people on earth.

To live through all this was exhilarating enough. Even more

exhilarating now is to watch a kid get their first smartphone and find it all – Bluetooth, GPS, 3G, wifi, streaming video, hi-res photography and heart-rate monitor – as if it had always been there.

The network economy emerged, and has become social. In 1997, just 2 per cent of the world's population had internet access. Now it is 38 per cent, and in the developed world 75 per cent. Today there are ninety-six mobile-phone subscriptions for every 100 people in the world, and 30 per cent of the earth's inhabitants have an active 3G (or better) mobile. The number of telephone landlines per person is actually falling.[26]

In the space of a decade, the network has pervaded our lives. The average teenager with a smart device is living a more psychologically connected life than the geekiest computer nerd fifteen years ago.

When Romer and Drucker made their contributions in the early 1990s, the issue was still the impact of intelligent machines. Today we understand implicitly that the network is the machine. And as software and data have moved into the network, the debate about the economic impact of information technology has also begun to focus on the network.

In 1997, Kelly proclaimed the existence of an emerging new economic order with three main characteristics: 'It is global. It favors intangible things – ideas, information, and relationships. And it is intensely interlinked. These three attributes produce a new type of marketplace and society.'[27]

Kelly accepted as commonplace what Romer had seen as new seven years before: the tendency of information technology to make data and physical products cheaper, so that the marginal cost of producing them declines towards zero. But, he assured his readers, there was a counterweight to endless supply and falling prices, namely endless demand: 'Technology and knowledge are driving up demand faster than it is driving down prices ... The extent of human needs and desires is limited only by human imagination, which means, in practical terms, there is no limit.'[28]

The solution, Kelly said, was to invent new goods and services faster than they could slide down the curve to worthlessness. Instead of trying to defend prices, you had to assume they would collapse over time, but build a business in the gap between one and zero. You had, he warned, to 'skate to the edge of chaos', to exploit the free knowledge customers donate when they interact with websites. By the late 1990s, the received wisdom among those who understood the problem was that capitalism would survive because innovation would counteract technology's downward effect on pricing. But nowhere did Kelly explore what might happen if this failed.

Then came the dotcom crash. The spectacular fall of Nasdaq, beginning in April 2000, changed the perception of the generation that had struggled with dial-up modems and got rich. Following the disaster John Perry Barlow, a cyber-rights campaigner who'd lost 95 per cent of his money, drew the harsh conclusion: 'The whole dot-com thing was an effort to use 19th and 20th century concepts of economy in an environment where they didn't exist, and the internet essentially shrugged them off. This was an assault by an alien force that was repelled by the natural forces of the internet.' And he pointed out where the debate might go next. 'In the long term it's going to be very good for the dot-communists.'[29]

A NEW MODE OF PRODUCTION?

In 2006 Yochai Benkler, then a law professor at Yale, concluded that the network economy was 'a new mode of production emerging in the middle of the most advanced economies in the world'.[30] Benkler had been trying to define a legal framework for Open Source publishing, known as the 'Creative Commons'. In *The Wealth of Networks*, he described the economic forces that were undermining intellectual property, causing common ownership models and unmanaged production to spread.

First, he said, the rise of cheap physical computing power and communications networks had put the means of production of intellectual goods into the hands of many people. People can blog, they can make movies and distribute them, they can self-publish e-books – in some cases creating a million-strong audience before the traditional publishers even know the authors exist: 'The result is that a good deal more that human beings value can now be done by individuals who interact with each other socially, as human beings and as social beings, rather than as market actors through the price system.'[31]

This, he argued, leads to the rise of non-market mechanisms: decentralized action by individuals, working through cooperative, voluntary forms of organization. It is producing new forms of 'peer-to-peer' economics, in which money is either absent or not the main measure of value.

Wikipedia is the best example. Founded in 2001, the collaboratively written encyclopaedia has, at the time of writing, 26 million pages and 24 million people registered to contribute and edit – with about 12,000 people regularly editing and 140,000 people vaguely taking part.[32]

Wikipedia has 208 employees.[33] The thousands who edit it do so for free. A user survey found 71 per cent of them do it because they like the idea of working for nothing, and 63 per cent because they believe information should be free.[34] With 8.5 billion page views per month the Wikipedia site is the sixth most popular in the world – just above Amazon, the most successful e-commerce company on earth.[35] By one estimate, if it were run as a commercial site, Wikipedia's revenue could be $2.8 billion a year.[36]

Yet Wikipedia makes no profit. And in doing so it makes it almost impossible for anybody else to make a profit in the same space. Furthermore, it is one of the most valuable learning resources ever invented and has (so far) defied all attempts to censor, subvert, troll or sabotage it, because the power of tens of millions of human eyeballs is greater than any government, stalker, interest group or saboteur can match.

The principle Wikipedia works on is the same the early Open Source programmers used on GNU and Linux, but applied to a mass consumer product. When we visit Amazon, and buy a camera or a book, our recorded choices help other users choose. In economics this is called a positive 'externality' – an unintended economic benefit.

With Amazon, it is the corporation that reaps most of the benefit, in the form of increased buying and selling power. With Wikipedia, there is only a human benefit: no kid ever again has to sit in a small town library, as I did, lost in a maze of mediocre and random knowledge, itself trapped for ever on sheets of paper that can never be updated or corrected without printing a completely new book.

Benkler draws out the economic lesson of a phenomenon like

Wikipedia: that the network makes it possible to organize production in a decentralized and collaborative way, utilizing neither the market nor management hierarchy.

Economists like to demonstrate the archaic nature of command planning with mind-games like 'imagine the Soviet Union tried to create Starbucks'. Now, here's a more intriguing game: imagine if Amazon, Toyota or Boeing tried to create Wikipedia.

Without collaborative production and Open Source there would be only two ways to do so: by using either the market or the command structures of a corporation. Since there are maybe 12,000 active writers and editors of Wikipedia, you could hire that number, and maybe get away with some of them being outworkers in the sweatshop economies of the world, controlled by a better-paid managerial layer in the American sun-belt. Then you could incentivize them to write the best possible encyclopaedia on the web. You would give them targets, bonuses, promote teamwork through quality circles, etc.

But you could not produce anything as dynamic as Wikipedia. Getting a 12,000-strong corporation to produce 26 million pages of Wikipedia would be as pointless as the Soviet Union trying to create its own version of Starbucks. A 208-strong foundation would always do it better. And even if you could produce something just as good as Wikipedia, you would face a massive problem: Wikipedia itself, your major competitor, doing it all for free.

So maybe, instead of using a corporation to command Wikipedia into existence, you could try using market forces to trade it into existence. After all, doesn't business school teach us the market is the most efficient system?

People would maybe pay small amounts of money for small chunks of knowledge, while being comfortable with the idea that the information rests in the public domain as free. Maybe the academics, amateurs and enthusiasts who write the pages would be glad to receive a small amount of money for each contribution.

This, in fact, is more like what actually happens – but it is not money the participants are exchanging. They are in effect exchanging gifts. And as anthropologists have long realized, the gift is only the physical symbol of something more intangible: call it goodwill, or happiness.

Wikipedia, like Linux, is radical in two ways. First, in the communal nature of what is produced: it is free to use but impossible to grab, own and exploit. Second, in the collaborative nature of the production process: nobody in a central office decides what the pages should be about; Wikipedia's employees simply regulate the standards of creation and editing, and defend the whole platform against erosion by property and management hierarchies.

Benkler defines this as 'commons-based peer production' – and the concept challenges the certainties of mainstream economics some more. Nothing has changed about humanity. It's just that our human desire to make friends, build relationships based on mutual trust and obligation, fulfilling emotional and psychological needs, has spilled over into economic life.

At the precise moment in history when it became possible to produce stuff without the market or the firm, significant numbers of people started doing so.

In the first place, the cheapening of computer power and network access puts the ability to produce information goods into the hands of many people, not the few. Next, you need what Benkler calls 'planned modularity': that is, a task is broken up into chunks small enough for people to complete on their own and then submit the outcome to a wider network. A Wikipedia page is a perfect example: adding a snippet of info or deleting an erroneous one is a modular task that can be done from the top deck of a bus on a smartphone, or from a PC in the web café of a Manila slum.

For Benkler, then, cheap technology and modular forms of production have driven us towards non-market, collaborative work. It is not a fad, he argues, but 'a sustainable pattern of human production'. Though he uses the words 'new mode of production' Benkler does not say that this is something different from capitalism. He argues instead that it will lead to a radically different and more sustainable form of capitalism. He predicts a redistribution of wealth and power from dominant firms and elites to a wider mixture of individuals, peer networks and businesses that can adapt to the new situation.

The problem is, Benkler is describing the new forms of info-capitalism without describing their dynamics, which are necessarily contradictory.

Info-tech drives labour out of the production process, reduces the market price of commodities, destroys some profit models and produces a generation of consumers psychologically attuned to free stuff. But in the first full decade of its existence it has helped fuel a global crisis during which the poorest citizens of developed countries were reduced to scrambling through dumpsters, even as they eked out the last few cents of credit on their mobile phones.

Info-capitalism is real, but if we analyse the whole thing – the collision of neoliberal economics with network technology – we must conclude it is in crisis.

THE ECONOMICS OF FREE STUFF

In the late nineteenth century economists began to notice that not all the effects of capitalism could be understood through the act of buying and selling. Given most factories were by then surrounded by slag heaps, slums and stinking rivers, it was hard not to notice that capitalism has effects external to what is done in the marketplace. They called these 'externalities', and a debate began over how to account for them.

At first they focused on 'bad' externalities: if I buy coal-fired power from an energy supplier and it pollutes the air, that pollution is an externality. The solution to bad externalities is easy: you work out a way to allocate the cost to the buyer and seller. So with the dirty power station, for example, you impose a pollution tax.

However, there are also 'good' externalities – such as the lower hiring costs that arise when similar businesses cluster in the same neighbourhood. There is no need for a solution to good externalities, but they often show up as reduction in cost and activity.

But in an information economy, the externalities become the major issue. In the old world, economists categorized information as a 'public good': the costs of science, for example, were borne by society – so everybody benefited. But in the 1960s economists began to understand information as a commodity. In 1962, Kenneth Arrow, the guru of mainstream economics, said that in a free-market economy, the purpose of inventing things is to create intellectual property rights.

'Precisely to the extent that it is successful there is an under-utilisation of information.'[37]

If you think about it this way, the purpose of patenting the advanced HIV drug Darunavir can only be to keep its price at $1095 a year, which is, as Médecins sans Frontières put it, 'prohibitively expensive'. The information exists to place millions of people on this advanced HIV treatment, but thanks to the patent it is underutilized. Conversely, because India famously prevented pharmaceutical companies slapping twenty-year patents on other advanced HIV treatments, their cost has slumped since the year 2000, and the information on how to make them has been utilized.

In an economy where information is everywhere, so are externalities. If we survey the giants of info-capitalism, almost the whole of their business model is about capturing good external side-effects.

Amazon works, for example, by offering to sell you things based on your previous choices – information you provided for free and could not choose to withhold. The whole business model is based on the one-sided capture of externalities by Amazon. It works for supermarkets too: by aggregating their customer data and preventing its utilization by everybody else, big supermarkets such as Walmart or Tesco gain a huge commercial advantage.

Now imagine Walmart or Tesco were prepared to publish their customer data (suitably anonymized) for free. Society would benefit: everybody from farmers to epidemiologists could mine the data, and make more accurate decisions; individual customers could see at a glance whether they'd been making rational or irrational shopping decisions. But the supermarkets would lose market advantage; their ability to manipulate consumer behaviour using price points, sell-by dates and two-for-one deals would be reduced. The whole point of their vast e-commerce systems is that customer data is, as Arrow would put it, 'underutilized'.

If we restate Arrow's observation in a different way, its revolutionary implications are obvious: if a free-market economy with intellectual property leads to the underutilization of information, then an economy based on the full utilization of information cannot have a free market or absolute intellectual property rights. And this is just another way of saying what Benkler and Drucker understood: that info-tech undermines something fundamental about the way capitalism works.

But what does it create in its place? For the term 'postcapitalism' to be meaningful, you would have to describe exactly how network technology triggers a transition to something else, and what the dynamics of a postcapitalist world would look like.

None of the writers I've surveyed above achieves that – and for a reason: none of them is working with a fully rounded theory of capitalism itself. But what if somebody did anticipate the information-driven fall of capitalism? What if someone had clearly predicted that the ability to create prices would dissolve if information became collectively distributed and embodied in machines? We would probably be hailing that person's work as visionary. Actually there is such a person. His name is Karl Marx.

THE GENERAL INTELLECT

The scene is Kentish Town, London, February 1858, sometime around 4 a.m. Marx is still a wanted man in Germany and has spent ten years becoming increasingly depressed about the prospects for revolution. But now Wall Street has crashed, there are bank failures across Europe and he is scrambling to finish a long-promised book on economics. 'I'm working like a madman right through the night' he confides, 'so that I'll at least have the outlines clear before the deluge.'[38]

Marx's resources are limited. He has a pass to the British Library, giving him access to the latest data. By day he writes articles in English for the *New York Tribune*. By night he is filling eight notebooks with near-illegible scrawl in German: free-flowing observations, thought experiments and notes-to-self.

The notebooks, known collectively as the *Grundrisse* (which translates as 'The Outline'), will be saved, but not read, by Engels. They will be stored in the HQ of the German social-democratic party until the Soviet Union buys them in the 1920s. They will not be read in Western Europe until the late 1960s, and in English not until 1973. When they finally get to see what Marx is writing on this cold night in 1858, scholars will admit that it 'challenges every serious interpretation of Marx yet conceived'.[39] It is called the *Fragment on Machines*.

The *Fragment on Machines* starts with the observation that as large-scale industry develops it changes the relationship between worker and machine. In early industry, there was a man, a tool worked by hand and a product. Now instead of a tool, the worker: 'inserts the process of nature, transformed into an industrial process, as a means between himself and inorganic nature, mastering it. He steps to the side of the production process instead of being its chief actor.'[40]

Marx had imagined an economy in which the main role of machines was to produce, and the main role of people was to supervise them. He was clear that in such an economy the main productive force would be information. The productive power of machines like the 'self-acting' cotton-spinning machine, the telegraph and the steam locomotive was 'out of all proportion to the direct labour time spent on their production, but depends rather on the general state of science and on the progress of technology, or the application of this science to production'.[41]

Organization and knowledge, in other words, made a bigger contribution to productive power than the labour of making and running the machines.

Given what Marxism was to become – a theory of exploitation based on the theft of labour time – this is a revolutionary statement. It suggests that – once knowledge becomes a productive force in its own right, vastly outweighing the actual labour spent creating a machine – the big question becomes not wages versus profits but who controls the 'power of knowledge'.

Now Marx drops a bombshell. In an economy where machines do most of the work, where human labour is really about supervising, mending and designing the machines, the nature of the knowledge locked inside the machines must, he writes, be 'social'.

Let's use a modern example. If, today, a software developer uses a programming language to write code linking a web page to a database, then she is clearly working with social knowledge. I'm not talking specifically here about Open Source programming, just an ordinary commercial software project. Every layer of the process has been created by sharing information, pooling it, tweaking the code and the interfaces.

The programmer herself doesn't own the code she's working on, obviously. But equally the company employing her can't own more than a fraction of it. It can legally patent every piece of code she outputs. It can even force her to sign an agreement that what she writes in her spare time belongs to them – but the code will still contain thousands of bits of previous code written by other people that cannot be patented.

Plus, the knowledge it took to produce the code is still in the programmer's brain. She can, if market conditions allow, move to a different workplace and execute the same solution, should it be required. With information, part of the product remains with the worker in a way it did not during the industrial era.

It is the same for the tool she's using: the programming language. It has been developed by tens of thousands of people contributing their knowledge and experience. If she downloads the latest update, it is sure to contain changes based on lessons learned by everyone else using it.

On top of that, the consumer data – the record left by each interaction with the website – may be wholly owned by a company. Yet it is socially produced: I send you a link, you click on it, or retweet it to 10,000 followers.

Marx couldn't imagine a web server. However, he could observe the telegraph system. By 1858 the telegraph, running alongside the world's railway lines and terminating at every railway station and business HQ, was the most important piece of infrastructure in the world. Britain alone boasted a network with 1,178 nodes outside London, and hundreds more linking the City, Parliament and the London docks.[42]

Telegraph operators were highly skilled but, as with the software programmer, the knowledge needed to work an electric key was insignificant alongside the knowledge embodied in the vast, cross-border machine they were actually supervising.

The memoirs of telegraph operators show clearly the social nature of the technology. Rule number one was that you could send information only as fast as the person on the other end could receive it. But in the complex telegraph systems, where rooms full of senders and receivers negotiated use of the crowded line capacity with far distant operators, 'handling egos was as much a part of an operator's work as handling a telegraph key. Considerate, helpful operators made work easier; domineering, cavalier, or self-righteous ones made work more difficult.'[43] Their work was social, the knowledge embodied in the machine was social.

In the *Fragment on Machines*, these two ideas – that the driving force of production is knowledge, and that knowledge stored in machines is social – led Marx to the following conclusions.

First, in a heavily mechanized capitalism, boosting productivity through better knowledge is a much more attractive source of profit than extending the working day, or speeding up labour: longer days consume more energy, speed-ups hit the limits of human dexterity and stamina. But a knowledge solution is cheap and limitless.

Second, Marx argued, knowledge-driven capitalism cannot support a price mechanism whereby the value of something is dictated by the value of the inputs needed to produce it. It is impossible to properly value inputs when they come in the form of social knowledge. Knowledge-driven production tends towards the unlimited creation of wealth, independent of the labour expended. But the normal capitalist system is based on prices determined by input costs, and assumes all inputs come in limited supply.

For Marx, knowledge-based capitalism creates a contradiction – between the 'forces of production' and the 'social relations'. These form 'the material conditions to blow [capitalism's] foundation sky-high'. Furthermore, capitalism of this type is forced to develop the intellectual power of the worker. It will tend to reduce working hours (or halt their extension), leaving time for workers to develop artistic and scientific talents outside work, which become essential to the economic model itself. Finally Marx throws in a new concept, which appears nowhere else – before or after – in his entire writings: 'the general intellect'. When we measure the development of technology, he writes, we are measuring the extent to which 'general social knowledge has become a force of production . . . under the control of the general intellect'.[44]

The ideas outlined in the *Fragment* were recognized in the 1960s as a complete departure from classic Marxism. In the twentieth century, the left had seen state planning as the route out of capitalism. They had assumed that capitalism's inner contradictions lay in the chaotic nature of the market, its inability to fulfil human need and its propensity to catastrophic breakdown.

In the 1858 *Fragment*, however, we are confronted with a different model of transition: a knowledge-based route out of capitalism, in which the main contradiction is between technology and the market mechanism. In this model, scribbled on paper in 1858 but unknown to the left for more than 100 years, capitalism collapses because it cannot exist alongside shared knowledge. The class struggle becomes the struggle to be human and educated during one's free time.

It was the Italian leftist Antonio Negri who described the *Fragment on Machines* as 'Marx beyond Marx'. Paolo Virno, one of his co-thinkers, pointed out that its ideas 'are not present in any of his other writings and in fact seem alternative to the habitual formula'.[45]

The question remains: why didn't Marx pursue this idea more widely? Why does the general intellect disappear as a concept except on this one unpublished page? Why does this model of the market mechanism being dissolved by social knowledge get lost in the writing of *Capital*?

The obvious answer – beyond all the textual discussions – is that capitalism itself at the time did not bear out the proposition. Once the 1858 panic was over, stability returned. The socialization of knowledge inherent in the telegraph and the steam locomotive were not sufficient to blow the foundations of capitalism sky-high.

In the following decade, Marx constructed a theory of capitalism in which the mechanisms of exchange are *not* exploded by the emergence of a general intellect, and in which no mention is ever made of knowledge being an independent source of profit. In other words, Marx retreated from the specific ideas in the *Fragment on Machines*.

The emergence of twentieth-century Marxism as a doctrine of state socialism and crisis-driven transition was no accident; it was grounded in the Marx of *Capital*.

Here, though, I am not concerned with a history of Marxism, but with the question: is there a route to postcapitalism based on the rise of information technology? It is clear from the *Fragment* that Marx had at least imagined such a route.

He imagined socially produced information becoming embodied in machines. He imagined this producing a new dynamic, which destroys the old mechanisms for creating prices and profits. He imagined capitalism being forced to develop the intellectual capacities of the worker. And he imagined information coming to be stored and shared in something called a 'general intellect' – which was the mind of everybody on earth connected by social knowledge, in which every upgrade benefits everybody. In short, he had imagined something close to the info-capitalism in which we live.

Furthermore, he had imagined what the main objective of the working class would be if this world ever existed: freedom from work. The utopian socialist Charles Fourier had predicted that labour would become the same as play. Marx disagreed. Instead, he wrote, liberation would come through leisure time: 'Free time has naturally transformed its possessor into a different subject, and he then enters into the direct production process as this different subject . . . in whose head exists the accumulated knowledge of society.'[46]

This is possibly the most revolutionary idea Marx ever had: that the reduction of labour to a minimum could produce a kind of human being able to deploy the entire, accumulated knowledge of society; a person transformed by vast quantities of socially produced knowledge and for the first time in history more free time than work time. It's not so far from the worker imagined in the *Fragment* to the 'universal educated person' predicted by Peter Drucker.

Marx, I think, abandoned this thought experiment because it had scant relevance to the society he lived in. But it has massive relevance for ours.

A THIRD KIND OF CAPITALISM?

To the neoliberals, the emergence of info-capitalism seemed like their greatest achievement. They could barely conceive that it might contain flaws. Intelligent machines, they believed, would create a post-industrial society in which everybody did high-value, knowledge-based work and in which all the old social conflicts died out.[47] Information would enable the idealized capitalism of the textbooks – with transparency, perfect competition and equilibrium – to become reality. In the late 1990s the literature of the mainstream – from *Wired* magazine to the *Harvard Business Review* – was filled with celebratory descriptions of the new system. But there was an ominous silence about how it worked.

Ironically, it fell to the people who had rediscovered the *Fragment on Machines*, the far left disciples of Antonio Negri, to make the first attempt at a theory of info-capitalism, which they dubbed 'cognitive capitalism'.

Cognitive capitalism, say its proponents, is a coherent new form of capitalism: a 'third capitalism', following the merchant capitalism of the seventeenth and eighteenth centuries and the industrial capitalism of the last 200 years. It is based on global markets, financialized consumption, immaterial labour and immaterial capital.

Yann Moulier-Boutang, a French economist, believes that the key for cognitive capitalism is the capture of the externalities. As people use digital devices, they become 'co-producers' with the companies they are dealing with: their choices, their apps, their friend lists on Facebook can all be given monetary value by the company that provides the service and harvests the information. 'Capturing positive externalities,' writes Moulier Boutang, 'becomes the number one problem of value.'[48]

In cognitive capitalism, the nature of work is transformed. Manual labour and industry don't stop, but their place in the landscape changes. Because profit increasingly comes from capturing the free value generated by consumer behaviour, and because a society focused on mass consumption has to be constantly fed coffee, smiled at, serviced by call centres, the 'factory' in cognitive capitalism is the whole of society. For these theorists, 'society as a factory' is a crucial concept – vital to understanding not just the nature of exploitation but resistance.

For a pair of Nike trainers to be worth $179.99 requires 465,000 workers in 107 factories across Vietnam, China and Indonesia to produce to the same exact standard. But it also requires the consumer to believe that the Nike swoosh makes these chunks of plastic, rubber and foam worth seven times the average US hourly wage.[49] Nike spends $2.7 billion a year on getting us to believe just that (compared to $13 billion actually making the shoes and clothing) – and that marketing budget buys way more than advertisements at the Superbowl.

In fact since Nike got its head around the rules of cognitive capitalism in the early 2000s, its spend on TV and press adverts has fallen by 40 per cent. Instead, the focus is on digital products: Nike+ for example, which uses an iPod to log runners' performances, has recorded – and fed back to Nike – 150 million individual jogging sessions since its launch in 2006.[50] Like all businesses, Nike is in the process of becoming, effectively, 'information plus things'.

This is what the cognitive capital theorists mean by the 'socialized factory'. We are no longer in a world of clearly delineated production and consumption, but one in which ideas, behaviours and customer interactions with the brand are critical to generating profit; production and consumption are blurred. This partly explains why struggles against the new capitalism are often focused on consumer issues, or brand values (e.g. corporate social responsibility), and why protesters behave more like the 'tribes' in marketing demographics than a unified proletariat. For cognitive capital theorists – as for Drucker – the primary activity of the new workforce is 'the production of knowledge by means of knowledge'.[51]

However, the cognitive capitalism theory contains a major flaw. It would be one thing to say 'a new kind of info-capitalism has been born within late industrial capitalism'. But the key cognitive capitalism theorists say the opposite: many of them believe cognitive capitalism to be a fully functioning system already. Factories in Shenzhen, slums in Manila, metal-bashing shops in Wolverhampton may look just as they did ten years ago – but to these theorists their economic functions are already transformed.

This is a technique common in European speculative thought: to invent a category and apply it to everything, thus reclassifying all existing things as sub-categories of your new idea. It saves you the trouble of analysing complex and contradictory realities.

It leads cognitive capitalism theorists to underestimate the importance of the rise of old-style industrial production in the BRIC (Brazil, Russia, India and China) countries, and for some to downplay the significance of the post-2008 financial crisis, or to see it as merely the teething troubles of the newborn system.

In fact, the system we live in is not a new, coherent and functioning form of capitalism. It is incoherent. Its tense, febrile and unstable character comes from the fact that we're living in an age of the network alongside the hierarchy, the slum alongside the web café – and to understand the situation we have to see it as an incomplete transition, not a finished model.

POSTCAPITALISM: A HYPOTHESIS

The debate on postcapitalism has come a long way since Peter Drucker, yet in another sense it has gone nowhere. It has been marked by speculative thinking, technobabble and a tendency to declare the existence of new systems rather than to explore their relationship to old realities.

Benkler, Kelly and Drucker each declared something akin to a 'new mode of production', but none advanced an explanation of what its dynamics might be. The Ontario-based economist Nick Dyer-Witheford, in his 1999 book *Cyber-Marx*, produced a decent speculative account of what information-based communism might look like.[52] But the debate on this has rarely achieved the status of economics.

Jeremy Rifkin, an influential management consultant, came closest to describing current reality in his 2014 book *The Zero Marginal Cost Society*.[53] Rifkin argues that peer-production and capitalism are two different systems; currently they coexist and even gain energy from each other, but ultimately peer-production will reduce the capitalist sector of the economy to a few niches.

Rifkin's most radical insight was to understand the potential of the Internet of Things. The most enthusiastic consultancies – for example McKinsey – have valued the impact of this process as up to $6 trillion a year, mainly in healthcare and manufacturing. But the vast majority of that $6 trillion is in reduced cost and increased efficiency: that is, it contributes to reducing the marginal cost of physical goods and services in the same way as copy and paste reduces the cost of information goods.

Rifkin points out that the impact of wiring every person and every object into an intelligent network could in fact be exponential. It could rapidly reduce the marginal cost of energy and physical goods in the same way as the internet does for digital products.

Like all books destined for the business shelves at airports, though, Rifkin's is light on the social dimension. He understands that a world of free stuff cannot be capitalist; that the free stuff is beginning to pervade the physical as well as the digital world, but the struggle between the two systems is reduced to a struggle between business models and good ideas.

Conducted among social theorists, lawyers and tech visionaries, the postcapitalism debate exists in a parallel universe to the debate among economists about the crisis of neoliberalism, and the debate among historians about the problematic takeoff of the fifth long wave. To move forward, we need to understand how the new economics of info-tech, the post-2008 crisis and the long-cycle pattern fit together. What follows below is a first attempt to do that. It's a hypothesis – but it is based on evidence and can be tested against reality.

Since the mid-1990s, a revolution in the way we process, store and communicate information has created the beginnings of a network economy. This has started to corrode the traditional property relations of capitalism in the following ways.

It corrodes the price mechanism for digital goods, as understood by mainstream economics, by pushing the cost of reproducing information goods towards zero.

It adds a high information content to physical goods, sucking them into the same zero-price vortex as pure information goods – and often, as with the trainers, making their value dependent more on socially created ideas (the brand) rather than the physical cost of production.

It makes financialization necessary, creating two streams of profit flowing to capital from the general population: as workers producing goods, services and knowledge; and as borrowers generating interest payments. So, while it's true to say 'the whole of society has become a factory', the mechanisms of exploitation are still first of all wages, then credit and only finally our mental collusion in the creation of brand value, or the giveaway of externalities to tech companies.

It is in the process of revolutionizing the productivity of physical things, processes and energy grids, as machine-to-machine internet connections begin to outnumber person-to-person links.

If information corrodes value, then corporations are responding with three types of survival strategy: the creation of monopolies on information and the vigorous defence of intellectual property; the 'skating to the edge of chaos' approach, trying to live within the gap between expanded supply and falling prices; and the attempt to capture and exploit socially produced information such as consumer data, or by imposing contracts on programmers that say the company owns code they write in their free time.

However, alongside the corporate response, we are seeing the rise of non-market production: horizontally distributed peer-production networks that are not centrally managed, producing goods that are either completely free, or which – being Open Source – have very limited commercial value.

Peer-produced free stuff drives out commercially produced commodities. Wikipedia is a space in which commerce cannot operate; with Linux or Android there is clearly commercial exploitation, but at the edges – not based on ownership of the main product. It is becoming possible to be both producer and consumer in the same process.

In response, capitalism is beginning to reshape itself as a defence mechanism against peer-production, through info-monopolies, through allowing the wage relationship to weaken and through the irrational pursuit of high-carbon business models.

Non-market forms of production and exchange exploit the basic human tendency to collaborate – to exchange gifts of intangible value – which has always existed but at the margins of economic life. This is more than simply a rebalancing between public goods and private goods: it is a whole new and revolutionary thing. The proliferation of these non-market economic activities is making it possible for a cooperative, socially just society to emerge.

The rapid change in technology is altering the nature of work, blurring the distinction between work and leisure and requiring us to participate in the creation of value across our whole lives, not just in the workplace. This gives us multiple economic personalities, which is the economic base on which a new kind of person, with multiple selves, has emerged.[54] It is this new kind of person, the networked individual, who is the bearer of the postcapitalist society that could now emerge.

The technological direction of this revolution is at odds with its social direction. Technologically, we are headed for zero-price goods, unmeasurable work, an exponential takeoff in productivity and the extensive automation of physical processes. Socially, we are trapped in a world of monopolies, inefficiency, the ruins of a finance-dominated free market and a proliferation of 'bullshit jobs'.

Today, the main contradiction in modern capitalism is between the possibility of free, abundant socially produced goods, and a system of monopolies, banks and governments struggling to maintain control over power and information. That is, everything is pervaded by a fight between network and hierarchy.

It's happening now because the rise of neoliberalism disrupted the normal fifty-year patterns of capitalism. And that's another way of saying that the 240-year lifecycle of industrial capitalism may be nearing its end.

So there are two basic possibilities ahead of us. Either a new form of cognitive capitalism does emerge and stabilize – based on a new mix of firms, markets and networked collaboration – and the remnants of the industrial system find an orderly place within this third capitalism. Or the network erodes both the working and the legitimacy of the market system. If so, a conflict will take place that results in the abolition of the market system and its replacement by postcapitalism.

Postcapitalism could take many different forms. We'll know it's happened if a large number of goods become cheap or free, but people go on producing them irrespective of market forces. We'll know it's underway once the blurred relationship between work and leisure, and between hours and wages, becomes institutionalized.

Because its precondition is abundance, postcapitalism will deliver some form of social justice spontaneously – but the forms and priorities of social justice will be negotiable. Whereas capitalist societies always had to worry about 'guns *vs* butter', postcapitalist societies might fight over growth *vs* sustainability – or the timeframe for delivery of basic social goals, or challenges like migration, women's liberation and demographic ageing.

So we have to *design* the transition to postcapitalism. Because most theorists of postcapitalism either just declared it to exist, or predicted it as an inevitability, few considered the problems of transition. So one of the first tasks is to outline and test a range of models showing how such a transitional economy might work.

Today we are used to hearing the word 'transition' to describe tentative local attempts to build a low-carbon economy; local currencies, time banks, 'transition towns' and the like. But transition, here, is a bigger project.

To make it happen we need to learn the negative lessons of failed transition in the USSR. After 1928, the Soviet Union tried to force a route through to socialism via centralized planning. This produced something worse than capitalism, but among the modern left there is a strong aversion to discussing it.

If we want to create a postcapitalist society, we have to know in detail what went wrong, and to understand the fundamental difference between the spontaneous non-market forms that I've been describing here and the Five Year Plans of Stalinism.

To go forward, we need to know how, exactly, information goods corrode the market mechanism; what might happen if this tendency was being promoted instead of restrained; and what social group has the interest to make the transition happen. We need, in short, a better definition of value and a more detailed history of work. What follows is an attempt to provide them.

6

Towards the Free Machine

There was a tent camp, a noisy crowd, the drift of tear gas and a small pile of free stuff: this was Gezi Park during the 2013 protest in Istanbul. The tent camp allowed people to live for a few days just how they wanted to; the free stuff was the ultimate gesture of hope.

On the first day the pile was small: packets of salami, cartons of juice, some cigarettes and aspirins. By the last day it had become a toppling pyramid of everything: food, clothes, medicines and tobacco. Young people would pick up armfuls of it and walk round the park in groups, insisting you take some. Of course none of the stuff was really free. It had been bought and donated. But it symbolized a desire to live in a society where some basic things are shared.

And that's an old desire. During the first decades of the nineteenth century, surrounded by a system determined to put a price on everything, the left formed utopian communities based on sharing, cooperation and collaborative work. They were mostly failures, for the ultimate reason that everything was scarce.

Today, not so many things are scarce. The ability of people in a city like Istanbul to build a mountain of free food testifies to that. The recycling dumps in European cities show it too: as well as outright rubbish, you will find people dumping wearable clothes, spotless books, usable electronics – items that once had value now have no selling price and are given away to be recycled or shared. Energy, of course, remains scarce – or rather the carbon-based energy we're addicted to does. But the most critical commodity of twenty-first-century life is not scarce at all. Information is abundant.

This advance from scarcity towards abundance is a significant development in the history of humanity, and the great achievement of fourth-wave capitalism. But it's a major challenge for economic theory. Capitalism made us see the price mechanism as the most organic, spontaneous, granular thing in economic life. Now we need a theory of its disappearance.

We need to start by getting past the issue of supply and demand. Supply-and-demand clearly works: if more garment factories open in Bangladesh, cheap clothes get cheaper. And if the cops arrest drug dealers just before the clubs open, ecstasy becomes more expensive. But supply and demand explains only why prices fluctuate. When supply and demand are equal, why isn't the price zero? Obviously it can't be. In a normal capitalist economy, based on scarce goods and labour, there has to be a more intrinsic price around which the selling price moves up or down. So what determines that?

Over the past 200 years, two completely different answers have been put forward. Only one of them can be right. Unfortunately it is not the one taught in economics courses.

In this chapter I am going to mount a sustained defence of something called the 'labour theory of value'. It's not popular because it's not very useful for calculating and predicting movements within a functioning and stable market system. But faced with the rise of info-capitalism, which is corroding price mechanisms, ownership and the connection between work and wages, the labour-theory is the only explanation that does not collapse. It is the only theory that allows us to properly model where value is created in a knowledge economy, and where it ends up. The labour-theory tells us how to measure value in an economy where machines can be built for free and last for ever.

WORK IS THE SOURCE OF VALUE

Amid the empty shops in the run-down high street of Kirkcaldy, Scotland, there is a branch of Gregg's. Gregg's sells high-fat food at low prices and is one of the few places busy at lunchtime. A glance at Scotland's poverty map gives the context: the town is dotted with areas of extreme deprivation and ill health.[1]

On the wall outside Gregg's is a plaque marking the house where Adam Smith wrote *The Wealth of Nations*. Nobody takes much notice. But this is where, in 1776, the economic principles of capitalism were first laid out. I'm not sure Smith would like the look of his home town today, blighted by de-industrialization, low pay and chronic sickness. But he would have understood the cause. The source of all wealth, said Smith, is work.

'It was not by gold or by silver but by labour that all the wealth of the world was originally purchased,' Smith wrote; 'and its value, to those who possess it, and who want to exchange it for some new productions, is precisely equal to the quantity of labour which it can enable them to purchase or command.'[2] This is the classic labour theory of value: it says the work needed to make something determines how much it's worth.

There is a raw logic to this. If you watch a water-wheel long enough, it helps you understand physics. If you witness workers sweating thirteen hours a day in a machine workshop, as Smith did, you will understand that it is the workers, not the machines, that produce the added value.[3]

Standard textbooks will tell you Smith thought the labour-theory was valid only for primitive societies, and that when it came to capitalism, 'value' was the combined product of wages, capital and land. This is incorrect.[4] Smith's labour theory of value was inconsistent, but on a detailed reading of *The Wealth of Nations* the argument is clear: labour is the source of value but the market can only reflect this roughly, through what Smith calls 'higgling and bargaining'. So the law operates beneath the surface in a full capitalist economy. Profits and rents are deductions from the value produced by labour.[5]

David Ricardo, the most influential economist of the early nineteenth century, created a more developed model. Published in 1817, it established the labour-theory as firmly in the public mind as supply and demand is now. Ricardo, who had witnessed the great upsurge of the factory system, ridiculed the idea that machines were the source of increased wealth. Machines merely transfer their value to the product; only labour adds new value, he said.

The magic of machinery lay in increased productivity.[6] If you can use less labour in making something, it should be cheaper and more profitable. If you cut the amount of labour needed to produce hats, he wrote, 'their price will ultimately fall to their new natural price, although demand should be doubled, trebled, or quadrupled'.[7]

After Ricardo, the labour-theory became the signature idea of industrial capitalism. It was used to justify profits, which rewarded the work of the mill owner; it was used to attack the landed aristocracy, who were living off rents instead of working; and it was used to resist workers' demands for shorter hours and union rights, which would hike the price of labour to 'artificial' levels, i.e. above the minimum needed to feed, clothe and house a working family.

However, despite its ultra-capitalist rationale, the labour-theory proved subversive. It created an argument about who gets what, which the factory owners immediately started to lose. Amid the candlelight of the pubs where the early trade unions met, David Ricardo suddenly had a whole new set of followers.

The worker-intellectuals of the 1820s understood the revolutionary implication of the labour-theory: if the source of all wealth is work, then there's a legitimate question about how that wealth should be distributed. Just as a rent-seeking aristocracy can be shown to be parasites on the productive economy, so too can capitalists be seen as parasites on the work of others. Their work is needed – but the factory system looks as if it is structured to deliver them excess rewards.

'There is nothing more than the knowledge, skill and labour requisite [to set up a factory] on which the capitalist can found a claim to any share of the produce,' wrote Thomas Hodgskin, a naval lieutenant turned socialist, in 1825.[8]

As illegal trade unions spread the doctrine of 'Ricardian socialism', the factory owners' enthusiasm for the labour-theory waned. By the time the British middle classes won the vote, in 1832, their need to justify capitalism with any kind of theory had vanished. Wages, prices and profits were no longer things to be investigated by social science, they were just there, to be described and counted. Ricardo was out, but all that replaced him was theoretical confusion.[9]

If, as a result, mid-nineteenth-century economics was reduced to 'describing and counting', there is a parallel with natural science. Charles Darwin formulated the theory of natural selection in 1844 and Alfred Russel Wallace three years later. Yet such were its implications – chiefly, rubbishing the Creation myth – that both men resorted to a routine of 'collecting, naming and categorizing' their specimens until 1858, when they both suddenly rushed to publication with an earth-shaking theory.

In economics, the earth-shaking theory arrives with Marx. It's often claimed that Marx built on the theories of Smith and Ricardo. In fact he demolished them. He described his project as a critique of political economy: of Smith, Ricardo, the Ricardian socialists, the liberal moralists and the bean counters. He said – long before mainstream economists did so in the 1870s – that Ricardo's version of the labour-theory was a mess. It would have to be rewritten from scratch.

Marx recognized in the labour-theory, despite all its flaws, something that could explain both how capitalism worked and why it might one day cease to work. The version he produced is coherent and has stood the test of time. There are thousands of tenured academics – including some of the world's most cited scholars – who teach that it is correct. The problem is, very few of them are allowed to teach economics.

THE LABOUR-THEORY BY NUMBERS

When a buyer from Primark signs a contract for 100,000 T-shirts with a factory in Bangladesh, that is a transaction. When a Bangladeshi worker arrives at the factory each morning, expecting the equivalent of $68 a month in return, that is also a transaction.[10] When she spends a fifth of her daily wage to buy 1kg of rice, that too is a transaction.[11]

When we make transactions, we have in our minds a rough idea of what the thing we're buying is worth. If the labour-theory is right, we are unconsciously judging its value against the amount of other people's work that thing, or service, contains.

What follows is a brief, simple explanation of the labour theory of value. Long, complicated versions are available but for the purpose of understanding how postcapitalism might work, only the basics are needed.

A commodity's value is determined by the average amount of labour hours needed to produce it.[12] It is not the *actual* number of hours worked that sets the value but the 'socially necessary' hours of work established across each industry or economy. So the basic unit of account here can be summed up as 'hours of socially necessary labour time'. If we know what an hour of basic labour costs – in Bangladesh the minimum wage pays about 28 US cents an hour – we can express it in money. Here I will just stick to hours.

Two things contribute to the value of a commodity: (a) the work done in the production process (which includes marketing, research, design, etc.) and (b) everything else (machinery, plant, raw materials, etc.). Both can be measured in terms of the amount of labour time they contain.

The labour-theory treats machines, energy and raw materials as 'finished labour' – transferring their value to the new product. So if the cotton for one garment took altogether thirty minutes average labour to grow, spin, weave and transport, it will transfer that value to the final shirt. But with machines and other big capital goods the process takes time; they transfer their value in small chunks. So if a machine took a million hours' worth of labour to make, and over its lifetime it makes one million objects, each object will carry a single hour of the machine's value into its final value.

Meanwhile, we treat the actual labour expended within the firm's production process as new value, added by what Marx called 'living labour'.

This underlying process – labour time determines the amount of new value – operates at a deep level, behind the backs of workers, managers, wholesale buyers and Primark shoppers. When we negotiate a price, it can be influenced by many other things – supply, demand, short-term usefulness, the lost opportunity if we don't buy, the cost of spending instead of saving – everything Adam Smith summed up in the evocative word 'higgling'. But at an aggregate level, the price of all the goods and services sold in a given economy is just a monetary expression of how much labour it took to produce them.

The problem is, we only know if we paid the right price after the event. The market acts like a giant calculating machine, rewarding those who guessed correctly what the socially necessary cost was, and penalizing those who used too much labour.

So prices always diverge from the underlying value of things, but they are ultimately determined by it. And value is determined by the amount of necessary labour it took to make the commodity.

But what determines the value of labour? Consistent with everything else, the answer is: other people's labour – the average amount of labour it takes to present each worker at the factory gate, ready for work. This includes the work that went into producing the food they consume, the electricity they use, the clothes a worker wears and – as society develops – the average amount of education, training, healthcare and leisure consumption needed for the worker to do their job.

Of course, the average cost of an hour's labour changes from one country to another. These differences are one of the reasons firms move production offshore. Childcare at a subsidized workplace nursery in Bangladesh costs the equivalent of 38 US cents a day, while in New York City a nanny costs $15 an hour.[13] In the past decade, global production chains have moved work from China to Bangladesh as workers in China achieved better pay rates, even though Bangladeshi productivity is lower. Bangladeshi labour was so cheap for a time that it offset the inefficiencies.[14]

So where does profit come from? In the labour-theory, profit is not theft – as in a rip-off. On average, a worker's monthly salary *will* reflect the amount of labour by others needed to produce their food, their energy needs, their clothes, etc. But the employer comes away with something more. My boss can pay me the true value of the eight hours work I just did. But that true value might be just four hours.

This mismatch between the inputs and outputs of human labour is the kernel of the theory, so let's look at an example.

Nazma at the Bangladeshi shirt factory agrees to work for a wage that seems roughly enough to pay for a month's food, rent, leisure, transport, energy and so on, plus a bit on top to put by as savings. She would like to earn more, but there's a relatively narrow range of wages for factory work, so she has a very clear implicit grasp of the average hourly wage possible with her skills.

But her employer is not buying her work *per se*: he is buying her *ability* to work.

If we forget money and measure everything in 'hours of necessary work', we can see how profit is generated. If the cost of putting Nazma at the factory gate six days a week is thirty hours work by other people spread across the whole of society (to produce her food, clothing, energy, childcare, housing and so on), and she then works sixty hours a week, her work is providing double the amount of output for the inputs. All the upside goes to the employer. Out of an entirely fair transaction comes an unfair result. This is what Marx calls 'surplus value', and is the ultimate source of profit.

Another way of putting this is to say: labour is unique. Of all the things we buy and sell, labour alone has the ability to add value. Work is not just the measure of value but the motherlode from which profit is mined.

One clue as to the truth of this is that wherever they can get labour for free – as in the American prison system or Nazi death camps – capitalists immediately take advantage of it. Another clue lies in the fact that, wherever they need to pay labour below its average value, as during the rise of the Chinese export industry, managers resort to providing the inputs collectively: dorms, uniforms and canteens. The labour of a dormitory workforce is much cheaper than the social average, which is based on the living costs of a family in a home – and of course dormitory workers can be disciplined more easily.

But why, if the real weekly value of my labour is thirty hours of other people's work, would I ever work sixty hours? The answer is: the labour market is never free. It was created through coercion and is re-created every day by laws, regulations, prohibitions, fines and the fear of unemployment.

At the dawn of capitalism, average working days of fourteen hours or more were imposed – not just on adults but on children as young as eight. A rigid system of timekeeping was implemented: rationed toilet time, fines for lateness, product defects or talking, enforced start times; and immovable deadlines. Wherever we see the factory system created afresh – whether in Lancashire in the 1790s or Bangladesh in the last twenty years – we see these rules enforced.

Even in advanced countries the labour market is built overtly on coercion. Just listen to any politician make a speech about welfare: cutting unemployment and disability benefits is designed to force people to take jobs at wages they can't live on. In no other aspect of the market does the government coerce us to take part; nobody says 'You must go ice skating or society will collapse.'

Work for a salary is the bedrock of the system. We accept it because, as our ancestors learned the hard way, if you don't obey, you don't eat.

So our work is precious. If you ever doubt this, study what happens in the fulfilment centre of an e-commerce retailer, or a call centre, or in the work schedule of a home-care worker. You will see work timed and targeted as if the minutes were gold dust. Which, to the employer, they are. Of course at the high-skill, high-wage end of the labour market it is not time or discipline, but targets and quality control that are the instruments of coercion.

There is more to explore about the labour theory of value but let's pause. We already know enough to start attacking it with the tools that are to hand in every economics department.

SOME VALID OBJECTIONS . . .

Here's why I like the labour theory of value. It treats profit as if it were made somewhere central within capitalism: the workplace, not the marketplace. And it treats one of the most basic things we do every day – work – as if it were important to economics. But there is also a long list of valid objections to the labour-theory:

Q: *Why do we need a 'theory' at all? Why not just the facts – as in the GDP figures, company accounts, the stock markets, etc.?*

A: Because we want to explain change. In science we want to go beyond a neat row of butterflies pinned under glass; we need a theory of why each sub-species looks slightly different. We want to know why, during a million repetitions of their normal lifecycles, small variations can emerge and then, suddenly, massive change.

Theories allow us to describe the reality we can't see. And they allow us to predict. All forms of economics accept the need for theory. But the difficulty of finding one, and confronting its implications, led economics in the late nineteenth century to retreat from the scientific method.

Q: *Why can't I 'see' value, surplus value and labour time? If they don't show up in the accounts of companies, and professional economists don't acknowledge them, aren't they just a mental construct?*

A: A more sophisticated way of putting it would be to say, as the

Cambridge economist Joan Robinson did in the 1960s, that the labour-theory is 'metaphysical' – a mental construct whose existence could never be disproved. For good measure she said the same about 'utility' – the key idea in mainstream economics – but accepted that metaphysics was better than nothing.[15]

Yet the labour-theory is more than metaphysics. Of course it works at a certain level of abstraction: that is, parts of reality are filtered out. For example, it is a model of a pure capitalism, in which everybody works for wages; there are no slaves, peasants, mobsters or beggars. It describes a process that works 'behind the backs' of economic agents: nobody can calculate whether they are spending more or less than the necessary labour time – though making a decent guess at it has become crucial to productivity management.

In the labour-theory, the market is the transmission mechanism between this deep, unknowable process and the surface outcome. Only the market can mediate the individual choices into an aggregate effect; only the market can tell us what the socially necessary labour time is. In this sense, the labour-theory is the greatest theory of the market ever written. It ascribes to the market, and *only* the market, the mechanism of making concrete the reality beneath.

So, yes, it is abstract – but no more abstract than Adam Smith's concept of the 'hidden hand' or Einstein's general theory of relativity, proposed in 1916 but not proved empirically until the 1960s.

The question remains: is it provable? Would it be possible to challenge the labour-theory in its own terms with evidence? Does it pass the test, laid down by philosopher Karl Popper, that if a single contrary fact were true, the theory would be false?

The answer is yes – once we understand the full theory. If you could say 'capitalism is crisis-free', the labour-theory would be false. If you could demonstrate that capitalism lasts for ever, it would also be false. Because, as we're about to see, the labour-theory describes at the same time both a regular cyclical process and one that leads eventually to long-term breakdown.

Q: *Why do we need this level of abstraction? Why can't the theory be constructed by collecting data and crunching it? Why leave the concrete world to mainstream economics?*

A: In answer to the last of these, you shouldn't. Marx recognized that to be rigorous the labour-theory should explain reality at the concrete level. He set about trying to build out the abstract model into a more concrete description of the real economy. This involved introducing a two-sector model of the economy (consumption and production) in the second volume of *Capital*, and a banking system in the third. Alongside this, he tried to show how the underlying values get transformed into prices at the concrete level.

There are inconsistencies in the way he worked out this so-called 'transformation problem', which led to a 100-year-long debate over whether the theory is inconsistent. Since this is an attempt to apply the whole theory to a specific issue, not a textbook on Marxism, I will avoid that debate here, saying simply that the 'transformation debate' has been resolved (to my satisfaction) by a group of academics known as the 'temporal single system' school.*

The point is that, even in its most consistent form, the labour-theory is not going to be a practical tool for measuring and predicting price movements. It is a mental tool for understanding what price movements are. It belongs to a class of ideas that Einstein described as 'principle theories': theories whose aim is to capture the essence of reality in a simple proposition, which may be removed from everyday experience. Einstein wrote that the aim of science is to capture the connection between all experiential data 'in their totality' – and to do this 'by use of a minimum of primary concepts and relations'. He pointed out that the more clear and logically unified these primary concepts were, the more divorced they would be from data.[16]

Einstein believed the truth of a theory is, for certain, borne out by whether it successfully predicts experience. But the relationship between the theory and the experience can only be grasped intuitively.

For reasons we discuss below mainstream economics evolved into a pseudo-science that can only allow for statements obtained through crunching the data. The result is a neat set of textbooks, which are internally coherent but which continually fail to predict and describe reality.

---

* They show that the alleged logical inconsistencies in Marx's calculations disappear once you understand this process takes place over time, not simultaneously as if in a single column of a spreadsheet.

Q: *Isn't this too ideological? Isn't the labour-theory too tainted with hostility to capitalism to be of any use?*

A: Yes, this is a problem. As a result of the ideological battles in economics since the 1870s, there's been a dialogue of the deaf. The outcomes, which we have to overcome today, were the inconsistency of mainstream economics and Marxism's lack of concreteness.

You'll often hear left wing economists decry mainstream economics as 'useless' – but it is not. In fact, once you understand its limitations, most of mainstream price theory maps very well on to the surface end of the labour-theory.

The problem is, mainstream economics does not understand its own limitations. The more complete it became as an academic discipline describing an abstract, static and immutable reality, the less it understood change. To see why, we will now consider the main source of change in capitalism – the force that makes expensive things cheaper and which has now begun to make some things free: productivity.

PRODUCTIVITY IN THE LABOUR-THEORY

According to the labour-theory, there are two kinds of productivity gain possible. First, the workers become more skilled. So the work of a trained metal press operator has more value than the work of some one who just arrived off the dole queue; either because they make an ordinary thing faster and with fewer defects, or because of their ability to make an extraordinary thing that the less well-trained worker could not.

But the cost of training skilled workers is usually higher by a proportional amount: their labour is worth more because it took more labour to produce and maintain. For example, the average earnings of graduates across the OECD countries are more than double those of people with only a basic education, and 60 per cent higher than of those who completed only 'upper secondary' education.[17]

The second kind of productivity gain is driven by new machinery, or a reorganization of the production process, or a new invention. This is the most common case and Marx deals with it as follows.

One hour of labour always adds one hour's worth of value to the products made. So the impact of rising productivity is to reduce the amount of value embodied in each product.

Suppose a factory produces 10,000 garments a day. Let's say the workforce is 1,000 people with average ability working ten hours each. So 10,000 hours of 'living' labour are going into the daily output. Let's assume that on top of that there are 10,000 hours of 'finished' labour going into each day's output as well – in the form of wear and tear to machinery, energy used, fabrics and other raw materials, transport costs, etc. The total daily output of the factory, as measured in labour time, therefore consumes 20,000 hours of labour, half living and half finished. So each garment contains two hours of labour time. On the market, it should exchange for the money equivalent of two hours' labour time.

Now, suppose a process is introduced that doubles labour productivity. For each batch of 10,000 garments you've still got roughly the same amount of finished labour going in (10,000 hours in this example). But the living labour component is cut to 5,000 hours. Now each garment contains ninety minutes' labour time.

Here's how the market rewards you. If your factory is the first to make the change, the garments go into a market where socially necessary labour time to make them is still 20,000 hours. That's the price you should get in the market. But you only needed 15,000 hours. So the factory reaps the productivity gain in the form of increased profit. The factory boss can cut prices and increase market share or take the above-average profit represented by the difference between two hours and ninety minutes. Eventually the whole industry will copy the innovation and the new normal price per garment will be ninety minutes' labour time.*

This brings us to the main point. To increase productivity, we

---

* One aspect of Marx's theory is counterintuitive. Surely increased productivity must increase the 'quality' of the labour? Almost all new machines and workplace reorganizations bring new qualities to our work. But insisting that the value of the labour remains unchanged by productivity gains is just a way of saying that it is *machines, management technique, and knowledge* that bring the productivity gain, not a change in the quality of labour itself. They become a 'force multiplier' for human labour, which remains the same basic thing.

increase the proportion of 'machine value' to the living human labour employed. We drive human beings out of the production process and in the short term – at the level of the firm or sector – profits rise. But since labour is the only source of extra value, once an innovation has been rolled out across the whole sector, and a new, lower social average set, there's less labour and more machine; the part of the operation producing the added value has got smaller; and if unchecked that would place downward pressure on the profit rate of the sector.

Innovation, which is driven by the need to minimize costs, maximize output and utilize resources, does bring rising material wealth. And it can lead to a rise in profits. But once it has been rolled out, it creates an inbuilt and perennial 'tendency for the rate of profit to fall' – if not offset by other factors.

Despite the doom-laden aura of this Marxist phrase 'tendency of the profit rate to fall', it is no real catastrophe for capitalism. As we saw in chapter 3, these offsetting factors are usually strong enough to balance out the effects of the falling labour content – above all, through the creation of new sectors which require higher-value inputs – either in the form of higher-value physical commodities or by the creation of service sectors.

So in the classic model of capitalism outlined by Marx, the pursuit of productivity drives material wealth higher but causes repeated short-term crises and then forces big mutations, whereby the system has to voluntarily raise the cost of labour. If it can't make workers rich enough to buy all the goods, or it can't find new consumers in new markets, this piling up of machine value versus labour value leads to a fall in the rate of profit.

And that was how all crises looked in the era of scarcity: mass unemployment and idle plant caused by a collapse in profitability, and all explicable using the labour theory of value.

But the labour-theory can also be used to explain something else, namely what happens when products and new processes can be made without any labour going into them at all.

Before we explore that, however, we have to deal with the alternative theory of price proposed by mainstream economics, known as 'marginal utility'.

THE AVOIDANCE OF
'FUTURE THINGS'

Like Marx, the founders of mainstream economics started by tearing holes in Ricardo. His explanation of profit was inconsistent, they said; nothing could be done to make it work. Their response was to move economics on to different terrain – that of observable movements in prices, supply and demand, rent, taxation and interest rates.

What they produced was the theory of marginal utility: that there is no intrinsic value to anything, except what a buyer will pay for it at a given moment. Léon Walras, one of the founders of marginalism, insisted: 'The selling prices of products are determined in the market ... by reason of their utility and their quantity. There are no other conditions to consider for these are the necessary and sufficient conditions.'[18]

This 'usefulness theory' of value had been deemed archaic since the days of Adam Smith. The crucial factor in its revival was the addition of the concept of marginality. 'The amount of value is determined not by average but by final or marginal utility,' wrote William Smart, an English popularizer of the theory.[19] Marginal simply means all the value is in the 'extra bit' you want to buy, not in the whole product. So the value of the last ecstasy tablet in the nightclub is higher than all the others.

For marginalists, the key psychological judgements we make when we buy things are reducible to the following question: 'Do I need to buy this next thing – glass of beer, cigarette, condom, lipstick, minicab ride – more than I need to keep this last €10 note in my pocket?'

William Stanley Jevons, the English pioneer of marginalism, demonstrated that in principle these fine judgements about utility – which he understood as choices between pleasure and pain – could be modelled using calculus. This sliding scale of momentary prices was the only thing needed to calibrate supply and demand. The only consistent meaning to value was 'ratio of exchange'; he proposed scrapping the term 'value' altogether.

On the face of it, the marginalists were trying to free economics from philosophy. You can't defend capitalism on the grounds that it is 'natural', said Walras, the only justification should be that it is efficient and increases wealth.

But there is a crucial piece of ideology built into marginalism: the assertion that the market is 'rational'. Walras was revolted by the idea that economic laws work independently of human willpower. This amounted to treating economics like zoology and the human race as animals. 'Alongside the many blind and ineluctable forces of the universe,' he wrote, 'there exists a force which is self conscious and independent, namely the will of man.'[20] The new science of economics should assume the market is an expression of our collective rational will, Walras argued. But it should be mathematical, making a one-time leap out of its ethical and philosophical roots by using abstract models and considering all cases in idealized form.

The achievement of marginalism was to show that markets governed by free and perfect competition must achieve 'equilibrium'. It was Walras who worked this into a demonstrable law: since all prices are the result of a choice by a rational individual (buy the lipstick or keep the €10 bill?), once the supply runs out the rational choice is to stop trying to buy it. Conversely, if the supply of something increases, it becomes rational for people to start wanting it, and to decide what price they will pay for it. Supply creates its own demand, says the theory; a freely operating market will 'clear' until demand matches supply, with prices changing in response.

Like Marx, Walras was working at a high level of abstraction. His model assumes that all agents have perfect information, that there is no uncertainty about the future and no extraneous factors influencing the market (such as monopolies, trade unions, import tariffs, etc.). These abstractions are not invalid, as long as we do not suggest that they represent reality. The question is: was marginal utility the *right* abstraction?

An early hint that it was not came in the marginalists' attitude to crisis. They were so convinced of capitalism's inner tendency towards equilibrium that they assumed crises must be produced by non-economic factors. Jevons, in all seriousness, suggested the Long Depression, beginning in 1873, was simply the latest in a series of regular fluctuations caused by 'some great and wide-spread meteorological influence recurring at like periods' – that is, by sun-spots.[21]

Textbook economics is today built on marginalism's discoveries. But in the pursuit of maths over 'political economy', the marginalists created a discipline which ignored the production process; reduced the psychology of the deal to a two-dimensional balance between pleasure and pain; saw no special role for labour;* discounted the possibility of economic laws acting at a deep, unobservable level, independent of the rational will of human beings; and reduced all economic agents to traders, abstracting away from class and other power relationships.

In its purest form, marginalism denied not only the possibility of exploitation, but of profit as a specific phenomenon. Profit was just the reward for the utility of something the capitalist was selling: their expertise or, in later forms of the theory, their abstinence – that is, the 'pain' they suffered during the act of accumulating their capital. Marginalism was, in short, highly ideological. It introduced a blindness to the problems of distribution and class that still blights professional economics, and a profound lack of interest in what goes on in a workplace.

Marginalism emerged because managers and policymakers alike needed a form of economics that was bigger than accountancy but smaller than a theory of history; it had to describe in detail the way the price system worked – and in a way that took no interest in class dynamics or social justice.

Carl Menger, the Austrian economist, summed up the inner psychological motivation for marginalism in a famous attack on Smith and Ricardo. They were obsessed with 'the welfare of man in the abstract, about remote things, about things which did not yet exist, about future things. In this effort [they] . . . overlooked the living, justified interests of the present.' The aim of economics, according to Menger, should be to study the reality that capitalism produces spontaneously, and to defend it against the 'one-sidedly rationalistic mania for innovation' which 'contrary to the intention of its representatives inexorably leads to socialism'.[22]

Marginalism's obsession with the continuous present, its hostility

---

* Labour, Jevons mused, is probably a mixture of pleasure and pain, but the fear of a bigger pain – hunger – drives us to work each day.

to future things, made it a brilliant model for understanding forms of capitalism that do not change, mutate or die.

Unfortunately these do not exist.

WHY IT MATTERS . . .

Why, in the era of big data, Spotify and high-frequency trading, should we be raking over a debate from the mid-nineteenth century?

For one thing, because it explains the pig-headedness of present-day economics in the face of systemic risk. Economics professor Steve Keen points out that present-day marginalism – by reducing everything to the doctrine of 'efficient markets' – actually contributed to the collapse. Mainstream economists made 'an already troubled society worse: more unequal, more unstable and less 'efficient'.[23]

But there is a second reason, to do with how we describe the dynamics of info-capitalism. The rise of information goods challenges marginalism at its very foundations because its basic assumption was scarcity, and information is abundant. Walras, for example, was categoric: 'There are no products that can be multiplied without limit. All things which form part of social wealth . . . exist only in limited quantities.'[24]

Tell that to the makers of *Game of Thrones*: the pirated version of Episode 2 of its 2014 series was illegally downloaded by 1.5 million people in the first twenty-four hours.[25]

Information goods exist in potentially unlimited quantities and, when that is the case, their true marginal production cost is zero. On top of this, the marginal cost of some physical info-tech (memory storage and wireless bandwidth) is also collapsing towards zero. Meanwhile, the information content of other physical goods is rising, exposing more commodities to the possibility that their production costs begin to plummet too. All this is eroding the very price mechanism that marginalism describes so perfectly.

The economy at present, consists both of scarce and abundant goods; our behaviour is a mixture of the old pleasure-*vs*-pain choices, made in our own self-interest, alongside sharing and cooperation, which seem to the marginalists like sabotage.

But in a full information economy – where much of the utility was provided through information and physical goods were relatively abundant – the price mechanism as described by marginalism would fall apart. Because marginalism was a theory of prices and prices only, it cannot comprehend a world of zero-priced goods, shared economic space, non-market organizations and non-ownable products.

But the labour-theory can. The labour-theory actually predicts and calibrates its own demise. That is, it predicts a clash between the social forms driving productivity and productivity itself.

The labour-theory, as outlined by Marx, predicts that automation can reduce necessary labour to amounts so small that work would become optional. Useful stuff that can be made with tiny amounts of human labour is probably going to end up being free, shared and commonly owned, says the theory. And it is right.

KARL MARX AND THE INFO-MACHINES

Let's restate what Marx called the 'law of value'. The price of everything in the economy reflects the total amount of labour used to make it. Productivity gains derive from new processes, machines, reorganizations – and each of these comes at a cost, in terms of the amount of labour it took to create it. In practice, capitalism escapes the tendency of innovation to shrink the labour content of the economy, and thus shrink the ultimate source of profit, because it creates new needs, new markets and new industries where labour costs are high, so there are more wages to drive consumption.

Info-tech is just the latest outcome of an innovation process lasting 250 years. But information injects a new dynamic. Because with info-tech you can have machines that cost nothing, last for ever and do not break down.

If somebody tried to sell the Bangladeshi factory boss a sewing machine that lasts for ever he would probably choke on his breakfast. However, he is quite happy to buy software. Software is a machine that, once built, will last for ever. Sure, it can be made obsolete by newer software, but the world is full of old software that – if the right hardware could be found to run it – could run for ever.

Once the design cost is incurred, the cost of producing software is reduced to the cost of the media it is stored on or flows through: the hard drive or the fibre network. That, plus upgrading it and maintaining it.

And these costs are plummeting exponentially. The cost of printing one million transistors on to a piece of silicon has fallen from a dollar to 6 cents in ten years. Over roughly the same period, the cost of one gigabyte of storage has fallen from a dollar to 3 cents; and the cost of a one megabit broadband connection has fallen from $1,000 in the year 2000 to $23 today. Deloitte, who did these calculations, describes the falling price of basic info-tech as exponential: 'The current pace of technological advance is unprecedented in history and shows no signs of stabilizing as other historical technological innovations, such as electricity, eventually did.'[26]

It has become commonplace to think of information as 'immaterial'. Norbert Wiener, one of the founders of information theory once claimed: 'Information is information, not matter or energy. No materialism which does not admit this can survive at the present day.'[27]

But this is a fallacy. In 1961, IBM physicist Rolf Landauer proved, logically, that information is physical.[28] He wrote: 'Information is not a disembodied abstract entity; it is always tied to a physical representation. This ties the handling of information to all the possibilities and restrictions of our real physical world, its laws of physics and its storehouse of available parts.'[29]

Specifically, he showed that information processing consumes energy and it should be possible to measure the amount of energy used in deleting one 'bit' of information. In 2012 a team of scientists built a tiny physical model demonstrating 'Landauer's Rule'.[30]

So information is a product that costs energy to produce and exists as matter. Bits take up room in reality: they consume electricity, give off heat and have to be stored somewhere. Google's famous Cloud is in fact acres of air-conditioned server farm space.

But Wiener was right to understand that the product of a computing process is qualitatively different from other physical products.

The real wonder of information is not that it is immaterial but that it eradicates the need for labour on an incalculable scale. It does all the things a machine does: it substitutes cheap labour for skilled labour; it eradicates labour altogether for some operations, and it makes new operations possible that no previous forms of labour could have achieved. The new information produced by a computer has a use value, or utility, massively in excess of its component parts.

But the amounts of labour value embodied in information products can be negligible. And once knowledge becomes truly social – as Marx imagined with the concept of the 'general intellect' – some of the value is contributed for free, as follows:

- Information goods naturally leverage general scientific knowledge
- Their users feed back, in realtime, data that allows them to be improved, for free
- Any improvement in knowledge somewhere can be implemented in every machine deployed everywhere, immediately.

For example, the internet protocol, invented in 1974 and published for free, is a 'standard', not a product. But it is not the same as, say, the safety standard the garment factory is supposed to adhere to. It is more like the electricity grid a factory draws power from: it is materially useful. And it is free.

What happens if you insert some of this free machinery into the labour theory of value? Marx, it turns out, had actually thought this through.

In the *Grundrisse*, Marx says: if a machine costs 100 days' worth of labour power to make, and wears out in 100 days, it's not improving productivity. Much better to have a machine that costs 100 days but wears out over 1,000. The more durable the machine, the smaller the amount of its value chipped off into each product. Taking this to its logical extreme, what you ideally want is a machine that never wears out, or one that costs nothing to replace. Marx understood that, in economic terms, they are the same thing: 'If capital could obtain the instrument of production at no cost, for 0, what would be the consequence? Surplus value [would be increased], without the slightest cost to capital.' He lists two ways in which, even in the nineteenth century, capitalism was getting just such a free hit: from the reorganization of workflow, and through scientific advances. Marx then writes: 'If machinery lasted for ever, if it did not itself consist of transitory material which must be reproduced . . . then it would most completely correspond to its concept.'[31]

We should shudder in awe at this incredible insight, written by gas-light in 1858: that the ideal form of a machine is one made of material that does not wear out, and which costs nothing. Marx is not here speaking about the immaterial but of non-transitory material: that is, something that does not degrade.

Machines where parts of the value are input for free by social knowledge and public science are not alien concepts for the labour-theory. *They are central to it.* But Marx thought that if they existed in large numbers they would explode the system based on labour values – 'blow it sky high', as he says in the *Fragment on Machines.*

The worked example Marx uses in the *Grundrisse* makes it clear: a machine that lasts for ever, or can be made with no labour, cannot add any labour hours to the value of the products it makes. If a machine lasts for ever, it transfers a near-zero amount of labour value to the product, from here to eternity, and the value of each product is thus reduced.*

Of course, in reality, physical machines do not yet last for ever; but what we've seen in the past fifteen years are machines whose utility derives from the information used to run them, design them or make them. And only the labour-theory can properly comprehend what it means economically, if the world of physical objects becomes alive with information.

WHEN MACHINES THINK

In 1981 I worked for a few months as a press operator in a small engineering factory next to the River Mersey. The stamping press worked on a mixture of electricity and compressed air: when you pulled a lever, it hammered a machine tool down on to a metal disc,

---

* Marx writes: 'Suppose a capitalist invests $1000, including $200 on machinery, and makes $50 a year. In four years the machine is paid for and thereafter, in value terms, it is as if the capital is only worth $800.'

bending it into shape. My job was to put the disc on the die, pull the lever and get my fingers out of the way before the guard came down. It was unskilled work, about ten repetitions per minute, and there were always a huge number of defective discs. There was no information feedback mechanism in the stamping press at all; and nothing was automated bar its single physical hammering motion.

Above me were two tool setters, semi-skilled men who fixed the tool in the machine and realigned it every few hours. In the next room were the skilled metalworkers who made the tools. They never spoke to us. However, what we all shared was this: without the skill of our fingers and a keen eye for defects, inherent danger and faulty processes, nothing in the factory worked.

Today, metal stamping is almost completely automated. The operation is first simulated on a computer, with thousands of datapoints on the metal modelled mathematically to understand the stress placed on the metal. Then a 3D design is fed directly into a computer, which controls the machine. The die and the machine tool are often much more intricate than the one I used in 1981; and now they are positioned by laser beams, allowing far greater accuracy. If something goes wrong, the computer controlling the machine knows about it. When the part comes out of the machine, it is picked up by a robot, analysed and placed precisely where it should go next. And when the tool needs changing, a robot arm does it.

Such machines can finish in an hour what we finished in a day, free of defects and with no fingertips accidentally left on the floor – because there are no workers. What makes this possible is numerous applications of IT: computerized analysis and 3D design in the preparation; realtime feedback and analytics during the process; and data retention to aid future refinements of the process. Researchers are now focusing on ways to automate the production of the tools themselves and even de-skill their design using computer models.

So the whole machine is alive with information and so is the product: automated factories require even small parts to be identifiable individually, through tags and numbers. The press can add these as well.

We have lived through a revolution in one of the most basic operations in industrial capitalism: metal bashing. But nobody has bothered to theorize it – the academic literature on the automated metal press belongs in the engineering department, not in economics.[32]

And that's because, as we've already seen, nobody knows how to measure the value of information economically. You can see the impact of buying an automated press on the company's bottom line; you can value the 3D designs and bespoke computer programs as assets, but as the SAS Institute research showed, you are basically guessing.

The labour-theory enables us to do something better than guess. It allows us to think of software as a machine; the information (3D designs, programs, monitoring reports) as finished labour in the same way the tools and metal dies are. And it allows us to trace the process by which the 'zero marginal cost' effect of pure information goods spills over into the world of physical products and the machines that make them.

My press shop in the early 1980s was staffed by maybe twenty-five workers. For a similar-sized operation today you would need fewer than five. The crucial difference is made by software, laser sensors and robotics.

The value of this industrial software is entirely reliant on the patent law that prevents it being used and replicated for free. Though it's harder to pirate than, say, the DVD of a feature film, the principle remains the same: the reproduction cost of industrial software is zero; the value added is contained in the work done to attach it to specific machines and processes.

Though a machine shop smells and sounds the same as it did thirty years ago, it is as different from the one I worked in as an iTunes track is from a vinyl record.

FREE MACHINES IN
A MIXED ECONOMY

We've seen what happens if you inject zero marginal cost products into the price model: it breaks down. We must now model what happens if you inject free machines into the cycle of capital investment.

For the sake of clarity I'm using an ultra-basic model here with all its attendant dangers of oversimplification.

Let's say there are four lines on a spreadsheet modelling the inputs to an economy in terms of labour value. The units could be millions of hours of labour time. Let's say the labour transferred to the final product in Period #1 looks like this:

- Capital: 200
- Energy: 200
- Raw materials: 200
- Labour: 200

The capital line of the spreadsheet is always different in the labour-theory, because machines transfer their value into the product over several years, while in the other three lines the value is consumed in the current period. So that capital line might represent machinery etc. costing 1000, chipping off 200 units of value each year into the total output over a five-year lifespan.

Now let's do something drastic to the capital line: let's assume it represents a single machine that lasts for ever. In the labour-theory that immediately slashes the labour transferred from the capital line to zero, for ever. No matter what the initial outlay was (in terms of hours spent to make the machine), if it lasts for ever it transfers almost no value – because even a billion divided by 'for ever' is zero.

The total labour hours transferred by all factors of production to the final output now fall to 600 hours (keen-eyed Marxists will spot I am not including profit in this model, but see below).

Now we run the spreadsheet over time: in Period #2, the zero-effect in the capital line spills over and reduces the number of labour hours transferred to the final product – because the hours needed to reproduce labour are reduced. If you keep on running this model, without doing anything to counteract the downward pressure on labour inputs, pretty soon it is not just capital costs that are zero, but labour/raw material costs fall rapidly. Of course, in a real economy machines don't last for ever. But insofar as they are pervaded by information, a part of the labour expended to make them ceases to circulate in the old way. The value vanishes.

Let's run this spreadsheet down to an end-state, over several time periods where capital and labour get shrunk towards zero marginal reproduction costs. Now the labour expended is mainly focused on providing energy and physical raw materials. If this happened in real life, because the law of value operates beneath the surface, it would be possible for the price system to carry on as normal, trying to calculate the marginal utility of things. As prices fell, corporations might react by trying to impose monopoly pricing – to stop the value embodied in the machine and its product falling towards zero. But mainstream economics would be puzzled. It would seem like whole swathes of economic activity were being 'stolen' from the normal market framework.

And even though we are far away from the pure information economy modelled crudely here, we can already feel these effects in reality: monopolies are arising to prevent software or information goods becoming free; accounting standards are becoming garbled as companies resort to valuation guesswork. There are attempts to stimulate wage growth, while most of the inputs to labour can now be produced with less labour.

In its first major macro-economic study of the internet, in 2013, the OECD admitted: 'While the internet's impact on market transactions and value added has been undoubtedly far-reaching, its effect on non-market interactions ... is even more profound. Non-market interactions on the internet are broadly characterised by the absence of a price and market-clearing mechanism.' Marginalism supplies no metric, no model to understand how a price economy becomes a substantially non-price economy. As the OECD team put it: 'Little attention has been paid to non-market interactions since few, if any, well-defined and well-grounded measurements have been commonly adopted.'[33]

Let's admit, then, that only marginalism enables us to build price models in a capitalist society where everything is scarce. In return, let us insist: only the labour-theory allows us to build models whereby zero-cost effects begin to cascade over from information into the sphere of machines and products, and from there into labour costs.

Once you introduce free machines and products into a model of capitalism that runs over time, even a crude one like this, it is as electrifying as introducing the figure zero into mathematics.

The four-line spreadsheet outlined above should really have an extra row for profit and instead of simply declining, each value should grow by perhaps 3 per cent a year, representing GDP growth. But suppose you did add profit and growth? Once the zero marginal cost effect kicks in, there would have to be tremendous profits and growth to offset the eventual impact on labour costs. In other words, there would have to be new industrial revolutions every fifteen years, very rapid nominal growth and ever bigger monopoly firms.

But that can't happen.

Capitalism worked as long as capital could move, when technological innovation brought lower costs in one sector, to sectors with higher wages, higher profits and higher-cost inputs. Capitalism does not self-reproduce in this way when the outcome is zero costs.

This simplified model also allows us to see really clearly how economics in a zero production cost society quickly comes to centre on energy and raw materials: they become the sector where scarcity still rules. Later we'll explore how modelling the disappearance of labour value like this could translate into the actual design of strategies for transition; and how issues around energy fit in. For now, however, let's look at how capitalism might evolve to meet these economic challenges.

WHAT WOULD INFO-CAPITALISM LOOK LIKE?

The rise of free information and free machines is new. But the cheapening of inputs through productivity is as old as capitalism itself. What stops capitalism from becoming a systemic race to the bottom is the creation of new markets, new needs, and raising the amount of socially necessary labour time used to meet these needs (fashion instead of rags, TVs instead of magazines); this in turn raises the amount of labour time embodied in each machine, product or service.

If this inbuilt reflex could work properly, faced with the information revolution, what we'd get is a fully fledged info-capitalism. But here's how it would have to work.

It would have to stop the price of information goods falling, by using monopoly pricing: think Apple, Microsoft and Nikon/Canon on steroids. It would have to maximize the capture of externalities by corporations. Every interaction – between producer and consumer, consumer and consumer, friend and friend – would need to be mined for value. (In labour-theory terms, our non-work activity has to be turned into work contributed to the corporation for free.) A thriving info-capitalism might seek to maintain artificially high prices for energy and physical raw materials, through hoarding and other monopolistic behaviour, so their cost fed through into higher average necessary labour time to reproduce labour. Crucially, it would have to create new markets beyond production, in the field of services. The 250-year history of capitalism has been about pushing market forces into sectors where they did not exist before. Info-capitalism would have to take this to its extremes, creating new forms of person-to-person micro-services, paid for using micro-payments, and mainly in the private sector.

And finally, for info-capitalism to succeed it would have to find work for the millions of people whose jobs are automated. These could not be in the majority low-paid jobs because the traditional escape mechanism needs labour costs to rise: human life has to become more complex, needing more labour inputs, not fewer, as in the four cyclical upswings described by long-cycle theory.

If all these things could happen, info-capitalism could take off. The elements of such a solution are there in modern economies: Apple is the classic price monopolist, Amazon's business model the classic strategy for capturing externalities; commodity speculation the classic driver of energy and raw material costs above their value; while the rise of personal micro-services – dog minding, nail salons, personal concierges and the like – shows capitalism commercializing activities we used to provide through friendship or informality.

But there are clear structural obstacles to making this work.

First, the normal escape route – innovation creates expensive new technologies that replace info-tech – is blocked. Information is not some random technology that just came along and can be left behind like the steam engine. It invests all future innovation with the zero-price dynamic: biotech, space travel, brain reconfiguration or nanotechnology, and things we cannot even imagine. The only way you could remove the information effect from these coming technologies would be, as in Frank Herbert's sci-fi novel *Dune*, to ban computers and replace them with expensive human experts in calculation.

The second obstacle is the scale of workforce redesign. In Marx's time, there were 82,000 clerical workers in the USA, 0.6 per cent of the workforce. By 1970, on the eve of the info-tech revolution, there were 14 million – almost one in five workers.[34] Today, despite the automation and disappearance of all kinds of brainwork jobs – such as bank teller, shorthand typist, comptometer operator and the like – 'office and admin support' remains the biggest job category in America, with 16 per cent of the workforce.[35] The second category is 'sales', with 11 per cent.

In 2013, a study by the Oxford Martin School suggested 47 per cent of all jobs in the US were susceptible to automation. Of these, it was admin and sales that stood the highest risk. They predicted two waves of computerization over the next twenty years: 'In the first wave, we find that most workers in transportation and logistics occupations, together with the bulk of office and administrative support workers, and labour in production occupations, are likely to be substituted by computer capital.'[36]

In the second wave, it is everything relying on finger dexterity, observation, feedback, or working in a cramped space that gets robotized. They concluded the jobs safest from automation were service jobs where a high understanding of human interaction was needed – for example, nursing – and jobs requiring creativity.

The study provoked an outcry along familiar under-consumptionist lines: robots will kill capitalism because they will create mass underemployment and consumption will collapse. That is a real danger. To overcome it, capitalism would have to greatly expand the human services sector. We would have to turn much of what we currently do for free, socially, into paid work. Alongside sex work we might have 'affection work': you can see the beginnings of it now in the hired girlfriend, the commercial dog-walker, the house cleaner, the gardener, the caterer and the personal concierge. Rich people are already surrounded by such post-modern servants, but to replace 47 per cent of all jobs this way would require the mass commercialization of ordinary human life.

And here's where you hit the third obstacle – what philosopher André Gorz called the 'limits of economic rationality'.[37] At a certain level, human life and interaction resist commercialization. An economy in which large numbers of people perform micro-services for each other can exist, but as a form of capitalism it would be highly inefficient and intrinsically low-value.

You could pay wages for housework, turn all sexual relationships into paid work, mums with their toddlers in the park could charge each other a penny each time they took turns to push the swings. But it would be an economy in revolt against technological progress.

Early capitalism, when it forced people into factories, had to turn large parts of the non-market lifestyle into a serious crime: if you lost your job you were arrested as a vagrant; if you poached game, as your ancestors had always done, it became a hanging offence. The equivalent today would be not just to push commercialism into the deep pores of everyday life, but to make resisting it a crime. You would have to treat people kissing each other for free the way they treated poachers in the nineteenth century. It is impossible.

Therefore the real danger inherent in robotization is something bigger than mass unemployment, it is the exhaustion of capitalism's 250-year-old tendency to create new markets where old ones are worn out.

And there's yet another obstacle: property rights. To capture the externalities in an information-heavy economy, capital has to extend its ownership rights into new areas; it has to own our selfies, our playlists, not just our published academic papers but the research we did to write them. Yet the technology itself gives us the means to resist this, and makes it long-term impossible.

So what we have in reality is an info-capitalism struggling to exist.

We should be going through a third industrial revolution but it has stalled. Those who blame its failure on weak policy, poor investment strategy and overweening finance are mistaking symptoms for the disease. Those who continually try to impose collaborative legal norms on top of market structures are missing the point.

An economy based on information, with its tendency to zero-cost products and weak property rights, cannot be a capitalist economy.

The usefulness of the labour-theory is that it accounts for this: it allows us to use the same metric for market and non-market production in a way that the OECD's economists could not. Crucially it enables us to design the transition process so that we know what we are trying to achieve: a world of free machines, zero-priced basic goods and minimum necessary labour time.

The next question is: who is going to make it happen?

7

Beautiful Troublemakers

In 1980, the French intellectual André Gorz announced that the working class was dead. It was permanently divided as a social group and culturally dispossessed, and its role as an agent of social progress was over.

The thought was spectacularly mistimed. Between then and now the global workforce has doubled in size. Offshoring, globalization and the entry of former communist countries into the world market have boosted the number of waged workers to above 3 billion.[1] In the process, what it means to be a worker has changed. For about 150 years, the word 'proletariat' meant a predominantly white, male, manual labour force located in the developed world. Over the past thirty years it has become a multicoloured, majority-female workforce, centred in the global south.

Yet in one sense Gorz was right. In the same thirty years we've seen a slide in trade union membership, the decline of labour's bargaining power in the developed world and a fall in wages as a share of GDP. This is the ultimate cause of the problem lamented by Thomas Piketty: the inability of workers to defend their share of the total product, and the rise in inequality.[2]

Alongside material weakness, the labour movement has suffered an ideological collapse – and one felt just as keenly in the factories of Nairobi and Shenzhen as in the rust-belt cities of Europe and America. The left's political defeat after 1989 was so complete that, as the philosopher Fredric Jameson wrote, it became easier to imagine the end of the world than to imagine the end of capitalism.[3] Put more brutally, it had become impossible to imagine *this* working class – disorganized, in thrall to consumerism and individualism – overthrowing capitalism.

The old sequence – mass strikes, barricades, soviets and working-class government – looks utopian in a world where the key ingredient, solidarity in the workplace, has gone AWOL.

The optimists among the left countered that the defeats were just cyclical. It was plausible: the history of the labour movement does show clear patterns of formation and decomposition that map closely to the Kondratieff long cycles.

But they were wrong. This is a strategic change. Those who cling to the idea that the proletariat is the only force that can push society beyond capitalism are ignoring two key features of the modern world: that the route to postcapitalism is different; and that the agent of change has become, potentially, everyone on earth.

The new workforce – in the factories of Bangladesh and China – is being formed by a process just as harsh as the one workers in England went through 200 years ago. Who can forget the contract issued at Apple's Foxconn plants in China, in 2010, forcing workers to sign a pledge not to commit suicide due to workplace stress?[4]

However, this time around, the process of industrialization is failing to blow away the social and ideological cobwebs of pre-industrial life. Ethnic rivalries, the village network, religious fundamentalism and organized crime are the obstacles labour organizers in the global south encounter constantly – and fail to overcome. And alongside these old problems there is a new phenomenon: what I've called the 'expanded footprint of the individual' and indeed the ability of networked people to maintain multiple identities.[5]

And though this new workforce of the global south was originally designated as peripheral in relation to the core workforce of Western capitalism twenty-five years ago, today it too is divided into core and periphery. When the ILO surveyed the workforce of the global south by income strata, it found that every income layer (from $2 a day to five times as much) contained the same percentage of industrial workers, meaning the modern industrial sector includes both poor and precarious workers and also those with better status and higher incomes. The factory in Nigeria is as stratified by skill and income as its sister factories in Cologne or Nashville.

The old labour movement thrived on cohesion. It flourished in local economies that were primarily industrial, and in communities with political traditions that could absorb and survive technological change. Neoliberalism has blown those communities apart in the developed nations and made them difficult to build in the world beyond.

On the subsoil of precarious work, extreme poverty, migrant labour and slum conditions it has been impossible for anything that matches the collectivity and consciousness of the Western labour movement at its height to grow in the global south. Only where a national elite has an organized support base in the unions does it wield the same influence it enjoyed in the twentieth century: Argentina under the Kirchners, for example, or South Africa under the ANC. Meanwhile, in the developed world, though a core of trade union activists clings to the old methods and culture, a rising class of young, precarious workers finds – as in Athens in December 2008 – it is easier to squat buildings and riot than to join a union.

André Gorz, who was wrong on many things, was right about the reason why. *Work – the defining activity of capitalism – is losing its centrality both to exploitation and resistance.*

The rapid increase in productivity brought about by computers and automation, Gorz argued, has turned the sphere *beyond* work into the primary battleground. All utopias based on work are finished, he said, above all Marxism. In their place, there would have to be new utopias – fought for without the comfort blanket of historical certainty, and without the help of a class designated as the unconscious agent of salvation. It was a bleak, and slightly crazy message to hear as you linked arms on the picket lines of the 1980s. But Gorz's insight can now be grounded in something more constructive than disillusion.

As we have seen, information technology expels labour from production, destroys pricing mechanisms and promotes non-market forms of exchange. Ultimately, it will erode the link between labour and value altogether.

If so, then there is something about the current decline of organized labour that is not just cyclical or the product of defeat, but as historic as its rise 200 years ago. If capitalism must have a beginning, middle and end, so must the story of organized labour.

As in nature – and as in dialectical logic – the end is usually a moment of 'sublation', a concept that combines the simultaneous destruction of something and its survival as something else. Though it is not dead, the working class is living through a moment of sublation. It will survive in a form so different that it will probably feel like something else. As a historical subject, it is being replaced by a diverse, global population whose battlefield is all aspects of society – not just work – and whose lifestyle is not about solidarity but impermanence.

Those who first spotted such networked individuals mistook them for nihilists who could never effect change. On the contrary, I have argued (in *Why It's Kicking Off Everywhere*, 2012) that the new wave of struggles beginning in 2011 is a signal that this group does fight, and does embody similar and technologically determined values, wherever it takes to the streets.

If so, it becomes necessary to say something that many on the left will find painful: Marxism got it wrong about the working class. The proletariat was the closest thing to an enlightened, collective historical subject that human society has ever produced. But 200 years of experience show it was preoccupied with 'living despite capitalism', not overthrowing it.

The workers were forced into revolutionary action by social and political crises, often provoked by war and intolerable repression. On the rare occasions when they achieved power, they couldn't stop it from being usurped by elites operating under a false flag. The Paris Commune of 1871, Barcelona in 1937, the Russian, Chinese and Cuban revolutions all demonstrate this.

The literature of the left is littered with excuses for this 200-year story of defeat: the state was too strong, the leadership too weak, the 'labour aristocracy' too influential, Stalinism murdered the revolutionaries and suppressed the truth. In the end, the excuses boil down to just two: bad conditions or bad leaders.

The labour movement created a breathing space for human values inside an inhuman system. It produced, out of the depths of squalor, makers of what we today call 'beautiful trouble': martyrs, autodidacts and secular saints. But far from being the unconscious bearers of socialism, the working class were conscious about what they wanted, and expressed it through their actions. They wanted a more survivable form of capitalism.

This was not the product of mental backwardness. It was an overt strategy based on something the Marxist tradition could never get its head around: the persistence of skill, autonomy and status in working-class life.

Once we have understood what really happened to work over the four long cycles of industrial capitalism, the significance of its transformation in the fifth cycle becomes clear. Info-tech makes the abolition of work possible. All that prevents it is the social structure we know as capitalism.

1771–1848: THE FACTORY AS BATTLEFIELD

The first real factory was built at Cromford, England in 1771. You can still see the stone pedestal where the first machine was set up. To any humanist, this dank stone hall should be hallowed ground. It is the place where social justice ceased to be a dream and could, for the first time in human history, be fought for as a possibility.

In the 1770s, the room would have been full of women and children, working amid thick dust from the cotton, forbidden to speak, tending complex spinning frames operated by adult men known as 'spinners'. Everybody in the factory had been forced to learn the new culture of work: to follow the employer's clock instead of the body clock; strict attention to the task; the non-negotiable nature of instruc tions and the need to risk serious injury for thirteen hours a day. Every other group in society had roots, cultures and traditions, but the factory workforce had none – it was new and unique. For the first thirty years, this allowed the system to be operated in a way that ruthlessly destroyed human life.

But the workers fought back. They organized; they built a culture of self-education and, as soon as the upswing of the first long cycle faltered – in 1818–19 – they launched mass strikes that linked wage issues with issues of democracy, throwing Britain into a twenty-year political crisis, which would see repeated outbreaks of revolutionary violence.

Marx and Engels, writing more than twenty years after the start of this movement, in the early 1840s, found in the working class a ready-made solution to a philosophical problem. The middle-class German left had become enthusiastic communists: they wanted a classless society, based on the absence of property, religion and total freedom from work. Suddenly, in the working class, Marx discovered a force that could make it happen.

Marx argued that it was the extreme negativity of the workers' lives that gave them their historic destiny. The absence of property; the absence of craft, skill, religion and family life – and their complete alienation from respectable society – made the proletariat, in the Marxist schema, the bearer of a new social system. It would first achieve class consciousness, and then take power – to abolish property, end alienation from work and inaugurate communism.

A better summary of the proletariat's relationship to destiny would be: it's complicated.

Workers certainly became conscious of their collective interests. But then, even amid the grossly negative situation of the 1810s, they created something positive: not a 'socialist consciousness' but a revolutionary republican movement, imbued with the principles of learning, humanity and self-help.

In 1818, the cotton spinners of Manchester struck en masse. Then, during 1819, all over northern England, workers set up night schools and clubs, debated politics, elected delegates to town-wide committees and formed women's groups. Out of these meetings, in the summer of 1819, they launched a mass movement for democracy: unofficial public gatherings to elect unofficial members of parliament. When 100,000 workers congregated at St Peter's Field in Manchester on 16 August 1819, in defiance of the law, they were mown down by a cavalry charge.

The Peterloo Massacre marked the true beginning of the industrial labour movement. It also prompted the first attempt to deal with social unrest through automation.

In theory, the majority of spinners had to be men because the spinning machine, known as a 'mule', needed a strong hand to pull and push an array of spindles back and forth, four times a minute. In practice, however, there were women strong enough to do this. The real purpose was social: it was easier to impose discipline in the factory through a layer of tough, better-paid working-class men rather than deal direct with women and children.[6]

Once the skilled men had turned militant, by the early 1820s, however, the only solution was to automate them out of existence. In 1824, a 'self-acting mule' was patented, and soon thousands had been deployed. The employers announced that in future the machines would be run entirely by women and children, since 'attendants have nothing to do but to watch its movements'.[7]

The exact opposite happened.

Male spinners staged repeated strikes after 1819 against the employment of women. They refused to train girls to do the jobs that gave access to higher skill, and insisted that their own sons be chosen. During the 1820s and 30s the minority of women who had kept hold of spinning jobs were driven from them; by the 1840s male domination was complete. And, as the historian Mary Friefeld has shown, the new machines did not abolish the need for high skill; they simply created a new technical skill to replace the old one: 'One highly complex task had been substituted for another, while the quality control and mental oversight functions remained unchanged.'[8]

I've described this episode at length because it would be repeated many times over the next two centuries. The real history of work cannot be written as 'economics plus technology'; it involves the interaction of technology with organizations created by workers, and it involves the creation of power relationships based on age, gender and ethnicity.

More specifically, this case study blows apart a cherished passage in Marx's *Capital* – for Marx, writing in the 1850s, would use the self-acting mule as the main example of capitalism's tendency to de-skill work to suppress the workforce. 'Machinery,' he wrote, 'is the most powerful weapon for suppressing strikes . . . We would mention above all the self-acting mule . . .'[9]

We can trace the source of confusion to his collaborator, Frederick Engels. When Engels arrived in Manchester in 1842, the entire workforce of the city had been on general strike, and had been defeated. Aided by his working-class lover Mary Burns, the 22-year-old Engels toured factories, slums, and cotton exchanges to gather evidence for the first serious work of materialist sociology: *The Condition of the Working Class in England.*

As an anthropologist, Engels gets a lot right: the slum conditions, the near-total absence of religious belief and deference among the workers, their addiction to drink, opium and casual sex. What he gets wrong is the impact of the self-acting mule. He wrote:

> Every improvement of machinery . . . transforms the work of full grown men into mere supervision which a feeble woman or a child can do quite as well and does for half or even one third the wages . . . grown men are constantly more and more supplanted, and not re-employed by the increase in manufacture.[10]

In his defence, Engels was drawing on evidence from radical spinners who, under conditions of downturn and defeat after the 1842 strike, were being thrown out of work. However, the long-term impact of automation was ultimately to reinforce the role of skilled male spinners and to increase their numbers.[11] Numerous studies, above all by University of Massachussetts professor William Lazonick, show how skill, male dominance and an intricate power structure among male workers survived the onset of mechanization.[12]

So Marxism's first contact with the organized working class led to a big misunderstanding, not just about skill but the kind of political consciousness it produces.

Marx argued that the workers would abolish property because they lacked property; abolish class stratification because they could not benefit from it – and they would do it without the need to build up an alternative economy within the old system.

Yet the history of the English labour movement before 1848 simply does not bear this out. It is a story of positivity, the survival and evolution of skill; of hillside mass meetings, study circles, cooperative stores. Above all, it produced a vibrant working-class culture – of song, poetry, folklore, newspapers and bookshops. In short, there was a 'one' where Marxist philosophy said there should be a 'zero'.

What this means has to be confronted squarely by anyone who wants to defend materialist thinking about history: Marx was wrong about the working class. He was wrong to think automation would destroy skill; wrong to say the proletariat could not produce an enduring culture within capitalism. They had produced one in Lancashire before he had even graduated from university.

Marx, as a follower of Hegel, always insisted that the subject matter of social science should be 'the whole thing': the thing in a process of becoming and dying; the thing in its contradictions; the official thing but also the subtextual, hidden thing. He followed this method rigorously with regard to capitalism, but not when it came to analysing the working class.

Engels' *anthropology* of the English working class in 1842 is detailed, complex and specific. The Marxist *theory* of the proletariat is not: it reduces an entire class to a philosophical category. And it was about to be totally disproved.

1848–98: MEN VERSUS MACHINES

By the end of the nineteenth century, trade unions had become woven into the industrial fabric. For the most part, they were led by skilled workers with a bias towards moderation but fiercely defensive of their autonomy in the workplace.

Engels's book on the English working class was not published in Britain until 1892, by which time it was a museum piece. His preface to the first UK edition recognized this, and stands both as a brilliant insight into capitalism's adaptive nature and as an act of self delusion about the sources of moderation among workers.

In Britain, after radical republicanism had fizzled out in 1848, the stable form of working-class organization was trade unions organized by skilled workers. Wherever the factory system was rolled out – particularly in metalwork and engineering – the autonomous skilled worker became the norm. Radicalism and utopian socialism were sidelined.

Engels rationalized this first through economics. After 1848, with new markets, new technologies and an expanded money supply, Engels recognized the takeoff of 'a new industrial era' – what Kondratieff would dub the second long cycle – which would run until the 1890s. And he identified something crucial to its technological paradigm: cooperation between labour and capital.

The system was now so profitable that the British bosses no longer needed to use the methods of *Oliver Twist*. The workday was limited to ten hours, child labour was reduced, diseases of poverty were suppressed by urban planning. Now, wrote Engels, employers were apt 'to avoid unnecessary squabbles, to acquiesce in the existence and power of trade unions'.[13]

The British workforce had expanded to include millions of unskilled, poor and precarious workers. But Engels recognized a 'permanent improvement' for two specific groups: the factory workers and those in 'the great trade unions' – by which he meant skilled jobs dominated by adult men.

Engels said workers had become moderate because they 'shared in the benefits' of Britain's imperial power. Not just the skilled workers – whom he described as 'an aristocracy of labour' – but also the broad mass of people, who Engels believed also benefited from falling real prices as a result of Britain's Empire. However, he thought Britain's competitive advantage was temporary and that skilled privilege would also be temporary.

Meanwhile, among the workers in the rest of the developed world, he could see only pre-1848 levels of rebellion and alienation. So Engels, in the late 1880s, begins a second attempt to rationalize the non-emergence of working-class communism: Britain had bought off its workers by exploiting its imperial power, but when the rest of the world caught up with Britain, moderation would disappear.

It was a near-total misreading of the situation. Skill, passivity and political moderation were pervasive *all across* the workforce of the developed world during the second half of the nineteenth century. We could draw on any number of case studies; some of the most detailed were written in Canada.

Gregory Kealey's account of Toronto's barrel makers shows how, in each workshop, the union set the price of labour. There was no wage bargaining. Coopers would meet, present a price list, and the bosses had to either accept it or start a lockout. Like skilled workers everywhere, though the working week was six days, they regularly took a 'Blue Monday' – that is an unofficial day off after getting drunk on Sunday night.

They had total autonomy over their own work. They owned their own tools – indeed the term for a strike was 'taking their tools out of the shop'. They controlled access to apprenticeships tightly. They would restrict output during downturns to keep wages up. They achieved all this through secret meetings, Masonic handshakes, oaths, rituals and total solidarity.

And the union was only the base-layer of a complex tapestry of institutions. 'The culture of the nineteenth-century working man,' writes Bryan Palmer in a study of workers in Hamilton, Ontario,

> embraced a rich associational life, institutionalised in the friendly society, the mechanics' institute, sporting fraternities, fire companies [i.e. volunteer fire brigades] and working men's clubs. Complementing these formal relationships were less structured but equally tangible ties of neighbourhood, workplace, or kin, manifesting themselves in the intimacy of the shared pail of beer, or the belligerence of the *charivari* [Punch & Judy] party.[14]

In the workplace, informal control – not just over wages but over the work itself – extended into even the newest industries.[15]

These extraordinary levels of informal workers' control were not residual, they were actually *created* by the new technological processes of the mid-century. The signature technologies of the second long wave – telegraphy, steam locomotives, printing, iron and heavy engineering – were heavily manual, which means that the strong hand and the experienced brain were vital. 'The manager's brain is under the workman's cap,' was a working-class slogan that reflected reality. To prevent skill constantly outpacing automation, the bosses would need 'a thinking machine', warned the leader of the Toronto coopers' union.[16] But that would take another 100 years.

Even during the downswing of the second long cycle, after 1873, as managers tried to impose low-skilled work and automation, they largely failed. As Kealey concludes of the skilled Toronto workforce in the 1890s: 'They had met the machine and triumphed.'[17] By the 1890s, the existence of a skilled, privileged and organized layer of workers was a general feature of capitalism – not the result of one nation's competitive advantage.

The combined impact of skilled autonomy, 'the rich associational life' and rising social-democratic parties would force capitalism into a new adaptation. Having 'met the machine and won', the organized worker would, in the first half of the twentieth century, meet the scientific manager, the bureaucrat and – eventually – the guard at the concentration camp.

1898–1948: PICK UP
A PIG AND WALK

In 1898, in the freight yard of Bethlehem Steel in Pennsylvania, a manager called Frederick Winslow Taylor came up with a new solution to the century-old problem of skilled worker autonomy.

'Pick up a pig and walk,' Taylor told his labourers – a 'pig' being a lump of iron weighing 92lbs. By studying not just the time it took them to move the iron, but the detailed motion of their bodies, Taylor showed how industrial tasks could be made modular. Jobs could be broken down into learnable steps, and then allocated to workers less skilled than those currently doing them.

Taylor's results were startling: productivity almost quadrupled. The incentive was a pay rise, from $1.15 to $1.85 a day.[18] The 'science', from Taylor's own scant description, seems to have involved putting a manager in strict control over the worker's rest periods, and even over his speed of walking. Taylor wrote that the type of man suited to such work was 'so stupid and so phlegmatic that he more nearly resembles in his mental make-up the ox than any other type'. On the basis of such insights, scientific management was born. Now Taylor applied his methods to other workplaces. At a ball-bearing factory, he introduced process changes that allowed the workforce to be cut from 120 to thirty-five, with the same output and increased quality. He observed: 'This involved laying off many of the most intelligent, hardest working, and most trustworthy girls merely because they did not possess the quality of quick perception followed by quick action.'[19]

Outwardly, Taylorism was about time and motion. But its real purpose was the selection and stratification of the workforce, creating a layer of better-educated workers to check, organize and train the lower layers, and then imposing rigid management control. This, Taylor boasted, 'rendered labor troubles of any kind or a strike impossible'.[20] The whole project was designed as an assault on skilled autonomy. The aim was to move the brain work as far away as possible from the manual work.

Though he had never heard of Taylor, in 1913 Henry Ford launched the second big innovation needed to enable semi-skilled work: the production line. At Ford, as at Bethlehem Steel, wages were hiked in return for absolute compliance. A ruthless anti-union hiring policy ensured management control. Three-quarters of Ford's early workforce were first-generation immigrants, and overwhelmingly young.

Taylor, Ford and those who followed them effectively redesigned the working class. The skilled manual layer would survive – with machine-tool makers at its core. But there would now be a white-collar elite within the working class too. The white-collar workers owed their higher wages to the new system, where management were in control. Entering the white-collar layer could be done on merit, not just through family ties and seven-year apprenticeships, as had been the case with the engineers and the spinners – and in certain industries, white-collar work was more open to women.

Semi-skilled workers brought a critical difference to the innovation process: they would generally adapt their skills to new machines free of the restrictions imposed by craft unions. There would still be unskilled general labourers, but the centre of gravity of the working class had moved upwards, towards manual semi-skilled workers.

If all this was designed to induce passivity, it failed. What nobody foresaw was that this reshaped working class would become educated, radicalized and political. Taylor's 'dumb oxen' would teach themselves to read – not just dime novels but philosophy. The white-collar secretaries and telephonists would become agitators and educators in mass socialist parties.

The raw facts of the labour upsurge of the 1900s are startling. An electoral breakthrough by the German SPD gave it 31 per cent of the vote in 1903. A clandestine labour movement in the tsarist empire formed itself into workers' councils (soviets) and armed militias in 1905. French industry was paralysed by strikes in 1905–6, while union membership doubled in a decade. The USA saw the tripling of trade union density in ten years, even as the workforce itself grew by 50 per cent.[21]

Working-class towns became centres of a sophisticated culture – of clubs, libraries, choirs and nurseries, the separate working-class lifestyle and, above all, of resistance inside the factory.

From 1910 to 1913, unskilled workers staged a strike wave that rolled across the globe and became known as the Great Unrest. At the centre of it was the struggle for control. The Welsh miners' union outlined a strategy that was being pursued everywhere: 'Every industry thoroughly organized, in the first place, to fight, to gain control of, and then to administer, that industry ... leaving to the men themselves to determine under what conditions and how, the work shall be done.'[22]

It was as if, through their offensive against the old craft control of workplaces, Taylor and Ford had created a new and more sophisticated demand for democratic control among the workforce.

What halted the Great Unrest was a combination of economic downturn, beginning in 1913, and high levels of repression. When war broke out in August 1914, it seemed as if the whole thing had been a blip. Before we consider what happened next, we should ask how the Marxists of that era understood this new configuration of the working class. In summary, they did not.

LENIN AND THE ARISTOCRATS

In 1902, the exiled Russian revolutionary Vladimir Lenin wrote a pamphlet that, although only mildly influential at the time, was to have huge significance for the far-left thinking of the twentieth century. In *What Is to Be Done?*, Lenin stated baldly that workers were incapable of understanding the role allocated to them in the Marxist project. Socialist consciousness 'would have to be brought to them from without'. 'The history of all countries shows that the working class, exclusively by its own effort, is able to develop only trade union consciousness,' he wrote.[23] The labour movement, he said, would have to be 'diverted' from its spontaneous moderate pathways and towards the seizure of power. This stands in total contradiction to Marx's understanding of the working class. For Marx, the working class was the self-contained agent of history; for Lenin it was more like a reagent – needing the catalyst of the intellectual-led vanguard party to set off the historical process.

But by 1914 Lenin had a new problem to address: why were the workers – so ferocious in their defence of wages and democracy during the Great Unrest – either enthused or paralysed by the patriotism that followed the outbreak of war?

To explain this, Lenin reached back to Engels's 'labour aristocracy' theory, which he turned inside out. Instead of abolishing the skilled elite in Britain, said Lenin, the dash for colonies by all industrial countries had made the labour aristocracy the permanent feature of modern capitalism. They were the source of patriotism and moderation polluting the labour movement. Fortunately, a larger pool of unskilled workers still remained to provide the raw material for revolution. The political split between reform and revolution, Lenin claimed, was the material result of this stratification of the working class.

By now, Lenin was a long way from both Marx and Engels. For Marx, the working class is capable of becoming communist spontaneously; for Lenin it is not. For Marx, skill is destined to disappear through automation; for Lenin, skilled privilege at home is the permanent result of colonialism abroad.

In Lenin, there is no discussion of the economic or technical basis of the skilled layer's privilege: it is as if they are simply awarded higher wages by the capitalists as a matter of policy. In fact, as we've seen, at this point the actual policy of the capitalists was focused on *destroying* skilled privilege and autonomy.

In 1920, Lenin restated the labour aristocracy theory, calling them 'the real agents of the bourgeoisie in the labour movement . . . the real carriers of reformism and chauvinism'.[24] But this was an utterly bizarre thing to write in 1920. By then, the working class was four years into a wave of revolutionary struggles *led* by skilled workers. Between 1916 and 1921, the working class launched a frontal assault on management control. It would reach revolutionary proportions in Germany, Italy and Russia, and prerevolutionary levels in Britain, France and parts of the USA. In each case, the struggles were led by the so-called 'labour aristocracy'.

I am loath to bolster the anti-Lenin industry. The man himself proved an adept revolutionary, ignoring in practice many of the strictures of his own theory. However, the labour aristocracy theory of reformism is rubbish. The source of patriotism is, unfortunately, patriotism, owing to the fact that just as classes are material, so are nations. In his prison notebooks, the Italian communist Antonio Gramsci recognized that developed capitalist societies have layer upon layer of defence mechanisms. The state, he wrote, was 'just a forward trench; behind it stood a succession of sturdy fortresses and emplacements'. And one of the strongest emplacements is capitalism's ability to grant reforms.[25]

The 1902 theory, however, does contain a grain of truth, though not one palatable to most Marxists. To understand it, we must watch an unprecedented global drama unfold.

A TERRIBLE BEAUTY: 1916–39

By 1916 the wheels had begun to come off the war machine. Dublin's Easter Rising – led by an alliance of socialists and nationalists – failed completely. But it fired the starting pistol for five years of worldwide unrest. The poet Yeats sensed its global significance when he wrote of the ordinary men who'd led it: 'All changed, changed utterly. A terrible beauty is born.'[26]

May Day 1916 saw Berlin's factory workforce on strike against the war, battling the police and led by a new kind of union activist: the shop steward – elected by the rank and file, independent of the pro-war trade union leaders and usually a left-wing socialist. In Glasgow, another rank and file shop stewards' group, the Clyde Workers Committee, were arrested en masse after leading strikes for workers' control in the arms industry.[27]

In February 1917 a strike wave in the arms factories of Petrograd, Russia, escalated to a nationwide revolution that forced the tsar to abdicate, bringing to power a provisional government of liberals and moderate socialists (Kondratieff was minister of agriculture). Russian workers created two new forms of organization: the factory committee and the soviet, the latter a geographically elected council of workers' and soldiers' delegates. And through the telegraph, the telephone and even military radio signals, the global unrest began to feed off itself. In May 1917 the French army mutinied. Of 113 divisions, forty-nine suffered disruption and nine were rendered incapable of fighting.

These events were shaped by a new sociology of the workplace and a new kind of war. From Seattle to Petrograd, as male workers joined the army, employers recruited women and unskilled teenagers into shipyards and engineering factories to work alongside the remaining skilled men whose jobs exempted them from military service.

With the unions supporting the war effort, and therefore opposed to strikes, shop stewards were a phenomenon that sprang up almost everywhere; they were drawn from the skilled layer but prepared to organize women and young men, across the old hierarchical boundaries, into 'industrial unions'. When the revolutions broke out, the shop stewards formed the grassroots leadership.

Parallel to this, another radicalization was taking place in the trenches, led by young men who had learned the cruelty of industrial-scale warfare. They had seen notions of courage, nation and 'manliness' – notions absolutely central to the culture of work before 1914 – destroyed.

Now a widespread collapse of workplace order happened. By June 1917, Petrograd had 367 factory committees representing 340,000 workers. At the Brenner engineering factory, for example, the committee resolved: 'In view of the management's refusal to go on with production, the workers' committee has decided, in general assembly, to fulfill the orders and to carry on working.'[28] No Bolshevik programme had ever called for workers' control. Lenin was wary of it, initially trying to explain it as 'a workers' veto on management' and later, as we will see, outlawing it.

The next great power to collapse was Germany; the German working class, having tried but failed to prevent the war starting, triggered its end. In November 1918, left-wing activists in the Imperial German Navy organized a mutiny which, within twenty-four hours, forced the ships back into port and sent thousands of rebel sailors speeding across Germany on armed trucks. Among their primary objectives was a radio tower in Berlin, from which they wanted to communicate with the revolutionary sailors of Kronstadt, Russia.

Across Germany, factory committees and soviet-style councils were formed. Within forty-eight hours of the mutiny, they had forced an armistice, the abdication of the Kaiser and the inauguration of a republic. Only by joining the revolution at the last moment did the moderate leaders of the mainstream socialist party head off a Russian-style revolution.

Then, in 1919, a mass strike in Italy led to a coordinated lockout of car workers in Turin, Milan and Bologna. They occupied the factories and – most significantly at Fiat in Turin – attempted to keep production going under their own control, with the help of allies among the technicians.

These events reveal a much more interesting sociology than the one Lenin imagined. In the first place, skilled workers were central. They fought for control in a new, explicit way. Workplace sociologist Carter Goodrich, observing the phenomenon in Britain, dubbed it 'contagious control':

> The old, craft control almost necessarily implies small groups of skilled workers; the advocates of contagious control are for the most part either members of industrial unions or strong advocates of industrial unionism; the temper of the old crafts is monopolistic and conservative; that of the latter, propagandist and revolutionary.[29]

The skilled layer had, in other words, consistently moved beyond 'pure trade unionism'. But at the same time they remained wary of those advocating all-or-nothing political revolution. Their objective was workplace control and the creation of a parallel society within capitalism.

For the next twenty years, these shop stewards would become the perennial floating voters of the far left – constantly searching for a third course between insurrection and reform. They understood (because they lived among them) that the majority of workers were not about to immediately embrace communism, that many Western societies had a political resilience unguessed at by Lenin, and that they, the militants, would need strategies to survive: to strengthen the autonomy of the working class, improve its culture and defend the gains already won.

The factional history of most communist parties in the inter-war years is of a recurrent clash between the Leninists, trying to force Moscow-inspired schemes, tactics and language on to these traditions, and the militant shop stewards trying to create an alternative society from within.

And here's the kernel of truth contained in *What Is to Be Done?*. Lenin was wrong to say workers can't spontaneously move beyond pure, reform-oriented trade unionism. He was right to say revolutionary communism was not their spontaneous ideology. Their spontaneous ideology was about control, social solidarity, self-education and the creation of a parallel world.

But capitalism could not grant that: the third long cycle was about to swing downwards, and spectacularly. After the Wall Street Crash of 1929, governments all over the world inflicted mass unemployment, welfare reductions and wage cuts on the working class. Where the stakes were highest, and the working class too strong, the ruling elites concluded it had to be smashed.

The stage was set for the decisive event of the 200-year history of organized labour: the destruction of the German workers' movement by fascism. Nazism was German capitalism's final solution to the power of organized labour: in 1933, unions were outlawed and socialist parties destroyed. Catastrophe followed in other countries. In 1934, the labour movement in Austria was crushed in a four-day civil war. Then in Spain, between 1936 and 1939, General Franco waged total war on organized labour and the radical peasantry, leaving 350,000 dead. In Greece, the Metaxas dictatorship of 1936 outlawed not just socialist parties and trade unions but even the folk music associated with working-class culture. The labour movement in Poland, Hungary and the Baltic states – including the massive Jewish labour movement – was first suppressed by right-wing governments and then wiped out during the Holocaust.

Only in three advanced economies did the labour organizations survive and grow in the 1930s: Britain and its Empire, France and the USA. In the latter two, the years 1936–7 saw a rash of factory occupations where the main issue was control.

The workers who fought fascism were the most class-conscious, self-sacrificing and highly educated generation in the entire 200-year history of the proletariat. But the first half of the twentieth century was the ultimate test bed for the Marxist theory of the working class – and it was disproven. Workers wanted something bigger than power; they wanted control. And the fourth long cycle would, for a time, provide it.

THE MASSACRE OF ILLUSIONS

In 2012, I went to a cemetery in Valencia to visit the mass graves of Franco's victims. In the years after Franco's fall, their families had erected small individual headstones containing sepia photographs of those murdered. When I tried to take a photo on my iPhone, the camera app recognized their faces as human, bracketing them with a small green square.

They were largely middle-aged men and women: councillors, lawyers, shopkeepers. Most of the younger men and women had been killed or executed on the battlefield. The mass graves were for those left over, shot by the truckload between 1939 – when the civil war ended – and 1953 when they ran out of people to murder.

George Orwell, who fought alongside them, was haunted by the idealism in these faces. They were, he wrote, 'the flower of the European working class, harried by the police of all countries . . . now, to the tune of several millions, rotting in forced-labour camps'.[30] And that figure was not hyperbole. The Soviet gulag contained 1.4 million prisoners, about 200,000 of whom were killed each year. At least 6 million Jews were murdered in the Nazi concentration camps, and an estimated 3.3 million Russian prisoners of war died in German camps between 1941 and 1945. The Spanish war itself accounted for maybe 350,000 dead.[31]

The scale of death during the Second World War makes it difficult to comprehend. So its impact on the politics and the sociology of the working class has been the subject of a horrified silence. But let us puncture it. The majority of the Jews killed in East Europe were from politicized working-class communities. Many were adherents either of pro-Soviet, left Zionist parties or the anti-Zionist *Bund*. The Holocaust wiped out an entire political tradition in the global labour movement in the space of three years.

In Spain, the unions, co-ops and militias of the left were destroyed by mass murder – and their traditions suppressed until the 1970s. Meanwhile, in Russia the working-class political underground was exterminated by the gulag and mass executions.

What Orwell called 'the flower of the European working class' was crushed. Even if it had only been a question of numbers, this deliberate slaughter of politicized workers – added to the tens of millions of people killed by military action – would have been a turning point in the story of organized labour. But there was a massacre of illusions going on as well. As the Second World War approached, the extreme left – the Trotskyists and anarchists – tried to maintain the old, internationalist line: no support for wars between imperialist powers, keep the class struggle going at home. But by May 1940 the war was a bigger fact than the class struggle.

As the Allied powers collapsed, with significant pro-Nazi wings emerging among the ruling class in the Netherlands, France and Britain, it was clear to any working-class family with a radio that the very survival of their culture would rely on the military defeat of Germany. Working-class politics would become dependent on an Allied military victory. After the war, those who survived the slaughter, conscious of how close organized labour had come to total obliteration, now sought a strategic accommodation.

1948–89: WORK BECOMES 'ABSURD'

The Second World War was punctuated by workers' uprisings – but of a different type from those of 1917–21. Beginning with the Dutch general strike in 1941, and reaching a climax with the strikes that brought down Mussolini in 1943 and 44, these were anti-fascist actions, not primarily anti-capitalist. Where workers' uprisings threatened the Allied plans – as they did in both Warsaw and Turin in 1944 – generals simply halted the military advance until the *Wehrmacht* had done its job. After that, the communist parties stepped in to limit all action to the restoration of democracy only.

There was no repeat of 1917–21. But fears of such a repeat would force a hike in workers' living standards and a tilt in the balance of wealth distribution towards the working class.

In the first phase, the rapid post-war expulsion of women from the industrial workforce – as depicted in the documentary film *The Life and Times of Rosie the Riveter* (1980) – allowed male wages to rise, causing a narrowing of wage differentials between workers and the middle class. The sociologist C. Wright Mills noted that, by 1948, while the income of American white-collar workers had doubled in ten years, that of manual workers had increased threefold.[32]

Additionally, the Allies actually imposed welfare states, trade union rights and democratic constitutions on Italy, Germany and Japan, as a punishment for their elites and as an obstacle to their re-emergence as fascist powers.

Demobilization saw the creation of a university-educated layer of working-class kids utilizing subsidized education. Policies pursued to promote full employment, together with the state-run labour exchanges, training boards and job demarcation rules further increased labour's bargaining power. As a result, once growth took off in the 1950s, the wage share of GDP in most countries rose significantly above pre-war levels, while the tax take from the upper and middle classes also rose, to fund health and welfare programmes.

The trade-off? Workers abandoned the ideologies of resistance that had sustained them in the third long wave. Communism, social-democracy and trade unionism became – whatever the rhetoric said – ideologies of coexistence with capitalism. In many industries trade union leaders effectively became an arm of management.

This is where the living memory of today's developed-world workers begins: with welfare, health, free education, public housing projects and with collective rights at work enshrined in law. During its upswing, the fourth long cycle would deliver material improvements previous generations could only dream of.

But for survivors of the pre-war period it was like waking up in a nightmare. In 1955, the US sociologist Daniel Bell argued that 'the proletariat is being replaced by a salariat, with a consequent change in the psychology of the workers'. Noting the massive rise in white-collar workers compared to blue-collar workers, Bell – at this point a leftist – warned: 'these salaried groups do not speak the language of labour. Nor can they be appealed to in the old class conscious terms.'[33] The social theorist Herbert Marcuse concluded in 1961 that new technology, consumer goods and sexual liberation had decisively weakened the proletariat's alienation from capitalism: 'The new technological work-world thus enforces a weakening of the negative position of the working class: the latter no longer appears to be the living contradiction to the established society.'[34]

In Italy, pioneering research by the shop-floor activist Romano Alquati discovered that new levels of workplace automation had left workers alienated from the factory as any kind of arena for political self-expression. For the generation that had overthrown Mussolini, the factories had been an iconic battlefield. But among the young, the word 'absurd' was the most common term used to describe the production process. They complained about a 'sense of ridiculousness surrounding their lives'.[35]

The most tangible effect of this new sociology of work was the global decline in class-based voting patterns, famously illustrated in the Alford Index.[36] Historian Eric Hobsbawm, surveying the process later, declared that 'the forward march of labour' was halted in the early 1950s. He cited the decline of a 'common style of proletarian life', the unprecedented rise in the number of women working and the replacement of large workplaces by an extended supply chain of smaller ones. Crucially, Hobsbawm noted that the new technologies of the 1950s and 60s had not only expanded the white-collar layer but had also decoupled high wages from manual skill. By taking on two jobs, working heavy overtime or outperforming in the piece-work system, a semi-skilled worker could earn nearly as much as an experienced electrician or engineer.[37]

The combined impact of these changes was that, from the war until the late 1960s, workers' struggles were, as Alquati complained, 'always functional to the system. Always atomised, always blind.'[38] Gorz wrote doomily that the post-war workplace 'will never produce that working class culture, which together with a humanism of labour constituted the great utopia of the socialist and trade union movements up until the 1920s'.[39]

It is startling how many of the 'working class decline' theorists had personal experience of the movement at its pre-war peak. Marcuse had been elected to a soldiers' soviet in Berlin in 1919; Hobsbawm joined the German communist party via its schoolchildren's branch in

1932; Bell joined the Young Socialists in the New York slums in the same year; Gorz had witnessed the workers' uprising in Vienna. Their disillusion was the product of long-term empirical knowledge.

Looking back we can see the changes they were responding to more clearly.

First, the working class expanded. Large numbers of the salariat were in fairly menial office jobs, getting lower pay than manual workers and subject to pointless discipline and routine. White-collar workers were definitely still workers. The level of their alienation was captured well by the popular novels of the 1950s: *Billy Liar* is an undertaker's clerk; Joe Lampton in *Room at the Top* is an accountant at the local council.

Next, stratification altered the consciousness of this expanded working class. White-collar workers, even unionized or alienated ones, do not think or act like manual workers. And the young manual workers, themselves increasingly alienated from work and the culture surrounding it, also formulated a different kind of rebellious consciousness – as captured perfectly in another popular novel of the 1950s, *Saturday Night and Sunday Morning*.

Access to consumer goods did not subdue militancy. It was a material change, but wholly containable within working-class culture. But automation triggered a long-term psychological change. If work seemed 'absurd, ridiculous and boring' to the Fiat workers Alquati interviewed in the early 1960s, there was a deeper reason. The automation levels of the time were crude, but advanced enough to illustrate what the future of work would be like. Though the actuality of a factory run by computer was decades away, and robotization even further, workers understood that these things were no longer science fiction but distinct possibilities. There would come a time when manual work was no longer necessary.

Subtly, the sense of what it meant to be 'a worker' changed. What united the young workers in the 1950s, Gorz believed, was their alienation from work: 'In short, for the mass of workers it is no longer the power of the workers that constitutes the guiding utopia, but the possibility of ceasing to function as workers; the emphasis is less on liberation within work and more on liberation from work.'[40]

Strikes would happen among the expanded service proletariat once the crisis began in the late 1960s, but they almost never reached the levels of total shutdown possible in factories, ports and mines. When they did, these strikes escalated into confrontations with the state, which the majority of service workers were not prepared to see through to resolution.

The decline theorists were ill-fated. Daniel Bell became a neo-con. Marcuse, Mills and Gorz argued for a 'New Left' based on the struggles of oppressed groups, not the workers. That's what we've ended up with – but only after two decades in which this new working class defied the decline theorists, staging an uprising that brought parts of the developed world close to chaos.

We, the militants of the mid-1970s and 80s, derided those who had declared the old forms of working-class struggle dead, but it was they who had glimpsed the future.

1967–76: THE HOT DECADE

The years 1967–76 saw Western capitalism in crisis and wildcat strike action on an unprecedented scale. In spite of their cars, televisions, mortgages and expensive clothes, the workers took to the streets. Social-democratic parties veered to the left and revolutionary groups gained footholds in the factories, where they recruited thousands of members.

Among those in power, there were serious fears of a workers' revolution; certainly in France and Italy – and, in their deepest nightmares, also Britain and the black cities of the USA. We know how it ended – with defeat and atomization – but to answer the question 'why?' I want to start with my own experience.

In 1980, the British TUC published a book of archive photographs.[41] When I took it home and showed it to my grandmother, one photograph had her mesmerized and physically shaken. It showed a naked girl in a tin bathtub, sometime before 1914. 'You don't have to tell me about that,' she said. 'I lived three months through the '26 strike and I got married in the '21 strike.' She had never before volunteered knowledge of these two big miners' strikes, nor had she ever spoken about them to my father. The tin bath triggered the memory of poverty;

the poverty triggered the memory of 1926, when a nine-day general strike turned into a three-month miners' strike during which, as she now revealed, she had starved.

The entire pre-1939 period was a sealed box for her: extreme hardship, humiliation, violence, stillbirths, debt and two giant strikes that she had tried to forget. There was more to this than suppressed trauma. I became certain, as we leafed together through the photographs of hunger marches, barricades and occupied coal mines, that these images were more startling to her than they were to me.

Born in 1899, she had lived through two world wars, a Depression and the heyday of Hobsbawm's 'common proletarian life'. But beyond her own memories, she had no general knowledge of the events, nor understanding of their significance. Yet she was possessed with a compulsive ideology of rebellion. Class consciousness, for my grandmother, was formed out of experience alone: through talking, listening and seeing. Discussions at the pub, slogans chalked on the walls, actions taken. So separate were working-class towns from the world in which newspapers were written, or radio bulletins made, that bourgeois ideology barely touched them.

Logic and detail were important for practical things: how to prune roses, house-train a puppy, assemble a mortar shell (which she taught me at the age of five using one stolen from her wartime factory work). But class consciousness was sub-logical and implicit. It was conveyed through sayings, songs, sighs, body language and constant acts of micro-solidarity. It was a solidarity preserved over generations through industrial and geographic stability.

She knew her family history from the names in the back of her Bible, going back to 1770. They were all silk weavers or cotton weavers including her own unmarried mother. None of them had lived further than five miles from the place she was born. In her own life she moved house just three times, always within the same square mile.

So when sociologists ask how important the 'common proletarian way of life' and its physical geography were to class consciousness before 1945, my answer would be: decisive.

Though it felt to the young workers of the 1960s that they lived within a stable, 200-year-old culture, its foundations were shifting so rapidly that when they tried to pull the traditional levers of solidarity and struggle, in the 1970s and 80s they didn't work.

The central change – as Richard Hoggart documented brilliantly in his 1957 study *The Uses of Literacy* – was the injection of formal knowledge into working class life: information, logic and the ability to question everything. Mental complexity was no longer the preserve of the Fabian schoolteacher or the communist agitator with his newspaper full of Moscow-speak. It was available to all.[42]

For my father's generation, knowledge arrived into the post-war working-class community not just through the expanded education system and the public library but through the television, the tabloid newspaper, the movie, the paperback book and the lyrics of popular songs, which sometime during the late 1950s began to take on the quality of working-class poetry.

And it was knowledge about a world that was suddenly complex. Social mobility increased. Geographical mobility increased. Sex – a taboo in the public discourse of the pre-war working class – was everywhere. And now, on the eve of the crisis, the biggest technological innovation of all was rolled out: the contraceptive pill, first prescribed in 1960 but mainly legalized for use by single women during the late 1960s and early 70s, producing what economists Akerlof, Yellen and Katz called a 'reproductive technology shock'.[43] Women surged into higher education: for example, 10 per cent of US law students in 1970 were female – this rose to 30 per cent ten years later. And with control over the timing of childbirth, the stage was set for a decisive increase in female participation in the workforce.[44]

In sum, what emerged was a new kind of worker. The generation that would wage class war in the 1970s began with higher incomes, higher levels of personal freedom, fragmenting social ties and much better access to information. Contrary to the decline theorists' beliefs, none of this would stand in the way of them fighting. But here is why, ultimately, they lost.

The post-industrial, free-market model which destroyed their economic power and the traditional narrative based around work had collapsed. A new capitalist strategy had emerged. There was also the emergence of a new kind of rebel consciousness, which was no longer negative, spontaneous or uninformed, but based on formal knowledge and more reliant on elite-controlled channels of mass communication. On top of this, we have to factor in the dead weight of both Stalinism and social-democracy, which worked virtually full-time during the 1970s upsurge to channel the class struggle into compromise and parliamentary politics. Finally, workers were held back by the knowledge that the revolutions of the 1920s and 30s had failed, and that fascism was beaten only with the help of democratic capitalism.

Each of the advanced economies went through extreme class warfare from the late 1960s to the mid-70s. We will take Italy as a case study as it is one of the best documented and most heavily discussed, and because it gave birth to some of the earliest conclusions about how we move on from defeat.

ITALY: A NEW KIND OF CONTROL

By 1967 Italy's economic miracle had pulled 17 million workers from the poor agrarian south to the industrial cities of the north. A shortage of public housing left many of the new migrant workers sleeping six or eight to a room, in shoddy tenements, with public facilities overburdened. But the factories had modern design, world-class technology and there was an *élan* attached to working there.

Real wages had risen 15 per cent in the decade to 1960.[45] The major industrial brands invested heavily in canteens, sports and social clubs, welfare funds and designer overalls. At an industry level, the unions and management jointly agreed wage rates, output and conditions. But at plant level, 'management absolutism is the rule', one study reported.[46]

This combination of rising incomes at work and shabby conditions outside was the first impact of the boom. A second was the surge in student numbers. By 1968 there were 450,000 students – double the number of a decade before. Most came from working-class backgrounds and had no money. They found the universities full of useless textbooks and archaic rules. The historian Paul Ginsborg wrote: 'The decision to allow open access to such a grossly inadequate university system amounted simply to planting a time bomb in it.'[47] A better analogy might have been 'a detonator'. Student occupations broke out in late 1967, flaring into street violence over the next year. Alongside them began a wave of workers' strike actions which was to culminate in the 'Hot Autumn' of 1969.

At Pirelli Bicocca in Milan, workers on strike formed a 'unitary base committee' – completely independent of the union. As the idea of the base committee spread, so did new kinds of industrial action: sequential one-hour strikes across different departments, sit-down strikes, go-slows specifically designed to reduce productivity and strikes spread by marching from one department to another in a so-called 'snake'. A worker at Fiat described one: 'We set off, just the seven of us. And by the time we got to the head offices where all the staff hung out, there were about seven thousand of us! . . . Next time we'll start with seven thousand and end up with seventy thousand, and that'll be the end of Fiat.'[48]

The Italian Communist Party rushed to create local bargaining committees but in many plants workers rejected them, drowning out the communists with the chant 'We are all delegates.'

At a bar outside the Fiat Mirafiori plant in Turin, students initiated a 'worker-student assembly'. On 3 July 1969 they marched from the factory into a running battle with the police, over the issue of rent increases, chanting a slogan that could have summed up the new mood: 'What do we want? Everything!'

The leftist group Lotta Continua summarized what the strikers themselves thought they were going through: 'They are slowly beginning to free themselves. They are destroying constituted authority in the factory.'[49]

If these developments had been limited to a few hot-headed suburbs in a perennially chaotic country, they would be of curiosity value and no more. But the Italian upsurge was symptomatic of a change taking place all across the developed world; 1969 was to be just the start of a period of contagious economic struggle, which continually spilled over into political conflict and which would trigger a total rethink of the West's economic model.

It's important to understand the sequence of events, because in popular literature the breakdown of Keynesianism often gets rolled into a single moment. In 1971, the long post-war upsurge ran out of steam. But the breakdown of fixed exchange rates, paradoxically, gave each country the ability to 'solve' wage and productivity pressures by allowing inflation to take off. Then, with the oil price hike of 1973, which triggered double-digit inflation, the old relationship between wages, prices and productivity simply fell apart.

Across the OECD, redistribution payments – family income supplements, welfare benefits and the like – which had averaged 7.5 per cent of GDP during the boom years, reached 13.5 per cent by the mid-1970s. Public spending – which had averaged 28 per cent of GDP in the 1950s – now hit 41 per cent.[50] The share of total wealth going to industrial profits collapsed by 24 per cent.[51]

To contain worker militancy, governments hiked the social wage to record levels and brought workers' representatives into government. In Italy this was in the context of the 1976 'historic compromise' that ended the period of unrest, tying the Communist Party and its trade unions to a conservative-led government. The same basic process can be seen in the Spanish Moncloa Pact of 1978, the 'social contract' of the Wilson–Callaghan governments (1974–9), and numerous attempts by the American unions to secure a strategic deal with the Carter administration.

By the late 1970s, all the actors in the old Keynesian system – the organized worker, the paternalist manager, the welfare politician and the state-owned corporation boss – were locked together in a bid to save the failing economic system.

The standardized production process of the post-war era – and the strict scientific management controls it had relied on – ended up creating a workforce it could not control. The mere fact that work-to-rule actions became the most effective form of sabotage tells the real story. It was the workers who really ran the production process. Any proposal to solve macro-economic problems without their consent was pointless.

In response, a new breed of conservative politicians decided the entire system would have to be dismantled. The second oil shock, after the Iranian revolution in 1979, gave them the opportunity. It triggered a new, deep recession and this time the workers faced corporations and politicians determined to try something new: mass unemployment, industrial closures, wage cuts and cuts in public spending.

They also faced the emergence of something they'd insufficiently prepared for in the years of radicalism: a part of the workforce prepared to side with conservative politicians. White southern workers put Reagan into power; many skilled British workers, tired of the chaos, swung to the Conservatives in 1979 to give Thatcher ten years in office. Outright working-class conservatism had never gone away: what it always wants is order and prosperity, and by 1979 it could no longer see these things being delivered by the Keynesian model.

By the mid-1980s, the working class of the developed world had moved in the space of fifteen years from passivity to strikes and semi-revolutionary struggles to strategic defeat.

Western capitalism, which had coexisted with organized labour and been shaped by it for nearly two centuries, could no longer live with a working-class culture of solidarity and resistance. Through offshoring, de-industrialization, anti-union laws and a relentless ideological warfare, it would be destroyed.

DIGITAL REBELS, ANALOGUE SLAVES

After more than thirty years of retreat and atomization, the working class survives, but massively transformed.

In the developed world, the core-periphery model first envisaged in Japan has become the norm, replacing 'unskilled vs skilled' as the most important division within the working class. The core workforce has been able to cling on to stable, permanent employment, with non-wage benefits attached to the job. The periphery must relate either as temporary agency workers, or via a network of contracting firms. But the core is shrunken: seven years into the post-2008 crisis, a permanent contract on a decent wage is an unattainable privilege for many people. Being part of the 'precariat' is all too real for up to a quarter of the population.

For both groups flexibility has become the key attribute. Among skilled workers, much value is placed on the ability to reinvent yourself, to align yourself with short-term corporate objectives, to be good at forgetting old skills and learning new ones, to be a networker and above all to live the dream of the firm you work for. These qualities, which would have attracted the word 'scab' in a Toronto print shop in 1890, are since the 1990s obligatory – if you want to stay in the core.

For the peripheral workforce, flexibility relies first on the general and abstract character of your work. Since much of the work is automated, you need to be able to learn an automated process quickly and follow a formula. While this may often involve boring and dirty manual work – say, personal home care delivered to a strict check-list in fifteen-minute slots for the minimum wage – at its extreme it involves submitting your personal and emotional behaviour to work discipline. At Pret A Manger, staff are required to smile and be cheerful, and are encouraged 'to touch each other'. The official list of forbidden activities include working 'just for the money' or to 'overcomplicate things'. One reported: 'After a day's trial, your fellow workers vote on how well you fit the profile; if your performance lacks sparkle, you're sent home with a few quid.'[52]

The workforce of all developed countries is now heavily service-oriented. Only in the export giants – Germany, South Korea and Japan – does the industrial workforce come close to 20 per cent of the whole; for the rest of the economically advanced countries it is between 10 per cent and 20 per cent.[53]

In the developing world too, only around 20 per cent of the workforce is industrial.[54] While the global workforce numbers around 3 billion, and across Asia and Latin America it is common for people to work in big production units, any idea that globalization has simply transported the Fordist/Taylorist model to the global south is illusory.

The global wage share of GDP is on a downward trend. In the USA it peaked at 53 per cent in 1970 and has now fallen to 44 per cent. Though the effect is lessened in countries with an export-oriented model, the social impact has been to push the workforce into financialized behaviour. And as we saw in Part I, the proportion of profits generated by the consumption and borrowing of the working class has risen in proportion to that generated through work.[55]

Costas Lapavitsas, a professor of economics at London University's SOAS (School of Oriental and African Studies), calls this 'financial expropriation', and its impact on the self-image of the working class has been profound.[56] For many workers, their primary physical and ideological relationship to capital is through consumption and borrowing rather than work.

This shines a new light on the long-observed tendency of post-1989 capitalism to blur the boundaries between work and leisure. In some sectors, and not all of them high-value, there is increasingly a trade-off between meeting a project target and leeway for personal activity at work (e-commerce, social media, dating); the deal is that the employee has to be answering emails at home, working while travelling, prepared to work long, unofficial hours to meet targets.

In highly information-centred work, especially with smart mobile devices, work and leisure time are substantially blurred. This has over a relatively short period loosened the bond between wages and working time. For the high-value worker you are paid, effectively, to exist, to contribute your ideas to your firm and to meet targets.

In parallel, the geography of working-class life has been transformed. Long commutes from suburbs whose culture bears no specific relationship to work are the new normal. Commuting originally required people to actively re-create a physical community through non-labour organizations: the gym, the nursery, the bowling alley, etc. With the rise of info-tech, a portion of this community-building activity has moved online, fostering even more physical isolation. As a result, the old solidarity – where workplace ties were reinforced by a socially cohesive community – exists far more sporadically than at any other time in capitalism's history.

To the younger, precarious workforce it is instead urban proximity that matters; they tend to cluster into city centres, accepting massively reduced living space as a trade-off for physical closeness to the network of contacts needed to find partners, sporadic work and entertainment. Their struggles – in places like Exharchea in Athens, or the London student uprising in 2010 – tend to focus on physical space.

As they tried to understand these qualitative transformations in working life, sociologists focused first on space. Barry Wellman chronicled the move from group-based communities to physical networks and then digital networks, terming the outcome 'networked individualism'[57] and linking it explicitly to greater job flexibility. LSE professor Richard Sennett meanwhile began to study the new characteristics of a hi-tech workforce.[58] If work rewards detachment and superficial compliance, values adaptability over skill and net-working over loyalty, Sennett found, this creates a new kind of worker: s/he is focused on the short term, in life as in work, and lacks commit-ment to hierarchies and structures, both at work and in activism.

Sennett and Wellman both noticed the tendency of people adapted to this networked lifestyle to adopt multiple personalities, both in reality and online. Sennett writes: 'The conditions of time in the new capitalism have created a conflict between character and experience, the experience of disjointed time threatening the ability of people to form their characters into sustained narratives.'[59]

The worker of the Keynesian era had a single character: at work, in the local bar, in the social club, on the football terraces, they were the same essential person. The networked individual creates a more com-plex reality: s/he lives parallel lives at work, in numerous fragmentary subcultures and online.

It is one thing to document these changes; the challenge is to under-stand their impact on humanity's capacity to fight exploitation and oppression. Michael Hardt and Antonio Negri summed it up well in their 2012 book *Declaration*:

> The center of gravity of capitalist production no longer resides in the factory but has drifted outside its walls. Society has become a factory . . . With this shift the primary engagement between capitalist and worker also changes . . . Exploitation today is based primarily not on (equal or unequal) exchange but on debt.[60]

If, in the 1970s, Negri and the Italian left were premature in declar-ing the workplace 'over' as a forum for class struggle and 'the whole of society' the new venue, they are today correct.

What is the future for the working class, if info-capitalism contin-ues along these lines?

In the first place, the current global division of labour can only be seen as transitional. The workforce of the global south will achieve higher living standards and at some point capital will react by intro-ducing greater automation and pursuing higher productivity in the emerging markets. This will place the workers of China and Brazil on the same overall trajectory as the rich-world workforce, which is to become service-dominated, split into a skilled core and a precariat, with both layers seeing work partially de-linked from wages. In addition, as the Oxford Martin School suggests, it is the low-skilled service jobs that stand the highest risk of total automation over the next two decades. The global working class is not destined to remain for ever divided into factory drones in China and games designers in the USA.

However, the struggle in the workplace is no longer the only, or most important, drama.

In many industrial and commercial cities around the world, the networked individual is no longer a sociological curiosity, s/he is the archetype. All the qualities the sociologists of the 1990s observed in the tech workforce – mercuriality, spontaneous networking, multiple selves, weak ties, detachment, apparent subservience concealing violent resentment – have become the defining qualities of being a young, economically active human being.

And – despite the oppressive conditions at work – you can find them even in China, whose factory workforce was supposed to be the alter ego of the feckless Western consumer. From the mid-2000s, internet cafés with hundreds of screens opened up in the workers' districts of the export-oriented cities. Sociologists who interviewed the young migrant workers back then found them using the web for two things: to build connections with other workers from their home towns and to let off steam by playing games. To young people who had only ever slept on a farm or in a factory dorm, the internet café was transformative. 'Our foreman is a tough guy. But when I meet him in the internet café I am not afraid of him,' one female worker told researchers in 2012. 'He has no right to control me here. He is an internet user. So am I.'[61]

That now feels like prehistory. Smartphones have put the internet café in every Chinese worker's overall pocket. Mobile internet connections outran desktop connections in China in 2012, and are now available to 600 million people. And the mobile internet means social networks. In 2014, 30,000 shoe workers at Yue Yuen factory in Shenzhen staged the first big strike to use group messaging and micro-blogging as organizational tools. The village networks, which in analogue form were used to recruit and divide jobs informally across a single factory, were now being used to check wage rates and conditions and spread information across whole industries.

Terrifyingly for the Chinese authorities, the factory workers in Shenzhen were using the very same technology as the liberal, networked students who in 2014 staged the democracy protest known as Occupy Central in Hong Kong.

If you accept that the main faultline in the modern world is between networks and hierarchies, then China is sitting right on top of it. And China's workers – who for now look like digital rebels but analogue slaves – are at the heart of the phenomenon of networked rebellion. These networked movements are evidence that a new historical subject exists. It is not just the working class in a different guise; it is networked humanity.

And this is the antidote to the pessimism of Gorz's generation. With the death of the 'real' working class, Gorz concluded, the prime mover in anti-capitalism had disappeared. If you wanted postcapitalism, you must pursue it as a utopia: a good idea, which might or might not come off, and with no major force in society to embody its values.

In the past twenty years, capitalism has mustered a new social force that will be its gravedigger, just as it assembled the factory proletariat in the nineteenth century. It is the networked individuals who have camped in the city squares, blockaded the fracking sites, performed punk rock on the roofs of Russian cathedrals, raised defiant cans of beer in the face of Islamism on the grass of Gezi Park, pulled a million people on to the streets of Rio and São Paulo and now organized mass strikes across southern China.

They are the working class 'sublated' – improved upon and replaced. They may be as clueless as to strategy as the workers of the early nineteenth century were, but they are no longer in thrall to the system. They are enormously dissatisfied with it. They are a group whose diverse interests converge on the need to make postcapitalism happen, to force the info-tech revolution to create a new kind of economy, where as much as possible is produced free, for collaborative common use, reversing the tide of inequality. Neoliberalism can offer them only a world of stagnant growth and state-level bankruptcy: austerity until death, but with an upgraded version of the iPhone every few years. And the freedom they cherish is perennially hemmed in by the neoliberal state – from the NSA's mass surveillance techniques to those of the Chinese internet police. Above their heads, politics in many countries has become infested by a kleptocratic mafia, whose strategy is to deliver growth at the price of suppressing freedom and expanding inequality.

This new generation of networked people understand they are living through a third industrial revolution, but they are coming to realize why it has stalled: with the credit system broken, capitalism cannot sustain the scale of automation that is possible, and the destruction of jobs implied by the new technologics.

The economy is already producing and reproducing a networked lifestyle and consciousness, at odds with the hierarchies of capitalism. The appetite for radical economic change is clear.

The next question is: what do we have to do to achieve it?

PART III

An all-round increase in wealth threatened the destruction –
indeed in some sense was the destruction – of a hierarchical
society.

Emmanuel Goldstein, in George Orwell,
Nineteen Eighty-Four[1]

8

On Transitions

It can be a shock to find out capitalism has not always existed. Economists present 'the market' as the natural state of humanity. TV
documentaries re-create in fantastic detail the Egyptian pyramids or
Beijing under the emperors, but gloss over the totally different economic systems that built them. 'They were just like us,' dads confidently
tell their kids as they wander around the Herculaneum exhibition in
the British Museum – until confronted by the statue of Pan raping a
goat, or the wall painting of a couple having a threesome with their
slave.

When you realize that capitalism, once, did not exist – either as an
economy or a value system – a more shocking thought arises: it might
not last for ever. If so, we have to get our heads around the concept of
transitions, asking: what constitutes an economic system and how
does one give way to another?

In the preceding chapters I've shown how the rise of information
technology disrupted the basic institutions of capitalism: price, ownership and wages. I've argued that neoliberalism was a false dawn;
that the post-2008 crisis is the product of flaws within the economic
model which prevent the exploitation of new technologies, and the
takeoff of a fifth long wave.

All this makes postcapitalism possible, but we have no model for
the transition. Stalinism left us with a blueprint for disaster; the
Occupy movement came up with some piecemeal good ideas; the
so-called P2P (peer-to-peer) movement has evolved collaborative
models on a small scale; while environmentalists have developed
pathways for the transition to a zero-carbon economy, but tend to see
these as separate from the survival of capitalism.

So when it comes to planning the transition from one kind of economy to another, all we have is the experience of two very different events: the rise of capitalism and the collapse of the Soviet Union. In this chapter I will focus on what we can learn from them, and in the final part of the book I will try to apply these lessons to the design of a 'project plan' for moving the economy beyond capitalism.

Twenty-five years of neoliberalism have forced our thinking about change to become small. But if we are bold enough to imagine we can rescue the planet, we should also imagine rescuing ourselves from an economic system that doesn't work. In fact, the imagination stage is critical.

A BOLSHEVIK ON MARS

In Alexander Bogdanov's vintage sci-fi novel, *Red Star* (1909), the hero – an organizer in the Russian Bolshevik party – gets taken to Mars on a spaceship. He finds the Martian factories modern and impressive but the most stunning thing is what he sees in the control room: a realtime display provides an hourly snapshot of labour shortages in every factory on the planet, together with a summary of sectors where there is a labour surplus. The aim is for workers to move voluntarily to where they are needed. Since there is no shortage of goods, demand is not measured. There is no money either: 'Everyone takes whatever he needs, in whatever quantities he wants,' explains the Martian guide. The workers, controlling but never touching giant pieces of machinery, also fascinate our earthling: 'They seem to be inquisitive, learned observers who had no real part in what was going on around them ... To an outsider the threads connecting the delicate brains of the men with the indestructible organs of the machines were subtle and invisible.'[1]

In *Red Star*, Bogdanov not only imagined how a postcapitalist economy could work, he imagined what kind of person would be needed to make it possible – information workers, their brains connected by something 'subtle and invisible'. But by portraying the communist future, he was defying the conventions of his time: all wings of socialism were opposed to discussing castles in the air. But this was no mere whimsy.

Bogdanov, a medical doctor, was one of the twenty-two founder members of Bolshevism. He had been imprisoned, exiled, led the party in the Petrograd soviet, edited its newspaper, managed its funds and organized the raising of them – through bank robberies. It is Bogdanov we see playing chess with Lenin in the famous photograph at the party's training school on Capri in 1908.[2] But within a year of that photo, Bogdanov would be expelled from Lenin's party. He had formed an opposition to Lenin, based on disagreements that prefigured the tragedy that was about to unfold.

The 1905 revolution, said Bogdanov, showed that workers were not ready to run society. Because he thought postcapitalist society would have to be a knowledge society, any attempt to create it through blind revolutionary action could only bring to power a technocratic elite, he warned. To prevent this, Bogdanov said, 'a new proletarian culture must be disseminated among the masses, a proletarian science developed, a proletarian philosophy worked out'.[3]

All this was anathema to Lenin. Marxism had become a doctrine of imminent breakdown and revolution, where the workers would make the revolution happen despite the ideas and prejudices in their heads. Bogdanov also had the temerity to suggest that Marxism should adapt to new ways of thinking in science. He predicted that mental labour would replace manual labour; that all labour would become technological. Once this happened, our understanding of the world would have to go beyond the dialectial methods of thinking Marx had inherited from philosophy. Science would replace philosophy, Bogdanov predicted; and we would come to see reality as connected 'networks of experience'. Separate sciences would become part of a 'universal organisational science' – the study of systems.

For becoming, effectively, the first systems theorist, and for his prescient warning about what might happen in Russia, Bogdanov was expelled – at a fractious meeting in Lenin's Paris apartment in 1909. Within months, his novel *Red Star* was published, and widely circulated among Russian workers. In the light of what actually happened under Stalinism, its treatment of the postcapitalist economy is far-sighted.

In the novel, Martian communism is based on abundance: there is more than enough of everything. Production takes place on the basis of realtime and transparent computation of demand. Consumption is free. It works because there is a mass psychology of cooperation among workers, based on their high education and the fact that their work is primarily mental. They shape-shift between male and female genders, remain calm and selfless in the face of stress and danger, and live an enriched emotional and cultural life.

Bogdanov's outline of the back-story is also provocative: Mars was industrialized under capitalism; a struggle for control of industry began, followed by a revolution – largely peaceful because it was conducted by workers rather than peasants. There had then been a 100-year-long transition period during which the need for work was progressively eroded, by shortening the compulsory working day from six hours to zero.

To anybody with a knowledge of orthodox Marxism, it is easy to read between the lines of *Red Star*. Bogdanov was using the novel to outline a complete alternative to the ideas that would dominate the far left in the twentieth century. He advocates technological maturity as the precondition for revolution, the peaceful overthrow of the capitalists by means of compromise and compensation, a focus on technology as a means to reduce labour to a minimum and a relentless insistence that it is humanity itself that has to be transformed, not just the economy. Furthermore, a major theme of *Red Star* is that post-capitalist society has to be sustainable for the planet. The Martians voluntarily commit suicide if they perceive there are too many of them for their planet to support. And as their natural resources fail, they begin an agonized debate about whether to colonize Earth.

If you are thinking: 'What might Russia have become if Lenin had fallen under a tram on his way to the meeting where they expelled Bogdanov?', you are not the first to do so. There is a whole literature of 'what if?' focused on Bogdanov – and rightly so. Though he could not imagine a computer, he had imagined the kind of communism that society based on mental labour, sustainability and networked thought might produce.

After 1909, Bogdanov retired from activism and spent ten years writing a pioneering book on systems theory. In the early years of the Soviet Union he formed a mass workers' cultural organization – the

Proletkult – which was shut down after it became allied with an opposition group advocating workers' control.[4] He returned to medicine and died in 1928 after subjecting himself to an experimental blood transfusion.[5]

When they began to construct socialism by diktat in the 1930s, Soviet planners were fond of citing *Red Star* as their inspiration.[6] But by then the facts and the utopia had diverged.

THE RUSSIAN NIGHTMARE

The Russian Revolution went wrong in stages. Under conditions of civil war, from 1918 to 1921, banks and major industries were nationalized, production was directed by commissars (with trade unions subject to military discipline), factory committees were banned and crops simply requisitioned from the peasants. As a result, output declined to 20 per cent of its pre-war level, famine spread through the countryside and the rouble collapsed; some companies resorted to barter and wages had to be paid in kind.

In March 1921, the USSR was forced to switch to a form of market socialism known as the 'New Economic Policy'. Letting the peasants keep and sell their crops revived the economy, but created two dangers that the beleaguered revolutionaries in Russia had trouble understanding. First, it channelled money towards the better-off peasants, known in slang as '*kulaks*', and gave the agricultural sector a *de facto* economic veto over the speed of industrial development – summarized in the slogan 'Socialism at a snail's pace'. Second, it solidified a privileged bureaucracy running factories, distribution organizations, the army, the secret police and government offices.

Against the rich peasants and the bureaucrats, the Russian working class pressed for more democracy, for rapid industrialization through central planning and for a crackdown on speculators. Soon this three-way struggle in society was reflected within the Communist Party itself.

A factional dispute broke out, between a left opposition led by Trotsky, arguing for more democracy and more planning; a pro-market wing led by Bukharin, who wanted to delay industrialization, telling the peasants 'enrich yourselves'; and in the centre Stalin himself, defending the interests of the bureaucracy.

In November 1927, at a parade celebrating the anniversary of the revolution, around 20,000 supporters of the left-wing faction carried banners calling for the party to suppress the *kulaks*, speculators and bureaucrats. When several Moscow factories marched out to join them, the police attacked and street fighting followed.

Stalin expelled Trotsky and the leaders of the left and sent them into forced exile. Then, in one of those U-turns that Orwell would later parody in *Nineteen Eighty-Four*, Stalin implemented the left's programme – but in a much more extreme form, with maximum violence and brutality. In 1928 it was Bukharin's turn to be purged, together with the market-oriented right of the party. The *kulaks*, were 'liquidated' in a programme of forced collectivization of their farms. Estimates vary, but a combination of famine and mass shootings in the countryside killed about 8 million people over three years.[7]

The scale of Stalin's ambition in the first Five Year Plan (1928–32) was captured in his statement: 'We are fifty or a hundred years behind the advanced countries. We must make good this distance in ten years. Either we do it, or they crush us.'[8]

The official figures show a massive growth in output during the first Five Year Plan: the doubling of coal, steel and oil production; colossal infrastructure projects completed ahead of time. But, unlike in the sci-fi world of *Red Star*, planners faced two absolute impediments. The economy was still dominated by agriculture, and the technical base of the industrial sector was weak and had been undermined by ten years of chaos. Far from planning in a situation of abundance, Stalin imposed planning on a society with high levels of scarcity and a semi-feudal farming system. To make any kind of progress, he needed a brutal process of reallocation: from the countryside to industry, and from consumption to the sectors producing heavy machinery. The industrial targets were met, but at the cost of mass starvation, mass executions, slave labour conditions in many workplaces and, in the end, a further economic crisis.[9]

The USSR did not catch up with the West in ten years. But by 1977 its GDP per head was 57 per cent of the USA's – which put it on a par with Italy. From 1928 until the early 1980s, the average growth in the USSR, according to a CIA-commissioned survey, was 4.2 per cent. 'This clearly qualifies as a sustained growth record,' concluded analysts at the RAND Corporation.[10]

But Soviet growth was never driven by productivity. The RAND study found only a quarter of the USSR's growth was driven by better technology, with the rest by rising inputs – of machinery, raw materials and energy. After 1970, there was no growth at all in productivity: if you needed double the number of nails produced, you built a new nail factory alongside the old one – productivity was off the agenda.

Economists call this 'extensive growth' – as opposed to the intensive growth that raises real wealth. In the medium term, a system based on extensive growth cannot survive. It is likely that, with flatlining productivity, the Soviet system would have collapsed at some point from its internal problems, even if it had not been confronted with pressure from the West in the 1980s.

One lesson – spelled out in advance by anarchists, agrarian socialists such as Kondratieff and dissident Marxists like Bogdanov – was: 'do not take power in a backward country'. A second lesson is: understand that planning is guesswork. As the economist Holland Hunter showed by data-mining the Soviet numbers, the targets of the first Five Year Plan were never achievable without a 24 per cent slump in consumption.[11] Soviet planners were flying blind: guessing at a target, erring on the upside to maintain pressure on their subordinates to deliver, and – when they failed – wasting huge amounts of effort trying to remedy the situation or cover it up. They refused to recognize that even transitional economies have objective laws: dynamics that work behind the backs of the economic players and confound their willpower. 'It is impossible to study the Soviet economy taking causality as one's axis,' announced the party's economics textbook in the mid-1920s.[12] In the fantasy world of Stalinism, even cause and effect were irrelevant.

Because Soviet growth outstripped that of the West for a time, Keynesian economics remained in awe of the planned economy. It was the prophets of neoliberalism – Mises and Hayek – who had from the very beginning predicted its chaotic demise. If we want to design a project of transition towards postcapitalism today, we have to take the criticisms of Hayek and Mises seriously. They were, at their sharpest, not just critics of Soviet reality; they insisted that – even in a developed country – all forms of planning must fail.

THE CALCULATION DEBATE

It's strange but true: the possibility of socialism was once a central tenet of mainstream economics. Because the marginalists thought the market was the perfect expression of human rationality, they had no problem – as long as it was only a thought experiment – with the idea that an all-knowing state could achieve the same results as a perfect market. 'Both systems are not different in form and they lead to the same point,' wrote the Italian economist Vilfredo Pareto in a celebrated textbook, 'the result is extremely remarkable.'[13]

In 1908, his colleague Enrico Barone wrote a detailed account of how a socialist state could calculate the exact same outcomes that the market achieves blindly. Barone showed how it would be possible to discover, using linear equations, the most efficient forms of production, consumption and exchange. 'It would be a tremendous – a gigantic – work . . . but it is not an *impossibility*,' he wrote.[14]

This was an article of faith for marginalists: in theory, a perfect plan – made by a state with perfect knowledge and the ability to calculate in realtime – was as good as a perfect market.

But there was a catch. In the first place, just like the market, the state can't calculate what's needed in advance. So each year's plan is in effect an experiment – and not on a small scale but on a very large one. The market could correct itself in realtime; the plan would take longer. A collectivist regime would be just as anarchic as the market, but on a bigger scale, according to Barone. And in practice the state can never have perfect knowledge, nor can it do the calculations fast enough, so the whole debate remained, literally, academic.

It was the upheaval of 1917–21 that made the issue of 'socialist calculation' a concrete question for economics. In 1919, Germany and Austria had begun their ill-fated 'socialization' drives, the early Soviet war economy was being hailed as a form of communism – and in the short-lived soviet republic of Bavaria they had seriously discussed trying to abolish money immediately. Planned economies were no longer a thought experiment, they were an imminent possibility, and being pursued with some fanaticism.

This was the context of Ludwig von Mises's book *Economic Calculation in the Socialist Commonwealth* (1920). The market, Mises said, acts as a calculating machine: people make choices, they buy and sell things at a given price, and the market works out whether their choices were correct. Over time, this ensures the most rational allocation of scarce resources. Once you remove private property and begin planning, the calculating machine breaks down: 'Without economic calculation there can be no economy. Hence, in a socialist state wherein the pursuit of economic calculation is impossible, there can be – in our sense of the term – no economy whatsoever.'[15]

As to the far left's determination to abolish money, Mises explained that it did not matter. If you go on using money while overriding the market mechanism through planning, you reduce money's ability to convey price signals. But if you abolish money, you abolish the measuring stick for supply and demand: distribution becomes inspired guesswork. 'Thus,' said Mises, 'in the socialist commonwealth every economic change becomes an undertaking whose success can be neither appraised in advance nor later retrospectively determined. There is only groping in the dark.'[16]

Mises targeted three critical weaknesses of planning in reality: a state can't calculate as fast as a market can; a state can't reward innovation; and when it comes to distributing capital between major sectors then, without a finance system, this becomes unwieldy and haphazard. Mises predicted that as a result planning would lead to chaos, specifically to the overproduction of shoddy goods that nobody wanted. It would work for a while because the 'memory' of the appropriate prices would be imprinted on to the system, but once that memory faded, it would collapse in chaos. Because his predictions were proved right, by both the life and death of the Soviet economy, his book has become a hallowed text of the free-market right. But it was not hugely influential at the time.

Only in the 1930s, amid the Depression, fascism and the USSR's second Five Year Plan, did the debate on socialist calculation take off. The USSR was inefficient for all the usual reasons cited, said Mises's pupil Friedrich Hayek: no consumer choice, clunky allocation of resources, no reward for innovation. But on Mises's main point – the inability of the state to calculate as well as the market – Hayek retreated. A socialist state *could* mirror the market effectively, as Barone had said, provided that it had the right information. The problem was that it could never do the calculations fast enough.

Hayek's collaborator, LSE professor Harold Robbins, complained that, to calculate the plan properly, 'would necessitate the drawing up of millions of equations on the basis of millions of statistical data based on many more millions of individual computations. By the time the equations were solved, the information on which they were based would have become obsolete and they would need to be calculated anew.'[17]

This sparked a brisk exchange. The left-wing Polish economist Oskar Lange pointed out Hayek and Robbins had effectively made a big concession to the left.[18]

Lange was part of a school of moderate socialists who rejected Marxism and believed socialism could be implemented using the principles of marginal utility theory. He showed that if you retain a consumer market, and leave people free to choose where they work, but plan the production of all goods, then the process of trial and error in a socialist economy is conceptually no different from the one that operates through prices. Instead of being signalled through price movements, the unmet needs of the economy are signalled through shortages and surplus goods. The central supply board simply reorders production quotas in response.

Most independent observers thought Lange had proved his point. After the war, even the CIA's expert on Soviet economics concluded: 'Of course socialism can work ... On this Lange certainly is convincing.'[19]

However, we need to revisit the calculation debate for a reason that should be obvious: technology is today eroding the price mechanism without the parallel rise of a planned economy. And supercomputers plus big data are putting within reach the kind of realtime calculations Robbins thought were impossible. Robbins asked for a million, million, million. That is a petabyte, which just happens to be the unit we use to measure the performance of a supercomputer: petabytes of instructions per second. This has revived the idea among some leftists that 'planning could work' – if only you could solve the problem of calculation through technology. In fact, however, there is no calculation problem in a postcapitalist economy – for a reason that was suggested by Mises in 1920.

In the 'calculation debate' of the 1930s, both sides rejected the labour theory of value. Lange the socialist and Hayek the ultra-capitalist both believed that marginal utility was the only explanation of what creates value. So for both sides, the idea of a *transition* – in which a system based on scarcity gives way to one based on abundance – is unexplored territory. If capitalism and state socialism are just two different ways of allocating goods rationally until you reach equilibrium, the transition between them is merely a technical challenge, not a revolution.

But as Mises had already pointed out, if the labour theory of value is correct, there is no calculation problem at all. The problems of allocating goods, deciding priorities and rewarding people who innovate can all be captured within a system based on labour values, because everything can be measured against the same yardstick. Socialism was possible, Mises admitted, but only if there was a 'recognizable unit of value, which would permit of economic calculation in an economy where neither money nor exchange were present. And only labor can conceivably be considered as such.'[20]

Yet Mises dismissed the labour-theory for the standard reasons accepted in Vienna in the 1920s: it can't be used to measure different skill levels, and it can't be used to apply a market value to natural resources. Both these objections are easily overcome; they are in fact misunderstandings of Marx's theory. Marx clearly explained how high-skilled work can be measured as a multiple of low-skilled work – and that the labour value embodied in raw materials was simply the work it took to extract and transport them.

And Mises's work on calculation contains a second valuable insight: it is not trading between enterprises that is the true mediator of supply and demand in a market economy, it is the finance system – which puts a price on capital. This was a perceptive insight, which has relevance today: if we want a postcapitalist economy, not only do we need something better than the market for distributing goods, we also need something better than the finance system for allocating capital.

TRANSITIONS HAVE THEIR OWN DYNAMICS

It was only the Russian left opposition – above all its leading economist Evgeny Preobrazhensky – which understood the centrality of the labour-theory to the transition. For them the goal of the transition was quite simply a rising supply of free, abundant things and the erosion of 'necessary labour' as the yardstick of exchange. As in *Red Star*, the early Soviet planners aimed to produce as much as possible so that work would be de-linked from wages and the ability to consume. In Marxist terms, this was understood as 'abolishing the law of value'.

But the Russian left could only achieve this by promoting heavy industry and state control. By the early 1920s, there was a shortage of everything: to make consumer goods you needed heavy industry and electrification; to feed people you needed to industrialize agriculture. So they urged the concentration of resources in the sectors that would become iconic in Soviet propaganda – power stations, steel works, big machinery. However, they showed great awareness that equilibrium was unlikely to be achieved, and that planning was likely to be anarchic.

In economic terms, the most important thing the Russian Trotskyists left us was probably the idea that a transition phase generates its own dynamics; it is never just the fading of one system and the rise of another.

Trotsky argued that in the first phase of the Soviet-style transition, both a private business and a consumer sector had to be maintained. It was hubris to suggest the plan could, at this stage, allocate better than the market in consumer goods. Plus, the rouble had to remain exchangeable on the world market. Furthermore, all plans were effectively hypotheses. 'The plan,' said Trotsky, 'is checked and, to a considerable degree, realized through the market.'[21]

To make even the crudest adjustment requires realtime information feedback. But in a heavily bureaucratic society, where to dissent was to invite a one-way ticket to the gulag, such feedback was strangled. Hence Trotsky's emphasis on reviving workplace democracy. You needed a rolling plan: a combination of plan and market, with money used as both a medium of exchange and store of value. And you needed workers' democracy.

Money, said Preobrazhensky, would function normally in those sectors you could not plan, while in the planned sector of the economy, money would start to function as a technical accounting device. And while the aim is for the plan to swamp the market, the market could be expected to constantly 'pollute' the plan.

In a memorable passage, whose relevance to the twenty-first century will be clear, Trotsky wrote:

> If a universal mind existed . . . that could register simultaneously all the processes of nature and society, that could measure the dynamics of their motion, that could forecast the results of their inter-reactions – such a mind, of course, could *a priori* draw up a faultless and exhaustive economic plan, beginning with the number of acres of wheat down to the last button for a vest.[22]

The absence of such a 'universal mind', he said, requires instead the promotion of workers' democracy – which had been abolished. Only if human beings, with freedom of speech, became the sensory and feedback mechanisms for the planning system could this crude calculating machine work.

Preobrazhensky, Trotsky and their collaborators were the last Marxists with any political power who conceived the transition in terms of labour value. Preobrazhensky was executed in 1936 and Trotsky assassinated in 1940. But their ideas contain powerful implications for the world we face today.

Under neoliberalism, the market sector is immensely more complex than in the 1920s and 30s. The USA in 1933 was vastly different from Russia in 1933 – but they were much closer to each other than the America of today is to the America of thirty years ago. Today's consumer sector is not only much bigger, it is much more atomized. Production and consumption overlap – and the economy already includes information goods whose marginal production cost is zero.

We also have Negri's 'social factory' to contend with: a highly financialized and granular consumer society, in which what we buy has become a question of identity.

So lesson one is: the market sector is much more complex and therefore more difficult to replicate or improve on through planning.

Next, we have to consider the state sector. The modern state as a service provider is massive compared to any capitalist state in the 1930s. Whether it spends its tax dollars on services from private companies or those provided by the state itself, the state pushes the true private economy – private companies producing for privately employed individuals – into a smaller space. In addition, the peer-to-peer economy is large, though not measured in terms of profit and GDP. So lesson two is: any attempt to move beyond the market is going to start from a different place than it would have in the 1930s.

But we can learn from both the calculation debate and from the Russian left's planning experts, if we know how to read them properly. Before that, however, we have to understand that, even with the best supercomputer and the biggest data farm, planning is not the primary route beyond capitalism.

ATTACK OF THE CYBER-STALINISTS

Over the past twenty years, Paul Cockshott and Allin Cottrell – a computer scientist and an economics professor – have worked tirelessly on a problem we thought we didn't have: how to plan an economy. Though not well known, their work is rigorous and performs an invaluable service; it is a textbook outline of what we should not do.

Cockshott and Cottrell argue that improvements in computer power, together with the application of advanced maths and information theory removes, in principle, the Hayek/Robbins objection: that the planner can never have better realtime information than a market. What's more, unlike the left in the calculation debate, they say the computer model we would need for planned production should use the labour theory of value, and not try to simulate the results of supply and demand.

This is a crucial departure from the work of Lange. Cockshott and Cottrell understand that the labour-theory gives you a measuring stick against which both market interactions and non-market ones can be compared, and a way of calibrating the transition. They see the planning process as similar to a modular computer program. It would collate the demands of consumers and producers; work out the cost and resources needed to meet them; formulate targets; calculate in advance the resource implications; check the feasibility of the plan; and then instruct producers and suppliers of services to hit the targets.[23]

But unlike the Russian left of the 1920s, Cockshott and Cottrell don't see the plan as provisional, or something for the state sector alone to execute; it has to be drawn up and tested in detail, down to enterprise level and individual products.

Once you remove the market, they argue, there are no other signals for the boss of a factory, or care home, or coffee bar to rely on. They have to know exactly what they're supposed to be producing. Theirs, in other words, is the methodology for a completely prescriptive plan, as imagined (and ridiculed) by Trotsky in the 1930s.

Historically, of course, sophisticated planning at this level is something the Soviet Union never achieved: by the 1980s there were 24 million different products in the USSR but the entire planning apparatus could track the price and quantity of only 200,000 of them, and the actual central plan just 2,000. As a result, factories met the targets for the small number of goods they were supposed to make, and fulfilled all other requests chaotically or not at all.[24]

In Cockshott and Cottrell's model, money exists in the form of 'labour tokens' which are paid to everybody according to the amount of labour they do, minus a flat tax to pay for state services. This allows for consumer choice. Where supply and demand for a product get out of kilter, the central planners adjust the price to achieve a short-term rebalancing. Then, over a longer period, they compare the prices commanded by a sector, or production unit, to the actual amount of labour it is doing. In the next round of the plan, they boost production in the areas where prices are higher than the labour used and cut them where lower. Planning is 'iterative'; it is adjusted constantly. But it is not mere trial and error: Cockshott and Cottrell believe the inputs and outputs can be calculated in advance, and they propose a detailed algorithm to do so.

The computing challenge is, first, to calculate what the value of an hour's labour should be. That is – how much work is going into each product, as listed on a giant spreadsheet. The researchers argue this is doable with a supercomputer, but only if it uses data-processing techniques that prioritize the most relevant information.

For Cockshott and Cottrell, working out the value of an hour's labour is the hard part. The plan itself – the allocation of resources – is an easier calculation to do, because you do not run the program blind. You ask it feasible questions such as: how much of a product is going to be sold this year; how much of the various inputs do we normally use; what's the seasonal variation, what's the expected demand, how much should we order within the boundaries of past experience? They conclude: 'With modern computers, one could envisage computing an updated list of labor values daily and preparing a new perspective plan weekly – somewhat faster than a market economy is able to react.'[25]

In an ambitious application of these principles, Cockshott and Cottrell proposed an outline for a planned economy in the European Union. They explained not just how you would calculate the plan, but also how you would have to restructure the economy to implement it. And it is here that the assumptions behind their methodology become clear: for all their dislike of what went wrong in the 1930s, this is still a form of cyber-Stalinism.

In their model, the de-marketization of Europe would be driven not primarily by nationalization, but by reforming the monetary system so that money began to reflect labour value.[26] Banknotes would be overprinted with a 'labour time figure', allowing people to see the mismatch between what they were being paid for their labour and what they were being charged for products. Over time, the authors expect people to choose products closer to their true value; consumer choice becomes a mechanism for squeezing profit out of the system. A law banning exploitation would allow workers to claim against excess profit-making; the final aim being to eradicate profit altogether. Banking would effectively cease to be a means of building up capital, which would be done by the state, using direct taxation. The finance industry would be wiped out.

The huge service Cockshott and Cottrell perform here is not the one they intend. They show that to fully plan an early-twenty-first-century developed economy, it would have to be stripped of its complexity, see finance removed completely, and have radical behavioural change enforced at the level of consumption, workplace democracy and investment.

Where the dynamism and innovation would come from is not addressed. Nor how the vastly enlarged cultural sector would come in. In fact, the researchers make a strong case that, because of its decreased complexity, a planned economy would need fewer calculations than a market one.

But that's the problem. In order for the plan to work, society in this project has to go back to being 'plannable'. Workers interface with every aspect of Cockshott and Cottrell's plan via 'their' workplace – so what happens to the precarious worker with three jobs; or the single mum doing sex work on a web cam? They can't exist. Likewise, the financial complexity that has come to characterize modern life has to disappear – and not gradually. There can be no credit cards in this world; no payday loans; probably a much-reduced e-commerce sector. And of course there are no network structures in this model and no peer produced free stuff.

Though the researchers decry the dogmatic idiocy of Soviet planning, their world view remains that of a hierarchical society, of physical products, of a simple system where the pace of change is slow. The model they've produced is the best demonstration yet of why any attempt to use state planning and market suppression as a route to postcapitalism is closed.

Fortunately, another route has opened up. To follow it we must exploit a granular, spontaneous micro-process, not a plan. Our solution must map comfortably on to a world of networks, info-goods, complexity and exponential change.

Of course, on the route to postcapitalism, we will have need of planning. Large parts of the capitalist world are effectively planned already – from urban design and construction projects through to the integrated supply chains of a large supermarket. It is the advance in processing power, the use of big data and the digital tracking of individual objects and components – using barcodes or RFID tags – that make this possible. That part of our project which requires planning would be well equipped because of this.

But the nature of modern society alters the problem. In a complex, globalized society, where the worker is also the consumer of financial services and micro-services from other workers, the plan cannot outdo the market unless there is a retreat from complexity and a return to hierarchy. A computerized plan, even if it measured everything against labour values, might tell the shoe industry to produce shoes, but it could not tell Beyoncé to produce a surprise album marketed only via social media, as she did in 2013. Nor would the plan be concerned with the most interesting thing in our modern economy: free stuff. Such a plan would see time spent curating a Wikipedia page, or updating Linux, exactly the same way as the market sees it: wasteful and incalculable.

If the rise of the networked economy is beginning to dissolve the law of value, planning has to be the adjunct of something more comprehensive.

André Gorz once wrote that the source of capitalism's superiority to Soviet socialism was its 'instability, its diversity ... its complex multiform character, comparable to that of an ecosystem, which continually triggers new conflicts between partially autonomous forces that can neither be controlled nor placed once and for all in the service of a stable order'.[27]

What we're trying to build should be even more complex, more autonomous and more unstable.

But change from one economic system to another takes time. If the postcapitalism thesis is right, what we're about to live through will be a lot more like the transition from feudalism to capitalism than the one the Soviet planners envisaged. It will be long; there will be confusion; and in the process the very concept of an 'economic system' will have to be redefined.

And that's why, whenever I want to stop myself being too Marxist about the future, I think about Shakespeare.

BIG CHANGE: SHAKESPEARE *VS* MARX

If you could watch Shakespeare's history plays back-to-back, starting with *King John* and ending with *Henry VIII*, it would at first sight seem like a Netflix drama series without a central plot: murders, wars and mayhem – all set within an apparently meaningless squabble between kings and dukes. But once you understand what a 'mode of production' is, the meaning becomes clear. What you are watching is the collapse of feudalism and the emergence of early capitalism.

The mode of production is one of the most powerful ideas to come out of Marxist economics. It influenced a wide range of historical thinkers, and has come to shape our view of the past. Its starting point is the question: what is the prevailing economic system based on?

Feudalism was a system based on obligation: peasants were obliged to hand part of their produce to the landowner and do military service for him; he in turn was obliged to provide the king with taxes, and supply an army on demand. In the England of Shakespeare's history plays, however, the mainspring of that system had broken down. By the time Richard III was slaughtering his rivals in real life, the power network based on obligation had been polluted by money: rents paid in money, military service paid for with money, wars fought with the aid of a cross-border banking network stretching to Florence and Amsterdam. Shakespeare's kings and dukes killed each other because money had made all power based on obligation susceptible to being overthrown.

Shakespeare managed to get to the essence of it long before the words 'feudalism' and 'capitalism' were even invented. The signal difference between his history plays and the comedies and tragedies is that the latter depict the contemporary society his audience lived in. In the comedies and tragedies we are suddenly in a world of bankers, merchants, companies, mercenary soldiers and republics. The typical setting for these plays is a prosperous trading city, not a castle. The typical hero is a person whose greatness is essentially bourgeois and self-made, either through courage (Othello), humanist philosophy (Prospero) or knowledge of the law (Portia in *The Merchant of Venice*).

But Shakespeare had no clue about where this was going to lead. He saw what this new kind of economy was doing to the human character: empowering us with knowledge, yet leaving us susceptible to greed, passion, self-doubt and power-craziness on a new scale. But it would be another 150 years until merchant capitalism, based on trade, conquest and slavery, paved the way for industrial capitalism.

If you interrogate Shakespeare through his texts, and ask him: 'what is between the past and the time you're living in?', the implicit answer is 'ideas and behaviour'. Human beings value each other more; love is more important than family duty; human values like truth, scientific rigour and justice are worth dying for – far more so than hierarchy and honour.

Shakespeare is a great witness to the moment when one mode of production begins to falter and another begins to rise. But we also need Marx. In a materialist view of history, the difference between feudalism and early capitalism is not just ideas and behaviours. Changes in the social and economic system are critical. And at root, the change is driven by new technologies.

For Marx, a mode of production describes a set of economic relationships, laws and social traditions that form the underlying 'normal' of a society. In feudalism, the concept of lordly power and obligation pervaded everything. In capitalism, the equivalent force is the market, private property and wages. To understand a mode of production, another revealing question is: 'what reproduces itself spontaneously?' In feudalism, it is the concept of fealty and obligation; in capitalism, it is the market.

And here's where the mode of production concept gets challenging: the changes are so huge that we are never comparing like with like. So when it comes to the economic system that replaces capitalism, we should not expect it to be based on something as purely economic as the market, nor on something as clearly coercive as feudal power.

For Marx, the modes of production concept led to a strict historical sequence: there are various pre-capitalist forms of society, where the rich get rich through legally authorized violence; then there is capitalism, where the rich get rich through technical innovation and the market; finally there is communism, where the whole of humanity gets richer because there is abundance instead of scarcity. That sequence is open to criticism from two angles. First, it can read like a quasi-mythology: human destiny looks pre-programmed to happen in three logical stages. Second, when used by historians looking backwards, it can lead to the application of simple labels to complex societies, or to imputing economic motives that simply didn't exist.

But if we avoid the myth of inevitability and assert simply, 'there must come a time when there is relative abundance, compared to the scarcity that has driven all previous economic models', then Marx was only saying the same thing as Keynes said in the early 1930s: one day there will be enough goods to go around and the economic problem will be solved. 'For the first time since his creation,' Keynes wrote, 'man will be faced with his real, his permanent problem – how to use

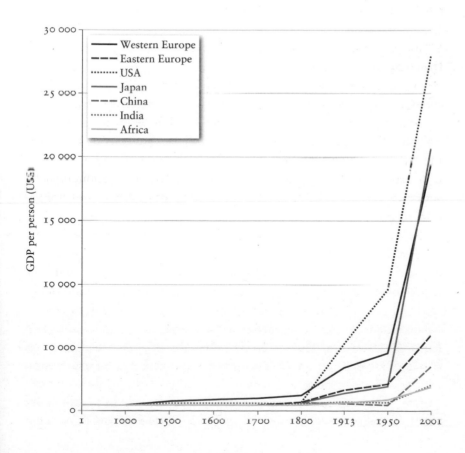

his freedom from pressing economic cares ... to live wisely and agree-
ably and well.'[28]

In fact, this three-phase view of world history is supported by data
we now possess (and that Marx and Keynes didn't) on population
and GDP. Until around the year 1800, only Western Europe experienced a tangible rise in GDP per person, mainly after the conquest of
the Americas; then, with the Industrial Revolution, per person growth
took off spectacularly in Europe and America until around 1950,
when its rate of acceleration increased again. Today, as the graph
above shows, GDP per person rates are rising all across the world.
The stage where all the lines go close to vertical is the one Keynes and
Marx allowed themselves to imagine – and so should we.[29]

DRIVERS OF TRANSITION

What caused feudalism to collapse and capitalism to rise? Naturally
that's the subject of a gigantic historical debate. But if we think the
transition to postcapitalism is going to be of a similar magnitude, then
there are lessons to learn about the interplay between internal and
external factors; the role of technology versus the importance of ideas;
and why transitions are so hard to understand when you're in the
middle of them.

Armed with new knowledge, from geneticists and epidemiologists
as well as social historians, we can list four probable causes for the
end of feudalism.

Up to about 1300, feudal agriculture had been dynamic, raising
GDP per head in Western Europe faster than anywhere else. But fam-
ines, beginning in the 1300s, signalled a decline in the efficiency of the
feudal systems of land use: productivity could not keep up with population growth. Then, in 1345, the English king Edward III defaulted
on his country's debts, wiping out the Florentine bankers who had
lent him the money. Though containable, this was just one symptom
of a general malaise, and a warning that crisis in one part of feudal
Europe might spread to all parts.

In 1347 the *Yersinia pestis* bacillus hit Europe. By 1353, the Black
Death had killed at least a quarter of Europe's population.[30] For those

who lived through it, the experience was spiritually transformative – like witnessing the end of the world. Its economic impact was stark: the supply of labour collapsed. Suddenly farm workers, who had been the lowest of the low, could command higher wages.

Once the plague was over a surge of economic struggles broke out – peasant revolts in France and England, worker rebellions in the key manufacturing towns of Ghent and Florence. Historians call this the 'general crisis of feudalism'. Though the revolts failed, the economic balance was now tipped in favour of the urban worker and the peasant. 'Agricultural rents collapsed after the Black Death and wages in the towns soared to two and even three times the levels they had held,' according to historian David Herlihy.[31]

With wool prices high, many landowners switched from crops to sheep pasture – and unlike wheat, wool was for trading, not consuming. The old tradition of peasants being forced to do military service was replaced increasingly by cash-based mercenary warfare. And with workers scarce, labour-saving devices began to be invented.

Basically, the rat that brought the Black Death into Cadiz in 1347 triggered an external shock that helped to collapse an internally weakened system.

The second driver of change was the growth of banking. Banking had already become the sure-fire way to amass a fortune in the undocumented space between the official classes of feudalism; nobles, knights, gentry, clerks, etc. The Medicis created a transnational super company in the fifteenth century, and the Fugger family of Augsburg overtook them once their influence declined.

Banking does not just systematically inject credit into feudal society, it injects an alternative network of power and secrecy. The Fugger and Medici families wielded unofficial leverage over kings through business – even as their activities were seen as borderline un-Christian. Everyone involved connived in the creation of a subtextual form of capitalism within the officially feudal economy.

The third big driver of capitalism's takeoff was the conquest and pillage of the Americas, beginning in 1503. This created a flow of money to non-aristocrats way in excess of anything generated internally by the market growing, organically, within late feudalism. In a single load, the *conquistadores* stole 1.3 million ounces of gold from

Peru. The huge amount of wealth imported into early modern Europe boosted market forces, craft manufacturing and banking. And it strengthened the power of monarchic states over the old independent towns and the now impoverished dukes in their castles.

Finally, there was the printing press. Gutenberg put the first one to use in 1450. In the following fifty years 8 million books were printed – more than all the scribes of Christendom had managed to produce since Roman times. Elizabeth Eisenstein, the great social historian of printing, points out the revolutionary nature of the print-shop itself: it brought together scholars, priests, authors and metalworkers into a business environment that no other social situation within feudalism could have created. Printed books established checkable knowledge and authorship. They fuelled the rise of Protestantism, the scientific revolution and humanism. If the medieval cathedral was full of meaning – an encyclopaedia in stone – printing destroyed the need for it. Printing transformed the way human beings think.[32] The philosopher Francis Bacon wrote in 1620 that printing, gunpowder and the compass 'have changed the whole face and state of things throughout the world'.[33]

If we accept the four-factor account given above, the dissolution of feudalism is not primarily a technology story. It is a complex interplay between failing economics and outside shocks. These new technologies would have been useless without a new way of thinking and the external disruptions that allowed new behaviours to flourish.

When we look at the possibility of transition beyond capitalism, we have to expect a similar complex interplay between technology, social struggle, ideas and external shocks. But our minds reel from the scale of it; just as they do when shown the size of our galaxy in the universe. We have a fatal tendency to push the dynamics of transition into simple categories and simple chains of cause and effect.

The classic Marxist explanation of what destroyed feudalism was 'its contradictions': the class struggle between peasant and nobility.[34] For later materialist historians, however, the emphasis was on the failure and stagnation of the old system, giving rise to a 'general crisis'. Perry Anderson, the New Left historian, drew an important general conclusion from this: that the key symptom of a mode of production transition is not the vigorous eruption of the new economic model.

'On the contrary, the forces of production typically tend to stall and recede within the existent relations of production.'[35]

What are the other general lessons we might draw?

First, that different modes of production are structured around different things: feudalism was an economic system structured by customs and laws about obligation. Capitalism was structured by something purely economic: the market. We can predict from this that postcapitalism – whose precondition is abundance – will not simply be a modified form of a complex market society. But we can only begin to grasp at positive visions of what it will be like.

I don't mean this as a cop-out: the general economic parameters of a postcapitalist society by, for example, the year 2075 will be clear from the next chapter. But if such a society is structured around human liberation, not economics, unpredictable things will begin to shape it. Maybe, for instance, the most obvious thing to the Shakespeare of 2075 will be the total upheaval in gender relationships, or sexuality, or health. Maybe there will not even be any playwrights: maybe the very fabric of the media we use to tell stories will change – just as it did for Shakespeare's generation when the first public theatres were built.

Marxism, with its insistence on the proletariat as the driver of change, tended to ignore the question: how will humans have to change in order for postcapitalism to emerge? Yet if we study the transition from feudalism to capitalism it's one of the most obvious issues.

Think of the difference between, say, Horatio in Shakespeare's *Hamlet* and a character like Daniel Doyce in Dickens's *Little Dorrit*. Both are secondary characters for the hero to use as a sounding board, both carry around with them a characteristic obsession of their age: Horatio is obsessed with humanist philosophy, Doyce is obsessed with patenting his invention. There can be no character like Doyce in Shakespeare; at best he would get a bit part as a working-class comic figure. Yet, by the time Dickens described Daniel Doyce, all his readers would have known somebody like him. Just as Shakespeare could not have imagined Doyce, so we too cannot imagine the kind of human beings society will produce once economics is no longer central to life.

Let's restate what we know about the way the last transition happened and spell out the parallels.

The feudal model of agriculture collided first with environmental limits and then with a massive external shock – the Black Death. After that, there was a demographic shock: too few workers for the land, which raised their wages and made the old feudal obligation system impossible to enforce. The labour shortage also made technological innovation necessary. The new technologies that underpinned the rise of merchant capitalism were the ones that stimulated commerce (printing and accountancy), the creation of tradable wealth (mining, the compass and fast ships) and productivity (mathematics and the scientific method).

Present throughout the whole process is something that looks incidental to the old system – money and credit – but which is destined to become the basis of the new system. Many laws and customs are actually shaped around ignoring money; in high feudalism credit is seen as sinful. So when money and credit burst through the boundaries and create a market system, it feels like a revolution. Then, the new system gains further energy from the discovery of a virtually unlimited source of free wealth in the Americas.

A combination of all these factors took a set of people who had been persecuted or marginalized under feudalism – humanists, scientists, craftsmen, lawyers, radical preachers and bohemian playwrights like Shakespeare – and put them at the head of a social transformation. At key moments, though tentatively at first, the state switched from hindering the change to promoting it.

There won't be exact parallels in the transition to postcapitalism but the rough parallels are there.

The thing that is corroding capitalism, barely rationalized by mainstream economics, is information. The equivalent of the printing press and the scientific method is information technology and its spillover into all other forms of technology, from genetics to healthcare to agriculture to the movies.

The modern equivalent of the long stagnation of late feudalism is the stalled fifth Kondratieff cycle, where instead of rapidly automating work out of existence, we are reduced to creating bullshit jobs on low pay, and many economies are stagnating.

The equivalent of the new source of free wealth? It's not exactly wealth: it's the externalities – the free stuff and wellbeing generated by networked interaction. It is the rise of non-market production, of un-ownable information, of peer networks and unmanaged enterprises. The internet, says French economist Yann Moulier-Boutang, is 'both the ship and the ocean' for the modern-day conquest of a new world. In fact, it is the ship, the compass, the ocean and the gold.

The modern-day external shocks are clear: energy depletion, climate change, ageing populations and migration. They are altering the dynamics of capitalism and making it unworkable in the long term. They have not yet had the same impact as the Black Death – but any financial collapse could easily wreak havoc on the highly fragile urban societies we've created. As Katrina demonstrated in New Orleans in 2005, it does not take the bubonic plague to destroy social order and functional infrastructure in a modern city.

Once you understand the transition in this way, the need is not for a supercomputed Five Year Plan, but for a gradual, iterative and modular project. Its aim should be to expand those technologies, business models and behaviours that dissolve market forces, eradicate the need for work and progress the world economy towards abundance. That is not to say we can't take urgent action to mitigate risk, or address burning injustices. But it does mean that we have to understand the difference between strategic goals and short-term actions.

Our strategy should be to shape the outcome of the process that has begun spontaneously so that it becomes irreversible and delivers socially just outcomes as quickly as possible. This will involve a mixture of planning, state provision, markets and peer production. But space must also be left for the modern equivalents of Gutenberg and Columbus. And for the modern Shakespeare.

Most twentieth-century leftists believed that they did not have the luxury of a managed transition. It was an article of faith for them that nothing of the coming system could exist within the old one – though, as I've shown, the workers always held the desire to create an alternative life despite capitalism. As a result, once the possibility of a Soviet-style transition disappeared, the modern left became preoccupied simply with opposing things: the privatization of healthcare, the reduction of union rights, fracking – the list goes on.

Today we have to relearn to do positive things: to build alternatives within the system; to use governmental power in a radical and disruptive way; and to focus all our actions towards the transition path – not the piecemeal defence of random elements of the old system.

The socialists of the early twentieth century were absolutely convinced that nothing preliminary was possible within the old system. 'The socialist system,' Preobrazhensky once insisted categorically, 'cannot be built up molecularly within the world of capitalism.'[36]

The most courageous thing an adaptive left could do is to abandon that conviction. It is entirely possible to build the elements of the new system molecularly within the old. In the cooperatives, the credit unions, the peer-networks, the unmanaged enterprises and the parallel, subcultural economies, those elements already exist. We have to stop seeing them as quaint experiments; we have to promote them with regulation just as vigorous as that which capitalism used to drive the peasants off the land or destroy handicraft work in the eighteenth century.

Finally, we have to learn what's urgent, and what's important, and that sometimes they do not coincide.

If it were not for the external shocks facing us in the next fifty years, we could afford to take things slowly: the state, in a benign transition, would act as the main facilitator of change through regulation. But the enormity of the external shocks means some of the actions we take will have to be immediate, centralized and drastic.

9

The Rational Case for Panic

Wherever I go, I ask questions about economics and get answers about climate. In 2011 in the Philippines, I met landless farmers living in rural slums. What had happened? 'The typhoons,' came the answer. 'With more typhoons the rice doesn't grow as well. There are not enough days of sunshine between planting and harvesting.'

In Ningxia Province, China, walled off from the Gobi desert by barren mountains, I met sheep farmers who'd become reliant on chemical pellets as the grassland died around them. When, back in 2008, scientists trudged the mountains to find out what had happened to the 144 springs and mountain streams marked on the map, they reported: 'With climate change and deterioration of the environment, the southern mountainous areas have no springs and no mountain streams.'[1]

In New Orleans, in 2005, I watched the social order of an already fragile modern city, in the richest country in the world, disintegrate. The proximate cause was a hurricane; the underlying problem was the failure of the city's infrastructure to deal with a change in weather patterns, and the inability of the poverty-stricken social and racial structure of the city to survive the blow.

There's a pointless argument between economists and ecologists over which crisis is more important – the ecosphere or the economy? The materialist answer is that their fates are interlinked. We know the natural world only by interacting with it and transforming it: nature produced us that way. Even if, as some supporters of 'deep ecology' argue, the earth would be better off without us, it is to us that the task of saving it falls.

In the world of suits and climate summits, a complacent calm rules.

245

The focus is on scenarios for 'what *will* happen', the climate catastrophe that awaits if we allow global temperatures to rise by more than two degrees Celsius above pre-industrial levels. But in the edge-places of the world the catastrophe is happening already. If we listened to those whose lives are being destroyed by floods, deforestation and encroaching deserts, we would better understand what is coming: the total disruption of the world.

The IPCC's fifth report, published in 2013, states unequivocally that the planet is warming. 'Since the 1950s,' say the world's most respected climate scientists, 'many of the observed changes are unprecedented over decades to millennia. The atmosphere and ocean have warmed, the amounts of snow and ice have diminished, [the] sea level has risen, and the concentrations of greenhouse gases have increased.'[2] The IPCC is confident that this is primarily caused by human beings using carbon to fuel economic growth – so much so that in this report it upgraded from 'likely' to 'very likely' the probability of hotter temperatures, more frequent hot days and more frequent heatwaves being caused by humans. Scientists do not use such terms lightly; they are the equivalent of a qualitative increase in their degree of certainty.

Because our ecosystem is so complex, we can't trace every disruption of the climate to a human cause with 100 per cent certainty. But we can, says the IPCC, be fairly certain that extreme weather – hurricanes, floods, typhoons, droughts – will increase in the second half of the century.

In its 2014 update, the IPCC warned unequivocally: failure to stop the rise in carbon emissions would increase the likelihood of 'severe, pervasive and irreversible impacts for people and ecosystems'. This, remember, is from a report by scientists. They do not sign off on words like 'severe, pervasive and irreversible' before weighing them carefully.

If you're a mainstream economist, what's coming will feel like an 'exogenous shock', an extra source of chaos within an already chaotic situation. For peasants in the Philippines, African-Americans in Louisiana and the people of Ningxia Province, the shock is already happening.

Climate policymakers and NGOs have produced numerous scenarios for what we need to do to stop it. But while they model the earth as a complex system, they tend to model the economy as a simple machine, with inputs/outputs, an energy requirement and a rational controlling hand – the market. When they speak of 'transition', they mean the phased evolution of energy policy towards burning less carbon, using a modified market mechanism.

But the economy itself is complex; just like the weather during the hurricane season, it is prone to reactions that accelerate uncontrollably and to complex feedback loops. Like the climate, the economy moves through a mixture of long- and short-term cycles. But, as I have shown, these cycles lead to mutations and ultimately to breakdown over timescales of fifty to 500 years.

In this book, I've avoided 'building in' the climate crisis until now. I wanted to show how the clash between info-tech and market structures is, on its own, driving us towards an important turning point. Even if the ecosphere was in a steady state, our technology would still be pushing us beyond capitalism.

But industrial capitalism has, in the space of 200 years, made the climate 0.8 degrees Celsius hotter, and is certain to push it two degrees higher than the pre-industrial average by 2050. Any project to move beyond capitalism has to shape its priorities around the urgent challenge of climate change. Either we react in time and confront it in a relatively orderly way, or we don't – and disaster follows.

It has become common to laugh at the absurdities of the climate-change deniers, but there is a rationality to their response. They know that climate science destroys their authority, their power and their economic world. In a way, they have grasped that if climate change is real, capitalism is finished.

The real absurdists are not the climate-change deniers, but the politicians and economists who believe that the existing market mechanisms can stop climate change, that the market must set the limits of climate action and that the market can be structured to deliver the biggest re-engineering project humanity has ever tried.

In January 2014, John Ashton, a career diplomat and formerly the British government's special representative on climate change, delivered the blunt truth to the 1 per cent: 'The market left to itself will not reconfigure the energy system and transform the economy within a generation.'[3]

According to the International Energy Agency, even if all the announced emissions-reduction plans, all the carbon taxes and all the renewables targets are achieved – that is, if consumers don't revolt against higher taxes, and the world does not de-globalize – then CO_2 emissions will still rise by 20 per cent by 2035. Instead of limiting the warming of the earth to only a two-degree increase, the temperature will rise 3.6 degrees.[4]

Faced with a clear warning that a 4.5-billion-year-old planet is being destabilized, those in power decided that a 25-year-old economic doctrine held the solution. They resolved to incentivize lower carbon use by rationing it, taxing it and subsidizing the alternatives. Since the market is the ultimate expression of human rationality, they believed it would spur the correct allocation of resources to meet the target of the two-degree cap. It was pure ideology and it has been proved plain wrong.

To remain under the two-degree threshold, we – as a global population – must burn no more than 886 billion tonnes of carbon between the years 2000 and 2049 (according to the International Energy Agency). But the global oil and gas companies have declared the existence of 2.8 trillion tonnes of carbon reserves, and their shares are valued as if those reserves are burnable. As the Carbon Tracker Initiative warned investors: 'they need to understand that 60–80% of coal, oil and gas reserves of listed firms are unburnable'[5] – that is, if we burn them, the atmosphere will warm to a catastrophic degree.

Yet rising energy prices are a market signal. They tell energy firms that it's a good idea to invest in new and more expensive ways of finding carbon. In 2011, they invested $674 billion on exploration and development of fossil fuels: tar sands, fracking and deep-sea oil deposits. Then, as global tensions increased, Saudi Arabia decided to collapse the price of oil, with the aim of destroying America's new hydrocarbon industries, and in the process bankrupting Putin's Russia.

This, too, acted as a market signal to American drivers: buy more cars and do more miles. Clearly, somewhere, the market as a signalling mechanism has gone wrong.

Look at it as an investment problem: either the global oil and gas companies are really worth much less than their share prices indicate, or nobody believes we're going to cut our carbon use. The stock market valuations of the top 200 carbon burners totals $4 trillion; much of that could be lost if we persuade ourselves to stop burning carbon. This is not just scaremongering by excitable climate NGOs. In 2014 the governor of the Bank of England, Mark Carney, warned the world's insurance giants that if the two-degree target is significantly breached it would 'threaten the viability of your business model'.[6]

The lesson is: a market-led strategy on climate change is utopian thinking.

What are the obstacles to a non-market-led strategy? First, the lobbying power of the carbon burners. Between 2003 and 2010, climate-denial lobby groups received $558 million from donors in the USA. ExxonMobil and the ultra-conservative Koch Industries were major donors until 2007, when there was a tangible shift to funds channelled through anonymous third parties, under pressure of journalistic scrutiny.[7] The outcome? The world spends an estimated $544 billion on subsidizing the fossil fuel industry.[8]

But that's just the most obvious part of climate lunacy. After the failure to agree a global path to the two-degree target at the 2009 Copenhagen Summit, energy companies realigned their efforts in order to pressure national governments for specific outcomes, always with the aim to slow the introduction of carbon targets, or to exempt specific firms.

Yet strong, positive action can work. In Germany, the sudden shutdown in 2011 of the nuclear programme after Fukushima, combined with heavy investment in renewable energy, has done to the power utilities what any hard application of carbon targets would do to market forces. It has shattered them.

In the German system, wind, solar and other renewable generators get the first opportunity to supply energy. If there's sun, and a healthy breeze, as there was on 16 June 2013, they can generate half of all demand. On that day, the gas and coal producers – who cannot easily adjust the output of their power stations, only switch them on and off – were forced to pay the German electricity grid €100 per megawatt to take unwanted electricity off their hands. The price of carbon energy had gone negative. As *The Economist* magazine put it: 'For established utilities . . . this is a disaster . . . you cannot run a normal business, in which customers pay for services according to how much they consume, if prices go negative.'[9]

In many countries, energy policy is paralysed – not just by the lobbying power of oil and gas, but also by the difficulty of forcing behaviour change using market forces – e.g. higher prices – rather than by undertaking a rational redesign of the whole system.

For the advocates of green capitalism, it is easier to imagine the end of the world than to imagine a non-market, low-carbon economy.

So we need to imagine better.

HOW TO AVERT CLIMATE DISASTER

Climate science tells us that, in order to keep the temperature rise to around two degrees, we need to halve the amount of CO_2 we burn by 2050. The IEA spelled out the importance of the timing: 'If emissions do not peak by around 2020 and decline steadily thereafter, achieving the needed 50% reduction by 2050 will become much more costly. In fact, the opportunity may be lost completely.'[10] The later emissions peak, the harder it is to halve them.

In response, various campaigns and research units have designed scenarios to show technically how this 50 per cent reduction might be achieved. Though they all differ as to the mix of alternative energy types and the way they model energy efficiency, they have one thing in common: nearly all of these scenarios conclude that it will be cheaper in the long term to go low carbon, than not.

The IEA's Blue Map Scenario, which halves CO_2 emissions by 2050, sees the world spending $46 trillion more on energy investments than it would if nothing changed. But because the scenario involves burning less fuel, even by the most conservative estimate it still saves $8 trillion.

Greenpeace, whose Energy Revolution Scenario is taken as a reference point in the wider industry debate, wants to achieve the target with no new nuclear power plants and less emphasis on carbon capture and storage, so that by 2050 85 per cent of all energy is produced from wind, wave, solar and biomass technologies. Even here, however, with much higher upfront investment costs and a bigger social change, the world saves money in the end.[11] In all the scenarios where carbon burning is halved, there is a spin-off benefit because the transition creates new jobs. Building and maintaining machines to generate electricity from wave, wind and solar power is a more technologically advanced solution than burning gas or coal.

Saving the planet, then, is technologically feasible and economically rational, even when measured in cash terms. What stands in the way is the market.

This is not to say we have achieved nothing. If you discount China – which distorted the global figures by building hundreds of coal-fired power plants in the 2000s – the amount of generating capacity coming online from renewables outstripped that from fossil fuels in 2009. This is a clear signal that state intervention into the market – through financial incentives for renewables and targets for reduced carbon emissions – can work.

The problem is, first, that the market-led transition is too slow and too vulnerable to pressure from consumers (who naturally want cheap energy) and from fossil-fuel producers. Secondly, as political pressure on governments rises, energy turns into geopolitics. Germany's move against nuclear energy came at the cost of giving Russia the power to hold the German economy to ransom during the Ukraine crisis. America's turn to fracking – in addition to its environmental impacts – altered the global balance of power so significantly that Saudi retaliation has in the space of a year collapsed the price of oil by more than half.

Seen against the rising geopolitical tensions, the prospects for a deal at the COP (Conference of Parties) in Paris, in December 2015, do not look positive. More and more, the climate talks conducted in these conferences come to resemble the peace treaties that paved the way to the Second World War.

Meanwhile even radicals in the environmental movement are confused about markets. Greenpeace, for example, compares China with Europe as follows: China's determination to fuel economic growth with coal boosted emissions, while privatization in Europe and the USA drove their switch to gas, which is less harmful than coal. This they see as proof that a market achieves better carbon outcomes than centralized control.[12]

However, to meet the critical emissions targets we are going to have to use some centralized control. Governments – at state and regional level – will need to take control, and probably ownership, of all big carbon producers. As the energy distribution grid becomes 'smart', using technology to predict and balance supply with demand, it makes sense for the grid to be a public resource.

If a state-influenced price mechanism can't achieve the right mix of investment in renewables, nuclear energy and residual carbon burners, then it will have to be done using state ownership, direct control and targets. This is the ultimate conclusion we have to draw from John Ashton's comments quoted above: if the market is not working then, given the urgency, state allocation must be tried.

Technically, if you use planning rather than market incentives, it will be easier to create a mix of 'base load' power generated by nuclear and cleaner carbon, with the rest coming from renewables: according to scenarios from Greenpeace to the IEA and other variants, that is what is needed to achieve the two-degree target.

The attempt to create a non-market economy and a low-carbon system are clearly interdependent. But while there are many routes to a postcapitalist economy, the potential variants of what we can do to address the climate emergency are limited.

There is, in short, a rational case for panic about climate change – and it is compounded when you consider the interrelatedness of climate and the other great uncontrolled variant: population.

A DEMOGRAPHIC TIMEBOMB

Being old was a privilege denied to most of our ancestors. If you take an urban history tour – whether in Manchester, Chicago or Shanghai – it's worth remembering, as you peer into the old industrial dwellings, that the life expectancy of those who lived there was forty years or less.[13] Go to a steel or mining town, from West Virginia to northern China, and you will see forests of gravestones marking the deaths of working-class men in their fifties – not in the distant past but in the post-1945 era. In the early years of capitalism, it was unsanitary urban life that killed you. In the twentieth century, it was chronic industrial diseases, stress, bad food and pollution.

Now though, we have a new problem: demographic ageing. There are no activists to drop banners from buildings to protest against ageing, there are no ministries for ageing, no prestigious scientific panel or global negotiations. Yet it is potentially as big an external shock as climate change – and its impact will be much more immediately economic.

The UN's projections are not disputed. The world's population, currently above 7 billion, will rise to 9.6 billion by 2050, with almost all growth occurring in the global south. By 2050, there will be more people in developing countries than there are people on earth right now. So the future story of humanity is mainly going to be told in cities like Manila, Lagos and Cairo.

Globally, the proportion of older people to those of working age will increase. In 1950, 5 per cent of the world's population was over sixty-five; by the mid-twenty-first century it will be 17 per cent. But it's in the rich world where the problems of ageing will turn into a shock.

Here, the crucial problem is the age-dependency ratio: the number of retired people compared to the number of those of working age. In Europe and Japan, there are currently three workers for every one retired person. By 2050 the ratio will be one-for-one. And though most developing countries will continue to have mainly young populations, China bucks the trend due to its one-child policy. By 2050 China will be the 'oldest' of the big economies in the world, with a projected median age of fifty-three.[14]

The growing age imbalance is irreversible. It's not just caused by people living longer due to better healthcare and higher incomes; the main driver of the imbalance is falling birth rates, as women gain control of their bodies through contraception, and as education, advances in human rights and urbanization give them greater independence.

The UBS economist George Magnus says rapidly ageing societies 'present us with an existential threat to the social and economic models we built after World War Two'.[15] In the developed world, demographic change will create stress in three critical areas of economic life: financial markets, public spending and migration.

During the post-war boom, private, corporate and state-mandated pension schemes grew massively. Though they sometimes included only a minority of the workforce, these schemes – in which savings deducted from wages were matched by company contributions and invested in the stock market – became the mainstay of the financial system. Before globalization, such schemes typically invested in their own country's debt and in the shares of major companies on their national stock exchange, with a small portion allocated tactically to meet projected needs. With tax breaks on the profits, and mandatory membership in some countries, it was the ultimate form of what Marx had called 'capitalist communism'.

But in the age of fiat money things changed. The repeated use of interest rate cuts when growth slowed made investing in shares a one-way bet, continually hiking the value of the stock market. The result was that, even as the demographic problem loomed, fund managers calculated that the financial system would still meet its commitments. Some even declared the projections were so positive that it was safe for the employer to take a 'contribution holiday' – leaving only the workforce to put money in.

The first country into the boom-bust vortex was Japan. The Nikkei 250 index of major companies trebled in value between 1985 and 1990. Then a crash began, and over the next ten years its value halved.

In the West, with above-average GDP growth in the late 1990s, stock markets surged again. The FTSE rose from 3000 in 1995 to peak at 6930 in December 1999. America's S&P 500 trebled in the same period; Germany's DAX index quadrupled. If you call up these indices' long-term charts since 2000, you will see a picture of three spiky mountains with steep sides. In the space of fifteen years, share prices have twice gone through boom and bust, with the current recovery – even though fuelled by trillions of confected dollars – pushing them barely above where they peaked in 2000.

The dotcom crash was the wakeup call. Where they could, companies scrambled to reduce their pension liabilities: transferring future pensioners to lower benefits, closing schemes to new workers – and sometimes going bust under the strain. In the search for higher returns on their investments, pension funds now diversified, pushing money into hedge funds, property, private equity and commodities. The aim in all cases was to make up the shortfall. We know the outcome. From the spectacular hedge fund implosions that started the credit freeze of August 2007 to the commodity price rises that triggered the Arab Spring, these big institutional investors collectively became – sometimes unwittingly – crucial drivers of instability.

In the aftermath of the crash, the typical big pension fund invests 15 per cent of its money in alternatives to shares (i.e. property or commodities) and lends more than 55 per cent of its money to governments in the form of bonds, which under quantitative easing pay zero or negative interest.

Overall, about $50 trillion is held in pension funds, insurance funds and public pension reserves across the OECD countries, well above their combined annual GDP. For all the reasons surveyed in chapter 1 – namely, a busted economic model on life support – the most recent survey describes the risk to that money as 'high' and pension liabilities as 'increased'.[16]

The problem is not the current position of this $50 trillion. The problem is that an ageing population means a smaller potential workforce, lower growth and lower output per head. Though the picture varies from one country to the next – with some smaller developed countries such as Norway extremely well provided for – the global situation is bleak: either the retired elderly must live on much less, or the financial system must deliver spectacular returns. But to deliver spectacular returns it must become more global and take more risks. If more pension provision could be moved into the public sphere, paid for with taxation, the impact of this dilemma would be softened. Instead, the opposite is happening.

The second area in which we are certain to face the stress of ageing populations is government debt. An ageing population boosts demand for spending on health, public pensions and long-term care. In 2010, Standard & Poor's calculated that unless governments across the world reined in public pension provision, their debts, by 2050, would sink the world.

Since then, governments have indeed slashed their pension liabilities: eligibility has been tightened, retirement ages raised and the link to inflation eroded in many countries. When, after this carnage of obligations, S&P recalculated the potential damage, it found the median net debt of developed countries was projected to be 220 per cent of GDP by 2050, with the big developing countries running average debts of 130 per cent. Japan still tops the league in 2050, at 500 per cent (compared to 250 per cent now) and America will be looking at a debt pile three times the current $17 trillion.

In this projection, demographic ageing is set to make state finances unsustainable all across the developed world. S&P's analysts predict that by 2050, even with pension cuts, 60 per cent of all countries in the world will have credit ratings below investment grade: it will be suicidal for anybody who does not want to risk losing their money to lend to them.

Are you panicking rationally yet? The scariest bit is coming up.

More than 50 per cent of all private pension money is currently invested in government debt. Furthermore, typically two-fifths of it is in foreign debt. No matter how safe a company pension fund looks now, if 60 per cent of all countries' bonds become junk – so that to lend to them becomes a crazy proposition – the private pension system will not survive.

Meanwhile, the social impact of the measures taken to date, says S&P, 'has already put the relationship between the state and the electorate under strain and severely tested social cohesion'.[17] All over the world, states have ripped up the last part of the implicit deal they made with their citizens during the post-war boom: that either the market or the state would provide a decent living for those in their old age. The impact of this broken promise will be felt over decades, not years. When governments claim they've stabilized their finances by raising the retirement age, or de-linking pensions to inflation, it is like congratulating yourself on buying a diet plan. The pain comes in the implementation.

The end result, as IMF economists put it, is 'unlikely to be socially and politically sustainable'.[18]

We have not yet considered the impact of migration. In 2013 I travelled to Morocco and Greece to hear the stories of migrants trying to move, illegally, to Europe. From Morocco, they were attempting to scale a three-metre-high razor wire fence into the Spanish enclave of Melilla; in Greece, they were enduring months of homelessness as they stalked the ferry ports in search of a ride to northern Europe. The insecurity of their daily lives made them prey to extortion, assault, sexual violence and extreme poverty. At the moment of attempted crossing they often risked death.

I asked them why, in the face of these hostile transit routes and the racism they would find in Europe, they were prepared to persist in trying to cross for months or years on end. They were incredulous: it was a stupid question. Compared to the lives they had left behind in the countries they came from, living on a concrete floor in a Tangier slum, or sleeping five to a room in a clandestine bunk-house in Marseilles was unequivocally better.

What I saw that summer, though, was nothing compared to what is coming. By 2050, there will be 1.2 billion more people of working age in the world than today – most of them living in the kind of circumstances those migrants were fleeing.

In Oujda, Morocco, I met two bricklayers from Niger in their early twenties, squatting on open ground, living on handouts from a mosque. Niger is a country so underdeveloped that you do not often meet its inhabitants on the roadsides of the world. When I talked to them, and looked at the UN's projections for their country, the scale of what's coming became clear.

By 2050, the population of Niger will have grown from its current 18 million to 69 million. Chad, the country they'd come through, will see its population treble, to 33 million. Afghanistan, whose troubles have sent its citizens into the people-trafficking systems that criss-cross Greece, Turkey and Libya, will rise from 30 to 56 million.

A stunning half of all the projected population growth between now and 2050 will take place in just eight countries,* six of which are in sub-Saharan Africa.[19] To find jobs, people from the population-boom countries will migrate to the cities; the land, as we've seen, is already under stress from climate change. In the cities, many will join the world's slum-dwelling population, which already stands at a billion – and increasing numbers will attempt illegal migration to the rich world.[20]

The World Bank economist Branko Milanovic, surveying the huge and growing inequality in developing countries, calls this a

* Nigeria, Tanzania, Congo, Ethiopia, Uganda, Niger, plus India and the USA.

'non-Marxian world' in which location, not class, is responsible for two-thirds of all inequality.'[21] His conclusion: 'either poor countries will become richer or poor people will migrate to rich countries'.

But for poor countries to become richer, they must break out of the so-called 'middle-income trap' – where countries typically develop to a certain point and then stall; both because they have to compete with the old imperial powers and because their corrupt elites strangle the emergence of functional modern institutions. Only thirteen countries out of 100 labelled 'middle-income' in 1960 had become high-income by 2012. These were mainly the Asian Tigers, led by South Korea, which ignored the development regime imposed by the global system and relentlessly built up their own industry and infrastructure with nationalist economic policies.

As George Magnus of UBS writes, the obstacles are more than economic: 'It gets progressively more difficult to raise income per head once you are a middle income country, and . . . doing so is not about drawing lines from spreadsheets, but about the economic benefits generated by continuously evolving, inclusive institutions.'[22] But the countries where population growth is biggest are the countries with the most corrupt and inefficient institutions.

If climate change, demographic ageing and a jobs-drought in the developing world were not interacting with a stagnant, fragile economic model, the problems might be solved separately. But they are. And the result is likely to place the whole global system under strain, and puts democracy itself in danger.

A GLOBAL ELITE IN DENIAL

'Ours is essentially a tragic age so we refuse to view it tragically. The cataclysm has happened, we are among the ruins . . . We've got to live, no matter how many skies have fallen.'[23] D. H. Lawrence was describing the English aristocracy after 1918, its ideology shattered, retreating into a world of stately homes and archaic manners. But the description could apply equally well to the modern elite after the catastrophe of 2008: a financial aristocracy determined to go on living as if the threats outlined above are not real.

In the late twentieth century, a generation of entrepreneurs, politicians, energy barons and bankers grew up in what felt like a friction-free world. Over the previous century or so, their predecessors had to watch a finely crafted order disintegrate, together with its illusions. From Imperial France in 1871 right through to the fall of Vietnam and the collapse of communism, the first lesson of statecraft for those born before 1980 was: bad stuff happens; events can overwhelm you.

By the year 2000 it felt different. It might not have been the 'end of history', but to the generation that built the neoliberal order it seemed as though history had at the very least become controllable. Every financial crisis could be met with monetary expansion, every terror threat obliterated with a drone strike. The labour movement as an independent variable in politics had been suppressed.

The psychological byproduct in the minds of the policy elite was the idea that there are no impossible situations; there are always choices, even if some of them turn out to be tough ones. There is always a solution, and it is usually the market.

But these external shocks should be the alarm call. Climate change does not present us with a choice of market or non-market routes to meeting carbon targets. It mandates either the orderly replacement of market economics or its disorderly collapse in abrupt phases. Ageing populations run the risk of tanking the world's financial markets, and some countries will have to wage a social war on their own citizens just to stay solvent. If that happens it will make what happened in Greece after 2010 look like just a few bad summers.

In the poorest countries, the combined impact of population growth, institutional corruption, skewed development and climate effects will create, for certain, tens of millions of landless poor people whose most logical choice will be to migrate.

You can see the defensive reflexes already in the developed West: the razor wire and the push-backs at the Spanish African enclave of Melilla; the violation of law by the Australian navy as it deals with migrant boats from Indonesia; America's breakneck charge into fracking in order to become energy self-sufficient; Russia and Canada's rival preparations to deploy military forces in the Arctic; China's determination to monopolize the Rare Earth metals vital to modern electronics. The common themes of these responses are withdrawal from multilateral collaboration and attempted self-sufficiency.

We have come to see the danger to globalization as *economic* nationalism, where the population of one or more advanced economy cannot take austerity and forces its political class – as in the 1930s – to pursue a 'beggar thy neighbour' solution to the crisis. But the external shocks create a dimension of instability beyond pure economic rivalry. The pursuit of energy self-sufficiency is creating regionalized global energy markets. Russia's diplomatic standoff with the West over Ukraine and its continued threat to deprive Europe of gas will, even if it does not blow up, lead Europe to seek its own self-sufficiency.

Meanwhile, the balkanization of the global energy market is mirrored by a similar process on the internet.

Already nearly one in five human beings has to put up with having their information filtered through the farcical controls erected by the Chinese communists. A politician is arrested for corruption? Naturally his name disappears from search engines. If that name happens to rhyme with the word for instant noodles (as was the case with Zhou Yongkang in 2014), the word for noodles disappears too, and so does the most popular noodle brand.[24]

Now the internet stands in danger of further fragmentation, as states react to the revelations of mass cyber-surveillance by the American National Security Agency. In addition, 2014 saw several governments, including Turkey and Russia, try to suppress dissent by forcing internet companies to register as entities under their domestic legal systems, opening them up to formal and informal political censorship.

So the first phase of the breakup of the global system is manifest through the breakup of information and the breakup of energy. But state-level fragmentation is on the agenda too.

I covered first-hand the Scottish independence referendum of 2014. Contrary to media myths, this was not a nationalist surge but a left-inclined plebeian movement. Handed the opportunity to break away from a neoliberal state committed to austerity for the next decade, the Scottish people came very close to doing so and breaking up the world's oldest capitalist economy in the proces. As the Spanish political system enters crisis, the momentum for Catalan independence may gather (it is stemmed currently by the sudden rise of Podemos). And we are just one political accident away from the collapse of the EU project itself. When a far-left party won the election in Greece, all the EU's institutions attacked it as white blood cells attack a virus. At the time of writing, the Greek crisis is in full swing – but it will look like small fry if, as is entirely possible, the far right comes to power in France.

In Beijing, Washington and Brussels, the next five years are likely to see the old rulers try one last time to make the old system work. But the longer we go on without calling an end to neoliberalism, the more its contingent crises will begin to collide and merge with the strategic ones I've outlined here.

On its own, the rise of info-capitalism would have offered a range of outcomes. You could – just – imagine a stagnant Western economy kept alive with high debt, bailed-out banks and printed money, were it not for the demographic crisis. You could – without climate change – imagine a postcapitalist transition path led by the gradual, spontaneous rise of non-market exchange and peer-production alongside a system faltering under its internal contradictions. More Wikipedias, more Linux, more generic drugs and public science, the gradual adoption of Open Source forms of work – and maybe a legislative curb on the info-monopolies. This is the airport book scenario for postcapitalism: a good idea. Implemented in a crisis-free environment, at a pace determined by ourselves.

But the external shocks call for action that is centralized, strategic and fast. Only the state, and states acting together, can organize such action. The starkness of the climate target and the clarity of the technical ways of responding to it mean it will require more planning and more state ownership than anybody expects or even wants. The possibility of a world in which 60 per cent of states are bankrupted by the cost of their ageing populations means we need structural solutions, not financial ones.

But the illusions bred during the past twenty-five years feed our paralysis. Confronted by emissions targets, we offset them, paying for trees to be planted in someone else's desert rather than changing our own behaviour. Confronted with evidence that the world is ageing, we spend $36 billion a year on cosmetic surgery.[25] If you placed the levels of risk evidenced in this chapter before any CEO, any software genius, any stress team in an engineering workshop, any quantitative analyst in a bank, they would say: act now! Mitigate the risk urgently.

If you used the method engineers use – root cause analysis – to ask why three systemic disruptions are happening at once (financial, climatic and demographic), you would quickly trace them to their cause: an economic system in disequilibrium with its environment and insufficient to satisfy the needs of a rapidly changing humanity.

Yet to say 'act now' on climate, the warped finance system or the impossible arithmetic of public debt is deemed revolutionary. It punctures the reverie of the Davos elite, poisons the atmosphere in Mediterranean yachting ports and disturbs the silence in the political mausoleum that is the Chinese communist HQ. Worse still, it destroys the illusion held by millions of people that 'everything is going to be OK'. And for activists it means something they are rightly scared of: engagement with the mainstream, involvement with political strategy, an enduring structural project more concrete than 'another world is possible'.

Faced with this situation, we need 'revolutionary reformism'. Even to say the words out loud is to realize how deeply they challenge both sides of political reality. Say it to a social democrat in a suit and watch them wince; say it in an Occupy camp and watch the activists wince – for exactly opposite reasons.

Panic would be rational faced with these challenges but the social, technological and economic changes underway mean we can meet them, if we can understand postcapitalism as both a long-term process and an urgent project.

So we need to inject into the environment and social justice movements things that have for twenty-five years seemed the sole property of the right: willpower, confidence and design.

10

Project Zero

If you believe there is a better system than capitalism then the past twenty five years have felt like being – as Alexander Bogdanov put it in *Red Star* – 'a Martian stranded on Earth'. You have a clear view of what society should be like, but no means of getting there.

In Bodganov's novel, the Martians decide to obliterate humanity because we have proved incapable of achieving the postcapitalist society they already possess. That was Bogdanov's metaphor of despair after the failure of the 1905 revolution.

The possibilities outlined in this book should provide an antidote to such despair. To understand why, let's update Bogdanov's metaphor: suppose the Martians really did arrive in orbit, ready to blast us to smithereens. What kind of economy would they see?

Just such a thought experiment was played out by Nobel laureate Herbert Simon in 1991, in a famous research paper entitled 'Organisations and Markets'. Simon proposed that the arriving Martians would see three kinds of things in our economy: organizations, which would look like big green blobs; markets, which appear like thin red lines between the green blobs; and a set of blue lines within the organizations showing their internal hierarchy. No matter where they looked, said Simon, the Martians would see a system whose dominant colour was green. The message they sent home would say: this is a society primarily made up of organizations, not markets.[1]

It was a highly political point to make, in the year the triumph of the market was declared. Simon's lifelong concern was to understand how organizations work. His paper has been used to demonstrate that, for all the rhetoric about free markets, the capitalist system is primarily made up of organizations that plan and allocate goods internally, in ways not directly driven by market forces.

But carried out with greater realism, Simon's model demonstrates something else: it shows how neoliberalism has opened up the possibility of postcapitalism. Let's add some detail:

1. The turnover of each green blob (the organization) determines its size; the money involved in each transaction determines the thickness of the red lines between them.

2. The blue lines, which show the internal hierarchy of a firm, have to end in dots as well – the workers: baristas, computer programmers, aircraft engineers, shirt factory employees. Simon didn't feel the need to model workers separately, but we do. Let's make them blue dots.

3. To be realistic, each blue dot is also at the centre of a web of thin red lines – connecting each wage earner, as a consumer, to retailers, banks and service companies.

4. Already, the globe looks a lot redder than Simon originally described it. There are trillions of thin red lines.

5. Now let's add the dimension of time: what happens during a typical twenty-four-hour cycle? If this is a normal capitalist economy we notice the blue dots (the workforce) oscillate in and out of the organizations once a day. As they leave work they start putting out red lines – spending their wages; when they go into the workplace they tend not to – this is a capitalist economy in 1991, remember.

Finally, let's run the model forward in time, from 1991 to now. What happens to the picture?

First, a lot more tiny red lines appear. A young woman leaves her farm in Bangladesh to work in a factory – her wages generate a new red line; she pays a local nanny to look after her kids, generating a new market transaction: a new red line. Her manager earns enough to start buying health insurance, paying interest to a bank, obtaining a loan to send his son to college. Globalization and free markets generate more red lines.

Secondly, the green blobs split, forming smaller green blobs as firms and states outsource non-core operations. Some of the blue dots turn green – i.e. workers become self-employed. In the USA, 20 per cent of the workforce are now self-employed 'proprietors'. They too generate more red lines.

Third, the red lines become longer, reaching out across the globe. And they don't stop when people go to work: buying and selling is now happening digitally, both inside and outside the working day.

Finally, the yellow lines appear.

'Whoa!' says the Martian fleet commander. 'What yellow lines?'

'It's interesting,' says the ship's economist. 'We have spotted a whole new phenomenon. The yellow lines seem to show people exchanging goods, labour and services but not through the market and not within typical organizations. A lot of what they are doing seems to be done for free, so we have no idea how thick these lines should be.'

Suppose, now, there's a Martian bombardier with her finger on the trigger, as in Bogdanov's novel, asking permission to nuke humanity as punishment for its inability to achieve communism.

Most probably, the fleet commander's response is: 'Wait! Those yellow lines are interesting.'

FIVE PRINCIPLES OF TRANSITION

The yellow lines in this construct are just a way of trying to visualize goods, labour and services provided collaboratively, beyond the market. They are weak – but they signal that a new route beyond capitalism has opened up, based on promoting and nurturing non-market production and exchange, and driven by information technology.

Up until this point, I've treated postcapitalism as a process emerging spontaneously. The challenge is to turn these insights into a project.

Almost everything that's driving the change is conceived as a project: Wikipedia, Open Source, open information standards, low-carbon energy installations. But few have bothered to ask what a high-level project would look like if we want to move the world economy beyond capitalism.

In part, that's because many of the old left are infected by the same despair as Bogdanov's stranded Martian. Others – in the green movement, or NGOs, or community activists and peer-to-peer economists – are so determined to avoid 'big narratives' that they've stuck to small-scale radical reforms.

In this chapter I will try to spell out what a large-scale postcapitalist project might involve. I call it Project Zero – because its aims are a zero-carbon energy system; the production of machines, products and services with zero marginal costs; and the reduction of necessary labour time as close as possible to zero. Before we start we should outline some principles based on the knowledge gleaned from past failure.

The first principle is to *understand the limitations of human will-power* in the face of a complex and fragile system. The Bolsheviks failed to understand it; to be fair, most mainstream politicians of the twentieth century also failed to understand it. Now we understand it well. The solution is to test all proposals at small scale and model their macro-economic impact virtually many times over before we attempt them at a large scale.

Evgeny Preobrazhensky, the murdered Soviet economist, predicted that as market forces began to disappear, economics would become a discipline for designing the future, not just analysing the past. 'This is quite a different science,' he said, 'this is social technology.'[2]

There's a chilling quality to that phrase, conjuring the dangers of treating society like a machine. But Preobrazhensky's description of the tools 'social technology' would use were prescient and subtle. He called for an 'extremely complex and ramified nervous system of social foresight and planned guidance'. Note the terms: foresight and guidance, not command and control. And note the simile: a nervous system, not a hierarchy. All the Soviets had was command, control and the bureaucratic hierarchy, but we have the network. When it comes to organizing change, the network can function better than a hierarchy, but only if we respect the complexity and fragility that comes with it.

The second principle for designing the transition is *ecological sustainability*. The external shocks discussed in chapter 9 will probably hit us in sequence: short-term localized energy shortages in the next decade; ageing and migration challenges over the next thirty years;

and the catastrophic outcomes of climate change after that. The task is to develop technologies that respond to these problems through sustainable growth; we do not have to go backwards in developmental time to save the planet.

The third principle I want to insist on is: *the transition is not just about economics*. It will have to be a *human* transition. The new kinds of people being created by networked economies come with new insecurities and new priorities. We already have a different perception of the self from the one in our grandfathers' and grandmothers' heads.[3] Our roles as consumers, lovers, communicators are as important to us as our role at work. So the project cannot be based purely on economic and social justice.

The French writer André Gorz was right to say that neoliberalism has destroyed the possibility of a utopia based on work. But we will still face a challenge similar to the one the early soviet republics faced with workers: specific social groups may have short-term priorities that clash with the wider priorities of the economy and the ecosystem. That's what networks are for: to argue things out and model the alternative possibilities. We will need new forms of democracy to arbitrate between valid competing claims. But it won't be easy.

A fourth principle should be: *attack the problem from all angles*. With the rise of networks, the capacity for meaningful action is no longer confined to states, corporations and political parties; individuals and temporary swarms of individuals can be just as powerful agents of change.

At present, the community of thinkers and activists around the peer-to-peer movement are heavily focused on experimental, small-scale projects – credit unions or co-ops, for example. When they think about the state, it is at the level of laws to protect and extend the peer-to-peer sector. With the exception of thinkers such as Michel Bauwens[4] and McKenzie Wark[5], few have bothered to ask what a whole new system of governance and regulation might look like in this new mode of production.

In response, we should broaden our thinking so that solutions can be found through a mixture of small-scale experiment, proven models that can be scaled up and top-down action by states.

So if the solution in finance is to create a diverse, socialized banking system, then setting up a credit union attacks the problem from one direction, outlawing certain forms of speculation attacks it from another, while changing our own financial behaviour attacks it from still another angle.

The fifth principle for a successful transition is that we should *maximize the power of information*. The difference between a smartphone app today and the programs on PCs twenty years ago is that the modern apps self-analyse and pool performance data. Almost everything on your phone and computer is feeding back information on your choices to a corporate owner. Soon the information will be flowing from 'smart' electricity meters, public transport passes and computer-controlled cars. The aggregated data of our lives – which will soon include our driving speed, our weekly diet, our body mass and heart rate – could be a hugely powerful 'social technology' in itself.

Once the Internet of Things is rolled out, we are at the real takeoff point of the information economy. From then on, the key principle is to create democratic social control over aggregated information, and to prevent its monopolization or misuse by states and corporations.

The Internet of Things will complete a vast social 'machine'. Its analytical power alone could optimize resources on a scale that significantly reduces the use of carbon, raw materials and labour. Making the energy grid, the road network and the tax system 'intelligent' are just the most obvious things on the task list. But the power of this emerging vast machine does not lie solely in its ability to monitor and feed back. By socializing knowledge, it also has the power to amplify the results of collective action.

The socialists of the *belle époque* eyed the monopolies and cartels with glee: seize them, and control of society from the centre becomes easy, they believed. Our project is to decentralize control – but there could be no better tool for doing so than the vast physical information machine that is being created.

Once we take hold of it, we can put much of social reality under collaborative control. For example, in epidemiology the focus is now on breaking the feedback loops that create poverty, anger, stress, atomized families and ill health.[6] Efforts to map these problems and mitigate them constitute the cutting edge of social medicine. How much more powerful would that medicine be if the poverty and disease that blight poor communities could be mapped, understood and collaboratively dismantled in realtime – with the micro-level participation of those affected?

Maximizing the power and openness of information needs to become an instinct, embedded in the project.

TOP-LEVEL GOALS

With the above principles in mind, I want to offer not a political programme, but something more like a distributed project. It is a set of linked, modular, non linear tasks that lead to a probable outcome. Decision-making is decentralized; the structures needed to deliver it emerge during the delivery; targets evolve in response to realtime information. And on the precautionary principle, we should use the new breed of simulation tools to model every proposal virtually before we enact it for real.

If I could write the rest of this chapter as post-it notes on a whiteboard, it would better express the modularity and interdependence. The best method for doing a distributed project is for small groups to pick a task, work on it for a bit, document what they've done and move on.

Absent the post-it notes, I'll stick to a list. The top level aims of a postcapitalist project should be to:

1. Rapidly reduce carbon emissions so that the world has warmed by only two degrees Celsius by 2050, prevent an energy crisis and mitigate the chaos caused by climate events.
2. Stabilize the finance system between now and 2050 by socializing it, so that ageing populations, climate change and the debt overhang do not combine to detonate a new boom-bust cycle and destroy the world economy.
3. Deliver high levels of material prosperity and wellbeing to the majority of people, primarily by prioritizing information-rich technologies towards solving major social challenges, such as ill health, welfare dependency, sexual exploitation and poor education.

4. Gear technology towards the reduction of necessary work to
   promote the rapid transition towards an automated economy.
   Eventually, work becomes voluntary, basic commodities and
   public services are free, and economic management becomes
   primarily an issue of energy and resources, not capital and labour.

In game terms, these are the 'victory conditions'. We may not
achieve them all but, as all gamers know, a lot can be achieved short
of total victory.

In pursuit of these goals, it will be important in all the economic
changes we make to send *transparent signals*. One of the most powerful aspects of the Bretton Woods system was the explicit rules it
enshrined. By contrast, throughout the twenty-five-year course of
neoliberalism, the global economy has been run on implicit rules or,
as with the Eurozone, rules that are always broken.

The sociologist Max Weber believed the rise of capitalism was
driven not by technology but by a 'new spirit' – a new *attitude* to
finance, machinery and work, not the things themselves. But for a new
spirit of postcapitalism to take off, we need to focus on where the
externalities are being generated and distributed – and to actively
propagate an understanding of the phenomena. We need to answer:
what is happening to the social benefit that network interactions produce, and which capitalist accounting can't usually see? Where does it
fit in?

Let's consider a concrete example. Coffee shops today often adver-
tise 'our beans are organic' – i.e. this is how we are serving a greater
social good. What they mean subtextually is 'and you are paying a
bit more for the feelgood factor'. But the signal is only partially
transparent.

Now reimagine the coffee shop as a co-op, paying its workers well,
ploughing profits back into activities that promote social cohesion, or
literacy, or post-prison rehabilitation, or better public health. The
important thing is to indicate – as clearly as the 'organic' label on the
coffee does – what social good is being produced and who will benefit
from it.

It's more than a gesture: it's a transparent signal, just as the loaded
cannon placed at the gate of the Cromford cotton factory in England

in 1771 was a transparent signal. You could erect a sign saying 'we sell coffee for a profit and that helps us give away psycho-social counselling for free'. Or as with the grassroots foodbank network sponsored by Syriza in Greece, you could just get on with it quietly.

What follows is my best guess at what a project plan would look like, if we were to follow these principles and aim for these five top-level goals. I will be more than happy to see it quickly torn apart and revised by the wisdom of angry crowds.

MODEL FIRST, ACT LATER

First, we need an open, accurate and comprehensive computer simulation of current economic reality. The sources could be the models macro-economists use – in banks and at the IMF and OECD – and the climate models that generate the IEA's and other scenarios. But their lopsidedness is striking.

Climate models tend to simulate the atmosphere using advanced maths but simulate the economy like a train set. Meanwhile, most professionally built economic simulators, known as DGSE models, are constructed on the twin fallacy that equilibrium is likely and that all agents in the economy are making simple pleasure-*vs*-pain choices.

For example, the European Central Bank's most advanced model of the Eurozone includes only three types of 'agents' – households, firms and the central bank. As current events show, it might have been useful to include in that model some fascists, or corrupt oligarchs, or several million voters prepared to put the radical left into power.

Given that we are decades into the info-tech era, it is startling that – as Oxford maths professor J. Doyne Farmer points out – there are no models that capture economic complexity in the way computers are used to simulate weather, population, epidemics or traffic flows.[7]

In addition, capitalist planning and modelling are typically unaccountable: by the time a major infrastructure project starts delivering results, ten or twenty years after its impact was first predicted, there is no person or organization still around to draw conclusions. Thus, most economic modelling under market capitalism is actually close to speculation.

So one of the most radical – and necessary – measures we could take is to create a global institute or network for simulating the long-term transition beyond capitalism.

It would start by attempting to construct an accurate simulation of economies as they exist today. Its work would be Open Source: anybody could use it, anybody could suggest improvements and the outputs would be available to all. It would most likely have to use a method called 'agent-based modelling' – that is, using computers to create millions of virtual workers, households and firms, and letting them interact spontaneously, within realistic boundaries. Even today such a model would be able to draw on realtime data. Weather sensors, city transport monitors, energy grids, postcode demographic data and the supply chain management tools of global supermarket groups are all giving off relevant macro-economic data in realtime. But the prize – once every object on earth is addressable, smart and feeding back information – is an economic model that does not just simulate reality but actually represents it. The agents modelled virtually are eventually substituted by granular data from reality, just as happens with weather computers.

Once we are able to capture economic reality in this manner, then planning major changes in an accountable way becomes possible. Just as aircraft engineers model millions of different stress loads on the tail-fin of a jet, it would be possible to model millions of variations of what happens if you reduce the price of Nike trainers to a point between their present $190 and their production price, which is likely to be lower than $20.

We would ask our supercomputer lateral questions: do young men get depressed because the Nike brand dies? Does the global sports industry suffer because Nike's marketing spend is gone? Does quality decline when there is no brand value to maintain in the production process? And what would the climate impact be? To promote its brand, Nike has worked hard to reduce carbon emissions. We might decide keeping the price of Nike trainers high is a good thing. Or not.

This, rather than the meticulous planning of the cyber-Stalinists, is what a postcapitalist state would use petaflop-level computing for. And once we had reliable predictions, we could act.

THE WIKI-STATE

The most challenging arena for action is the state; we need to think positively about its role in the transition to postcapitalism.

The starting point is: states are enormous economic entities. They employ about half a billion people globally, and on one measure make up an average 45 per cent of economic activity across all countries' GDP (from 60 per cent in Denmark to 25 per cent in Mexico). Plus, through what they choose to procure, and by signalling their future behaviour, they can have a decisive influence on markets.

In the socialist project, the state saw itself as the new economic form. In postcapitalism, the state has to act more like the staff of Wikipedia: to nurture the new economic forms to the point where they take off and operate organically. As in the old vision of communism, the state has to 'wither away' – but here the economic withering has to be front and centre, not just the functions of law enforcement and defence.

There's one change which anybody in charge of a state could implement immediately, and for free: switch off the neoliberal privatization machine. It's a myth that the state is passive in neoliberalism; in reality the neoliberal system cannot exist without constant, active intervention by the state to promote marketization, privatization and the interests of finance. It typically deregulates finance, forces government to outsource services and allows public healthcare, education and transport to become shoddy, driving people to private services. A government that was serious about postcapitalism would give a clear signal: there will be no proactive extension of market forces. Simply for attempting this, the relatively conventional leftists of Syriza in Greece were overtly sabotaged. The ECB staged a run on the Greek banks and, as the price for stopping it, demanded more privatization, more outsourcing, more degradation of public services.

The next action the state could undertake is to reshape markets to favour sustainable, collaborative and socially just outcomes. If you set the feed-in tariff on solar panels high, people will install them on their roofs. But if you don't specify they have to come from a factory with high social standards, the panels will get made in China, generating fewer wider social benefits beyond the energy switch. If you incentivize the creation of local energy systems, so that excess power generated can be sold to nearby businesses, you create further positive externalities.

We need a new understanding of the state's role in an economy that includes capitalist and postcapitalist structures. It should act as an enabler of new technologies and business models, but always with an eye on how they fit with the strategic aims and principles outlined earlier.

Peer-to-peer projects, collaborative business models and non-profit activities are typically small scale and fragile. A whole community of economists and activists has grown up around them, but the actual raw material is so meagre, compared to the market sector, that one of the first things you have to do is clear a space in the capitalist jungle for these new plants to grow.

In the postcapitalist project, the state must also coordinate and plan infrastructure: today this is done haphazardly and under heavy political pressure from the carbon lobby. In future, it could be done democratically and with radically different outcomes. From social housing in cities blighted by speculative development to cycle lanes or healthcare provision, even the most progressive infrastructure designs are moulded around the interests of the rich – and assume the market will last for ever. As a result, infrastructure planning remains one of the disciplines least transformed by networked thinking. This needs to change.

In addition, because of the global nature of the problems we face, the state has to 'own' the agenda for responses to the challenges of climate change, demographic ageing, energy security and migration. That is to say, whatever micro-level actions we take to alleviate these risks, only national governments and multilateral agreements can actually solve them.

The most pressing issue, if states are to help drive the transition to a new economic system, is debt. In today's world, developed countries are paralysed by the size of their debts. These are, as we saw in chapter 9, projected to become stratospheric as a result of ageing populations. Over time, there is a danger that austerity plus stagnation will shrink the size of the economies from which the debts have to be repaid.

Therefore governments have to do something clear and progressive about debts. They could be written off unilaterally – and in countries like Greece, where they are unpayable, that might be required. But the outcome would be de-globalization, as countries and investors holding the worthless debt retaliated, cutting off market access or kicking the defaulting countries out of various currency and trading zones.

Some of the quantitative easing money could be used to buy and bury the debts – but even this so-called 'monetization' of debt, using the $12 trillion created so far, would not reduce global sovereign debts enough compared to GDP as these stand at $54 trillion and rising, and the global stock of all debts is approaching $300 trillion.

It would be more sensible to combine controlled debt write-offs with a ten- to fifteen-year global policy of 'financial repression': that is, to stimulate inflation, hold interest rates lower than the inflation rate, remove people's ability to move money into non-financial investments or offshore, and thus inflate away the debts, writing off the part that remained.

To be brutally clear, this would reduce the value of assets in pension funds, and thus the material wealth of the middle classes and the old; and by imposing capital controls you would be partially deglobalizing finance. But this is only a controlled way of doing what the market will do via chaos if, as S&P predicts, 60 per cent of all countries see their debt reduced to junk by 2050. In conditions of near-stagnation and long-term zero interest rates, the income generated by pension fund investments is in any case already minimal.

But the state is not even half of the story.

EXPAND COLLABORATIVE WORK

To promote the transition, we need a decisive turn to collaborative business models. To achieve this requires the removal of the uneven power-relationships that have sabotaged them in the past.

The classic workers' co-ops always failed because they had no access to capital and when crisis hit they couldn't persuade their members to take lower wages or work fewer hours. Successful modern co-ops, such as Mondragon in Spain, work because they have the support of local savings banks and because they're complex structures – able to redeploy workers from one sector to another, or soften short-term underemployment through non-market perks for those laid off. Mondragon is no postcapitalist paradise, but it is the exception that illustrates the rule: if you look at a list of the top 300 co-ops in the world, many of them are simply mutual banks that resisted corporate ownership. In most respects, they play the game of financial exploitation – though with a social conscience.

In a network-based transition, collaborative business models are the most important thing we can foster. They, too, have to evolve, however. It is not enough for them to be just non-profit businesses; the postcapitalist form of the co-op would try to expand non-market, non-managed, non-money-based activity against the baseline of market activity it starts from. What we need are co-ops where the legal form is backed up by a real, collaborative form of production or consumption, with clear social outcomes.

Likewise we should not fetishize the non-profit aspect of things. There can be profitable peer-to-peer lenders, cab companies and holiday rental firms, for example, but they would have to operate under regulations that limited their ability to contribute to social injustice.

At the government level, there could be an Office of the Non-Market Economy, tasked to nurture all businesses where free stuff is produced, or where sharing and collaboration are essential, and maximizing the amount of economic activity that takes place beyond the price system. With relatively small incentives, this could create big synergies and restructure the economy.

For example, lots of people form startup businesses – of which about one in three fails – because the tax system incentivizes startups. Often, they create cheap-labour businesses – such as fast-food outlets, building contractors and franchise shops – because, again, the system is stacked in favour of a cheap-labour economy. If we reshape the tax system to reward the creation of non-profits and collaborative production, and reshape company regulations to make it hard to form low-wage businesses but very easy to form living-wage ones, we could achieve a big change for little outlay.

Large corporations could also be very useful for driving change, as much as anything else because of their sheer scale: McDonald's, for example, is the thirty-eighth biggest economy in the world – bigger than that of Ecuador – and is also the biggest toy distributor in America. In addition, one in eight people in the USA has worked for McDonald's. Imagine if, on induction day for new employees, McDonald's had to give you a one-hour course in trade unionism. Imagine if Walmart, instead of advising people to claim in-work benefits to reduce the wage bill, advised them on how to increase their wages. Or imagine simply if McDonald's stopped dispensing plastic toys.

What could induce corporations to do any of this? Answer: law and regulation. If we legally empowered the workforces of global corporations with strong employment rights, their owners would be forced to promote high-wage, high-growth, high-technology economic models, instead of the opposite. The low-wage, low-skill and low-quality corporations that have flourished since the 1990s exist only because the space for them was ruthlessly carved out by the state. All we need to do is throw that process into reverse gear.

It may sound radical to outlaw certain business models, but that's what happened with slavery and with child labour. These restrictions, in the teeth of protest from the factory bosses and plantation owners, actually regularized capitalism and forced it to take off.

Our aim would be to regularize postcapitalism: to privilege the free wifi network in the mountain village over the rights of the telecoms monopoly. Out of such tiny changes, new systems can grow.

SUPPRESS OR SOCIALIZE MONOPOLIES

The creation of monopolies to resist prices falling towards zero is capitalism's most important defence reflex against postcapitalism.

To promote the transition, this defence mechanism has to be suppressed. Where possible, monopolies would be outlawed and rules against price fixing strictly enforced. For twenty-five years, the public sector has been forced to outsource and break itself into pieces; now would come the turn of monopolies such as Apple and Google. Where it's dysfunctional to break up a monopoly – as for example with an aircraft manufacturer or a water company – the solution advocated by Rudolf Hilferding 100 years ago would suffice: public ownership.

When pursued in its original form – i.e. the public non-profit corporation – public ownership delivered a huge social benefit to capital by cheapening the input costs of labour. In the postcapitalist economy it would deliver this and more. The strategic aim – shining in big letters from a PowerPoint projector in every public sector boardroom – would be to cheapen the cost of basic necessities, so that the total socially necessary labour time can fall and more stuff gets produced for free.

If true public provision of water, energy, housing, transport, healthcare, telecoms infrastructure and education was introduced into a neoliberal economy, it would feel like a revolution. Privatizing these sectors over the past thirty years was the means by which the neoliberals pumped profitability back into the private sector: in countries stripped of productive industries, such service monopolies constitute the core of the private sector and, with the banks, the backbone of the stock market.

And providing these services at cost price, socially, would be a strategic act of redistribution, vastly more effective than raising real wages.

In summary: under a government that embraced postcapitalism, the state, the corporate sector and public corporations could be made to pursue radically different ends with relatively low-cost changes to regulation, underpinned by a radical programme to shrink debt.

It is not in this area, though, that true postcapitalist economic forms emerge. Just as the British state fostered the growth of industrial capitalism in the early nineteenth century by setting new rules, today a mixture of government and highly regulated corporations would create only the framework of the next economic system, not its substance.

LET MARKET FORCES DISAPPEAR

In a highly networked, consumer-oriented society, where people have an individual-centred model of economic need, markets are not the enemy. This is the major difference between a postcapitalism based on info-tech and one based on command planning. There is no reason to abolish markets by diktat, as long as you abolish the basic power imbalances that the term 'free market' disguises.

Once firms are forbidden to set monopoly prices, and a universal basic income is available (see below), the market is actually the transmitter of the 'zero marginal cost' effect, which manifests as falling labour time across society.

But in order to control the transition, we would need to send clear signals to the private sector, one of the most important of which is this: profit derives from entrepreneurship, not rent.

The act of innovating and creating – whether it be a new kind of jet engine or a hit dance music track – is rewarded, as now, by the firm's ability to reap short-term gains, either from higher sales or lower costs. But patents and intellectual property would be designed to taper away quickly. This principle is already recognized in practice, despite the protestations of Hollywood lawyers and pharmaceutical giants. Drug patents expire after twenty years, often becoming undermined before then because of production in countries where the patent is not recognized, or because – as in the case of HIV – the patent holders agree to allow generic drug use in the face of pressing human need.

Simultaneously, the increased use of Creative Commons licences – where inventors and creators voluntarily waive some rights in advance – would be promoted. If, as suggested above, governments insisted that the results of state-funded research should be essentially free at the point of use – moving everything produced with public funding into the public sphere – the balance of intellectual property in the world would quickly tilt from private to common use. People who are driven only by material reward would go on creating and innovating – because the market would still reward entrepreneurship and genius. But, as befits a society where the rate of innovation is becoming exponential, the reward period is going to be shorter.

The only sector where it is imperative to suppress market forces completely is wholesale energy. To meet climate change with urgent action, the state should take ownership and control of the energy distribution grid, plus all big carbon-based suppliers of energy. These corporations are already toast, as the majority of their reserves cannot be burned without destroying the planet. To incentivize capital investment in renewables, this technology would be subsidized and the companies providing it remain outside state ownership where possible.

This could be done while keeping the overall energy price to consumers high – in order to suppress demand and force them to change behaviour. But it's equally important to reshape the way households consume energy. The aim would be to decentralize the consumer side of the energy market, so that technologies such as combined heat and power and local generation grids could take off.

At every stage, energy efficiency would be rewarded and inefficiency punished – from building design, insulation and heating to transportation networks. There is a wide range of proven techniques to choose from, but by decentralizing and allowing local communities to keep the efficiency gains they make, market forces in the retail energy market could be used to achieve a defined and measurable goal.

But beyond energy and the strategic public services, it is important that a large space be left for what Keynes called the 'animal spirits' of the innovator. Once information technology pervades the physical world, every innovation brings us closer to the world of zero necessary work.

SOCIALIZE THE FINANCE SYSTEM

The next big piece of social technology would be focused on the finance system. Financial complexity stands at the heart of modern economic life. This includes financial instruments like futures and options, and highly liquid twenty-four-hour global markets. It also includes the new relationship that we, as workers and consumers, have to financial capital. It is for this reason that states are forced with each financial crisis to ratchet up the implicit bailout guarantee that stands behind banks, pension funds and insurers.

Morally, if the risks are socialized, then the rewards should be socialized too. But there is no need to abolish all financial complexity. Where complex financial markets lead to speculation and make the velocity of money needlessly high, they can be tamed. The following measures would be more effective if undertaken globally, but it's more likely, given the scenario spelled out in chapter 1, that individual states will have to implement them, and with some urgency. They are:

1. Nationalize the central bank, setting it an explicit target for sustainable growth and an inflation target on the high side of the recent average. This would provide the tools to stimulate a socially just form of financial repression, aimed at a controlled write-down of the massive debt overhang. In a global economy made up of states, or currency blocs, this is going to cause antagonism but ultimately, as under Bretton Woods, if a systemic economy did it, other countries would have to follow suit.

   In addition to its classic functions – monetary policy and financial stability – a central bank should have a sustainability target: all decisions would be modelled against their climatic, demographic and social impacts. Its bosses would, of course, have to be democratically elected and scrutinized.

   The monetary policy of central banks – probably the most powerful policy tool in modern capitalism – would become overt, transparent and politically controlled. In the late stages of the transition the central bank and money would have a different role, which I will return to.

2. Restructure the banking system into a mixture of utilities earning capped profit rates; non-profit local and regional banks; credit unions and peer-to-peer lenders; and a comprehensive state-owned provider of financial services. The state would stand explicitly as lender of last resort to these banks.

3. Leave a well-regulated space for complex financial activities. The aim would be to ensure the global finance system could, in the short to medium term, return to its historic role: efficiently allocating capital between firms, sectors, savers and lenders, etc. The regulations could be a lot simpler than the Basel III Treaty, because they would be backed up by strict criminal enforcement and professional codes in banking, accountancy and law. The guiding principles would be to reward innovation and to penalize and discourage rent-seeking behaviour. For example, it would

become a breach of professional ethics for a chartered accountant or qualified lawyer to propose a tax avoidance scheme, or for a hedge fund to store uranium in a warehouse to drive its spot price higher.

In countries such as the UK, Singapore, Switzerland and the USA with globally oriented finance sectors, governments could offer a deal whereby, in return for coming clearly and transparently onshore, some limited lender of last resort facilities were made available to the remaining high-risk, profit-oriented finance firms. Those which did not come onshore and become transparent would be treated as the financial equivalent of Al-Qaeda. After a suitable amnesty offer, they would be tracked down and suppressed.

These short-term, strategic measures could dismantle the ticking time-bomb of global finance, but they do not yet constitute a design for a true postcapitalist finance system.

A postcapitalist project would not seek – as the money fundamentalists do – the end to fractional reserve banking. In the first place, if it was attempted as a short-term remedy to financialization, it would cause demand to slump. Also, we need credit creation and an expanded money supply to wear down the debt pile that is strangling growth.

The most immediate objective is to save globalization by killing neoliberalism. A socialized banking system and a central bank attuned to sustainability could do this using fiat money – which, as we discussed in chapter 1, works as long as people believe in the credibility of the state.

However, over the long transition to postcapitalism, an elaborate finance system is going to run into a brick wall. Credit creation works only if it makes the market sector grow – so the borrower can repay the loan with interest. If the non-market sector begins to grow faster than the market sector, the inner logic of banking would break down. At this point, if we want to maintain a complex economy, where the finance system acts as a realtime clearing house for a multitude of needs, then the state (via the central bank) would have to take on the task of creating money and providing credit, as advocated by supporters of so-called 'positive money'.[8]

But the aim here is not to achieve some kind of mythical, steady state capitalism. The aim is to promote the transition to an economy where many things are free, and where returns on investment come in a mixture of money and non-monetary forms.

By the end of the process, decades in the future, money and credit would have a much smaller role in the economy, but the accounting, clearing and resource mobilization functions currently provided by banks and financial markets would have to exist in a different institutional form. This is one of the biggest challenges for postcapitalism.

Here's how I think it could be solved.

The objective is to maintain complex, liquid markets in tradable instruments, while removing the possibility that there will ever be payback in monetary form (because the profit and ownership system disappears). One model could be what's happened with carbon.

Though the creation of a carbon market has not achieved enough progress against climate change, it has not been useless. In future we might see all kinds of socially benign instruments traded – health outcomes, for example. If the state can create a market in carbon, it can create a market in anything else. It can use market forces for behaviour change, but ultimately there must come a time when it imbues these instruments – which effectively form a parallel currency – with greater purchasing power than actual money.

As people are dumping money – because the market sector is being replaced by collaborative production – it is possible that they will accept what is effectively 'techno-scrip' until the moment when a state-administered bid/offer system for goods and services comes into being, as Bogdanov envisaged in *Red Star*.

In the short term, the intention is not to reduce complexity – as the money fundamentalists want – nor simply to stabilize banking, but to promote the most complex form of capitalist finance compatible with progressing the economy towards high automation, low work and abundant cheap or free goods and services.

With energy and banking socialized, the aim in the medium term would be to retain as extensive as possible a private sector in the non-financial world, and to keep it open to a diverse and innovative range of firms.

Neoliberalism, with its high tolerance for monopolies, has actually stifled innovation and complexity. If we break up the tech monopolies and the banks, we could create an active space for smaller companies to replace them and deliver – at last – on the unfulfilled promise of info-tech.

The public sector could, if we wished, outsource functions to the private sector, provided that the latter is not allowed to compete through differential wages and conditions. One byproduct of promoting competition and diversity in the service sector is that, once you can't relentlessly drive down wages, there would have to be a surge of technical innovation, the outcome of which would be to reduce the number of work hours needed across society overall.

And that leads us to what is probably the biggest structural change required to make postcapitalism happen: a universal basic income guaranteed by the state.

PAY EVERYONE A BASIC INCOME

The basic income, as a policy, is not that radical. Various pilot projects and designs have been touted, often by the right, sometimes by the centre-left, as a replacement for the dole with cheaper administration costs. But in the postcapitalist project, the purpose of the basic income is radical: it is (a) to formalize the separation of work and wages and (b) to subsidize the transition to a shorter working week, or day, or life. The effect would be to socialize the costs of automation.

The idea is simple: everybody of working age gets an unconditional basic income from the state, funded from taxation, and this replaces unemployment benefit. Other forms of needs-based welfare – such as family, disability or child payments – would still exist, but would be smaller top-ups to the basic income.

Why pay people just to exist? Because we need to radically accelerate technological progress. If as the Oxford Martin School study suggested, 47 per cent of all jobs in an advanced economy will be redundant due to automation, then the result under neoliberalism is going to be an enormously expanded precariat.

A basic income paid for out of taxes on the market economy gives people the chance to build positions in the non-market economy. It allows them to volunteer, set up co-ops, edit Wikipedia, learn how to use 3D design software, or just exist. It allows them to space out periods of work; make a late entry or early exit from working life; switch more easily into and out of high-intensity, stressful jobs. Its fiscal cost would be high: that's why all attempts to enact the measure separately from an overall transition project are likely to fail, despite the growing number of academic papers and global congresses dedicated to it.[9]

As a worked example, the UK's benefits bill is £160 billion a year, of which maybe £30 billion is targeted at the disabled, pregnant, sick and so on. The poorest recipients are pensioners, who get about £6,000 a year as basic pension. To give 51 million adults £6,000 a year, as of right, would cost £306 billion – which is nearly twice the current welfare bill. This might be affordable if you abolished a range of tax exemptions and at the same time delivered cost-saving changes to other public spending, but it would represent a significant claim on resources.

A basic income says, in effect, there are too few work hours to go round, so we need to inject 'liquidity' into the mechanism that allocates them. The lawyer and the daycare worker both need to be able to exchange hours of work at full pay, for hours of free time paid for by the state.

Suppose, in the UK, we set the basic income at £6,000 and hike the minimum wage to £18,000. The advantages of working remain clear, but there are also advantages to be gained through not working: you can look after your kids, write poetry, go back to college, manage your chronic illness or peer-educate others like you.

Under this system, there would be no stigma attached to not working. The labour market would be stacked in favour of the high-paying job and the high-paying employer.

The universal basic income, then, is an antidote to what the anthropologist David Graeber calls 'bullshit jobs': the low-paid service jobs capitalism has managed to create over the past twenty-five years that pay little, demean the worker and probably don't need to exist.[10] But it's only a transitional measure for the first stage of the postcapitalist project.

The ultimate aim is to reduce to a minimum the hours it takes to produce what humanity needs. Once this happens, the tax base in the market sector of the economy would be too small to pay for the basic income. Wages themselves would increasingly be either social – in the form of collectively provided services – or disappear.

So as a postcapitalist measure, the basic income is the first benefit in history whose success measure is that it shrinks to zero.

THE NETWORK UNLEASHED

In the socialist project, there was to be a long first stage in which the state had to suppress the market by force; the outcome was supposed to be a gradual reduction of the hours of work necessary to maintain and supply humanity. Then technological progress might begin to make some things at negligible cost or for free, and you could move to phase two: 'communism'.

I am certain the workers of my grandmother's generation cared more about phase one than phase two – and that was logical. In an economy based primarily on physical goods, the way to make houses cheaper was for the state to build them, own them and supply them at cheap rents. The cost was uniformity: you were forbidden to maintain the house yourself, or improve it, or even to paint the door a different colour. For my grandmother, who had lived in a stinking slum, being banned from painting the door was not a major concern.

In the postcapitalist project the task in the first phase is to deliver things just as tangible and life-changing as my grandma's council house, with its garden and solid walls, was to her. To this end, a lot can be achieved by changing the relationship between power and information.

Info-capitalism is based on asymmetry: the global corporations get their market power from knowing more – more than their customers, suppliers and small competitors. The simple principle behind postcapitalism should be that the pursuit of information asymmetry is wrong – except when it comes to privacy, anonymity and security issues.

In addition, the aim should be to push information and automation into types of work where they are held back at present because cheap labour removes the need to innovate.

In a modern car factory there is a production line, and there are still workers with spanners and drills. But the production line is intelligently managing what the workers do; a computer screen tells them which spanner to use, a sensor warns them if they pick up the wrong one, and the action is recorded somewhere on a server.

There is no reason other than exploitation why world-class techniques of automation cannot be applied, for example, to the labour of the sandwich factory or the meat-packing plant. In fact, it is only the availablity of cheap, unorganized labour, supported by in-work benefits, that permits these business models to exist. In many industries old disciplines of work – time, obedience, attendance, hierarchy – are enforced only because neoliberalism is suppressing innovation. But they are technologically unnecessary.

In information-based businesses, old style management begins to look archaic. Managing means organizing predictable resources – people, ideas and things – to produce a planned outcome. But many benign outcomes of network economies are unplanned. And the best human process for dealing with volatile outcomes is teamwork – which used to be called 'cooperation'.

Let's spell out what this means: cooperative, self-managed, non-hierarchical teams are the most technologically advanced form of work. Yet large parts of the workforce are trapped in a world of fines, discipline, violence and power hierarchies – simply because the existence of a cheap labour culture allows it to survive.

A crucial goal for the transition process would be to trigger a third managerial revolution: to enthuse managers, trade unions and industrial system designers about the possibilities inherent in a move to networked, modular, non-linear team work.

'Work cannot become play,' Marx wrote.[11] But the atmosphere in the modern video game design workshop shows that play and work can alternate quite freely and produce results. Among guitars, sofas, pool tables covered in piles of discarded pizza boxes, there is of course still exploitation. But modular, target-driven work, with employees enjoying a high degree of autonomy, can be less alienating, more social, more enjoyable – and deliver better results.

There is nothing other than our addiction to cheap labour and inefficiency that says a meat-packing operation cannot enjoy the same kind of unmanaged, modular work – where work is literally interspersed with play, and access to networked information is a right. One of the most telling signs that neoliberalism is a dead end is the hostility of many twenty-first century managers and most investors to the ideal of highly productive, fulfilling work. Managers in the pre-1914 era were obsessed with it.

As we pursue these goals, a general pattern is likely to emerge; the transition to postcapitalism is going to be driven by surprise discoveries made by groups of people working in teams, about what they can do to old processes by applying collaborative thinking and networks.

What we are looking for are rapid technological leaps that make things cheaper to produce and benefit the whole of society. The task of the decision-making nodes in a networked economy (from the central bank to a local housing co-op) is to understand the interplay between networks, hierarchies, organizations and markets; to model them in different states, to propose a change, monitor its effects and adjust their intentions accordingly.

But for all our attempts at rationality, this is not going to be a controlled process. The most valuable things that networks (and the individuals within them) can do is to *disrupt everything above*. Faced with group-think and convergence, either in the design stage of an economic project or in its execution, networks are a brilliant tool for allowing us not just to dissent, but to secede and start our own alternative.

We need to be unashamed utopians. The most effective entrepreneurs of early capitalism were exactly that, and so were all the pioneers of human liberation.

What is the end state? That is the wrong question. If you study the graph of GDP per head in chapter 8, it is horizontal for the whole of human history until the Industrial Revolution, then it takes off rapidly, and after 1945 it turns exponential in some countries. Postcapitalism is just a function of what happens when it goes completely vertical everywhere. It is a beginning state.

Once exponential technological change cascades over from silicon chips to food, clothing, transport systems and healthcare, then the reproduction cost of labour-power is going to shrink dramatically. At this point, the economic problem that has defined human history will shrink or disappear. We will probably be preoccupied by problems of sustainability in economics and the interplay of competing patterns of human life beyond it.

So instead of looking for an end state, it's more important to ask how we might deal with reverses – or escape a dead end.

One specific problem is how to record the experience of failure into persistent data that allows us to retrace our steps, amend them and roll out the lessons across the whole economy. Networks are bad at memory; they are designed so that memory and activity sit in two different parts of the machine. Hierarchies were good at remembering – so working out how to retain and process lessons will be critical. The solution may be as simple as adding a recording and storing function to all activities, from the coffee shop to the state. Neoliberalism, with its love of creative destruction, was happy to dispense with the memory function – from Tony Blair's 'sofa' decision-making to the tearing up of old corporate structures, nobody wanted to leave a paper trail.

In the end, all we're trying to do is move as much of human activity as possible into a phase where the labour that's necessary to support very rich and complex human life on the planet falls, and the amount of free time grows. And in the process, the division between the two gets even more blurred.

IS THIS FOR REAL?

It's easy to recoil from the scale of these proposals. To ask ourselves: can it really be that – on top of a fifty-year crisis – a 500-year change is under way? Can laws, markets and business models really evolve dramatically to match the potential of info-tech? And could it be true that we as puny individuals can have any real impact?

Yet, every day, a large part of humanity participates in a much bigger change, triggered by a different kind of technology: the contraceptive pill. We are living through the one-time and irreversible cancellation of male biological power. It's causing major trauma: watch the Twitter and Facebook trolling of powerful women, the attempts by cults like

GamerGate to get into their mindspace and destroy their mental health. But the advance towards liberation is happening.

It is absurd that we are capable of witnessing a 40,000-year-old system of gender oppression begin to dissolve before our eyes and yet still seeing the abolition of a 200-year-old economic system as an unrealistic utopia.

We lie at a moment of possibility: of a controlled transition beyond the free market, beyond carbon, beyond compulsory work.

What happens to the state? It probably gets less powerful over time – and in the end its functions are assumed by society. I've tried to make this a project usable both by people who see states as useful and those who don't; you could model an anarchist version and a statist version and try them out. There is probably even a conservative version of postcapitalism, and good luck to it.

LIBERATE THE 1 PER CENT

What happens to the 1 per cent? They become poorer and therefore happier. Because it's tough being rich.

In Australia, you see the women of the 1 per cent jog from Bondi to Tamarama beach each morning, decked out in cheap lycra made expensive by the addition of – what else? – gold lettering. Their ideology tells them it is their uniqueness that has made them successful, yet they look and behave the same.

As the world turns, dawn-lit gyms halfway up the skyscrapers of Shanghai and Singapore see businessmen pound the treadmills in anticipation of a day spent in competition with people exactly like them. The bodyguarded rich of Central Asia begin another day of ripping off the world.

Above it all, in the first-class cabins of long-haul flights, drift the global elite, their faces composed into a routine frown over their laptops. They're the living image of how the world is supposed to be: educated, tolerant, prosperous. Yet they are excluded from this great experiment in social communication that humanity is staging.

Just 8 per cent of American CEOs have a real Twitter account.

Sure, an underling can run one for them, but because of rules on making financial statements, and because of cyber-security, the social media accounts of the powerful can never be real. When it comes to ideas, they can have any ideas they like as long as they conform to neoliberal doctrine: that the best people win because of their talent; that the market is the expression of rationality; that the workers of the developed world are too lazy; that taxing the rich is futile.

Convinced that only the smart succeed, they send their kids to expensive private schools to hone their individuality. But they come out the same: little versions of Milton Friedman and Christine Lagarde. They go to the elite colleges but the fancy names on the college hoodies – Harvard, Cambridge, MIT – mean nothing. You might as well just print Standard Neoliberal University. The Ivy League hoodie is simply a badge of entry to this tawdry world.

Beneath it all lies lingering doubt. Their self-belief tells them that capitalism is good because it is dynamic – but its dynamism is only really felt where there are plentiful supplies of cheap labour, repressed democracy – and where inequality is rising. To live in a world so separate, dominated by the myth of uniqueness but in reality so uniform, constantly worried you're going to lose it all, is – I am not kidding – tough.

And to cap it all, they know how close it came to collapsing; how much of every single thing they still own was actually paid for by the state, which bailed them out.

Today, the ideology of being bourgeois in the Western world means social liberalism, a commitment to fine art, to democracy and the rule of law, giving to charity and hiding the power you wield beneath a studied personal restraint.

The danger is that as the crisis drags on the elite's commitment to liberalism evaporates. The successful crooks and dictators of the emerging world have already bought influence and respectability: you can feel their power as you walk through the door of certain law firms, PR consultancies and even corporations.

How long will it take before the culture of the Western elite swings towards emulating Putin and Xi Jinping? On some campuses you can already hear it: 'China shows capitalism works better without democracy' has become a standard talking point. The self-belief of the 1 per cent is in danger of ebbing away, to be replaced by a pure and undisguised oligarchy.

But there is good news.

The 99 per cent are coming to the rescue.

Postcapitalism will set you free.

Notes

INTRODUCTION

1. http://www.worldbank.org/en/country/moldova/overview
2. 'Policy challenges for the next 50 years', OECD, 2014
3. http://openeurope.org.uk/blog/greece-folds-this-hand-but-long-term-game-of-poker-with-eurozone-continues/
4. L. Cox and A. G. Nilsen, *We Make Our Own History* (London, 2014)
5. http://oll.libertyfund.org/titles/2593#Thelwall_RightsNature1621_16
6. M. Castells, *Alternative Economic Cultures*, BBC Radio 4, 21 October 2012
7. D. Mackie et al, 'The Euro-area Adjustment: About Halfway There', JP Morgan, 28 May 2013

PART 1

1. C. Kindleberger, *Comparative Political Economy: A Retrospective* (Cambridge, MA, 2000), p. 319

1. NEOLIBERALISM IS BROKEN

1. P. Mason, 'Bank Balance Sheets Become Focus of Scrutiny', 28 July 2008, http://www.bbc.co.uk/blogs/newsnight/paulmason/2008/07/bank_balance_sheets_become_foc.html
2. http://money.cnn.com/2007/11/27/news/newsmakers/gross_banking.fortune/
3. P. Mason, *Meltdown: The End of the Age of Greed* (London, 2009)
4. http://www.telegraph.co.uk/finance/financetopics/davos/9041442/Davos-2012-Prudential-chief-Tidjane-Thiam-says-minimum-wage-is-a-machine-to-destroy-jobs.html

5. http://ftalphaville.ft.com/2014/02/07/1763792/a-lesson-from-japans-falling-real-wages/; http://www.social-europe.eu/2013/05/real-wages-in-the-eurozone-not-a-double-but-a-continuing-dip/; http://cep.lse.ac.uk/pubs/download/cp422.pdf

6. D. Fiaschi et al, 'The Interrupted Power Law and the Size of Shadow Banking', 4 April 2014, http://arxiv.org/pdf/1309.2130v4.pdf

7. http://www.theguardian.com/news/datablog/2015/feb/05/global-debt-has-grown-by-57-trillion-in-seven-years-following-the-financial-crisis

8. http://jenner.com/lehman/VOLUME%203.pdf p 742

9. http://www.sec.gov/news/studies/2008/craexamination070808.pdf p12

10. http://www.investmentweek.co.uk/investment-week/news/2187554/-done-for-boy-barclays-libor-messages

11. J. M. Keynes, *The General Theory of Employment, Interest and Money* (Cambridge, 1936), p. 293: http://www.marxists.org/reference/subject/economics/keynes/general-theory/ch21.htm

12. http://www.ftense.com/2014/10/total-global-debt-crosses-100-trillion.html

13. http://www.internetworldstats.com/emarketing.htm

14. http://cleantechnica.com/2014/04/13/world-solar-power-capacity-increased-35-2013-charts/

15. L. Summers, 'Reflections on the New Secular Stagnation Hypothesis', in C. Teulings and R. Baldwin (eds.), *Secular Stagnation: Facts, Causes, and Cures*, VoxEU.org (August 2014)

16. R. Gordon, 'The Turtle's Progress: Secular Stagnation Meets the Headwinds' in Teulings and Baldwin (eds.), *Secular Stagnation*

17. http://www.constitution.org/mon/greenspan_gold.htm

18. http://www.treasury.gov/ticdata/Publish/mfh.txt

19. R. Duncan, *The New Depression: The Breakdown of the Paper Money Economy* (Singapore, 2012)

20. http://www.washingtonpost.com/blogs/wonkblog/wp/2013/01/18/breaking-inside-the-feds-2007-crisis-response/?wprss=rss_ezra-klein

21. http://www.economist.com/blogs/freeexchange/2011/08/markets-and-fed

22. http://www.multpl.com

23. http://www.federalreserve.gov/boardDocs/speeches/2002/20021121/default.htm

24. http://www.economist.com/blogs/freeexchange/2013/11/unconventional-monetary-policy

25. D. Schlichter, *Paper Money Collapse: The Folly of Elastic Money* (London, 2012), loc 836

26. D. Graeber, *Debt: The First 5000 Years* (London, 2011)

27. G. R. Krippner, 'The Financialization of the American Economy', *Socio-Economic Review*, 3, 2 (May 2005), p. 173

28. C. Lapavitsas, 'Financialised Capitalism: Crisis and Financial Expropriation', RMF Paper 1, 15 February 2009

29. A. Brender and F. Pisani, *Global Imbalances and the Collapse of Globalised Finance* (Brussels, 2010)

30. F. Braudel, *Civilization and Capitalism, 15th–18th Century: The Perspective of the World* (Berkeley and Los Angeles, 1992), p. 246

31. IMF, 'World Economic Outlook', October 2013

32. Brender and Pisani, *Global Imbalances*, p. 2

33. B. Eichengreen, 'A Requiem for Global Imbalances', *Project Syndicate*, 13 January 2014

34. http://www.tradingeconomics.com/china/foreign-exchange reserves

35. http://www.imf.org/external/np/sta/cofer/eng/

36. L. Floridi, *The Philosophy of Information* (Oxford, 2011), p. 4

37. M. Foucault, *The Birth of Biopolitics: Lectures at the Collège de France, 1978–79*, trans. G. Burchell (New York, 2008)

38. http://www.techopedia.com/definition/29066/metcalfes-law

39. 'Measuring the Internet Economy: A Contribution to the Research Agenda', OECD, 2013

40. H. Braconier, G. Nicoletti and B. Westmore, 'Policy Challenges for the Next 50 Years', OECD, 2014

2. LONG WAVES, SHORT MEMORIES

1. N. Kondratieff, Letter, 17 November 1937, in N. Makasheva, W. Samuels and V. Barnett (eds.), *The Works of Nikolai D. Kondratiev* (London, 1998), vol. IV, p. 313

2. Makasheva, Samuels and Barnett (eds.), *Nikolai D. Kondratiev*, vol. I, p. 108

3. E. Mansfield, 'Long Waves and Technological Innovation,' *The American Economic Review*, 73 (2) (1983), p. 141, http://www.jstor.org/stable/1816829?seq=2

4. G. Lyons, *The Supercycle Report* (London, 2010)

5. C. Perez, 'Financial Bubbles, Crises and the Role of Government in Unleashing Golden Ages', FINNOV, London, January 2012

6. N. Kondratieff, 'The Long Wave Cycle', trans. G. Daniels (New York, 1984), pp. 104–5. (I have chosen to use the Daniels translation of the 1926 paper because on several issues of terminology it is in better English than the one in Makasheva et al.)

7. Ibid., p. 99

8. Ibid., p. 68

9. Ibid.

10. Ibid., p. 93

11. https://www.marxists.org/archive/trotsky/1923/04/capdevel.htm

12. Kondratieff, 'The Long Wave Cycle', p. xx

13. Makasheva, Samuels and Barnett (eds.), *Nikolai D. Kondratiev*, vol. I, p. 116

14. Ibid., p. 113

15. J. L. Klein, 'The Rise of "Non-October" Econometrics: Kondratiev and Slutsky at the Moscow Conjuncture Institute', *History of Political Economy*, 31:1 (1999), pp. 137–68

16. E. Slutsky, 'The Summation of Random Causes as the Source of Cyclical Processes', *Econometrica*, 5 (1937), pp. 105–46, quoted in V. Barnett, 'Chancing an Interpretation: Slutsky's Random Cycles Revisited', *European Journal of the History of Economic Thought*, 13:3 (September 2006), p. 416

17. Klein, 'Rise of "Non-October" Econometrics'; p. 157

18. Slutsky, quoted in ibid., p. 156

19. For a summary of statistical critiques of Kondratieff see R. Metz, 'Do Kondratieff Waves Exist? How Time Series Techniques Can Help to Solve the Problem', *Cliometrica*, 5 (2011), pp. 205–38

20. A. V. Korotayev and S. V. Tsirel, 'A Spectral Analysis of World GDP Dynamics: Kondratieff Waves, Kuznets Swings; Juglar and Kitchin Cycles in Global Economic Development and the 2008–09 Economic Crisis', *Structure and Dynamics*, 4 (1) (2010)

21. C. Marchetti, 'Fifty Year Pulsation in Human Affairs: An Analysis of Some Physical Indicators', *Futures*, 17 (3) (1987), p. 376

22. J. Schumpeter, *Business Cycles: A Theoretical, Historical and Statistical Analysis of the Capitalist Process* (New York, 1939), p. 82

23. Ibid., p. 213

24. C. Perez, *Technological Revolutions and Finance Capital: The Dynamics of Bubbles and Golden Ages* (Cheltenham, 2002), p. 5

3. WAS MARX RIGHT?

1. K. Marx, *Capital*, vol. 3 (Chicago, 1990), http://www.marxists.org/archive/marx/works/1894-c3/ch15.htm

2. https://www.marxists.org/archive/marx/works/1894-c3/ch27.htm

3. K. Marx, Preface to *A Contribution to the Critique of Political Economy* (Moscow,1977), http://www.marxists.org/archive/marx/works/1859/critique-pol-economy/preface-abs.htm

4. K. Kautsky, *The Class Struggle* (1892), trans. by William E. Bohn and Charles H. Kerr (Chicago, 1910), p. 83

5. H. and J. M. Tudor, *Marxism and Social Democracy: The Revisionist Debate, 1896–8* (Cambridge, 1988)

6. G. Kolko, *The Triumph of Conservatism: A Reinterpretation of American History 1900–1916* (New York, 1963)

7. http://www.slate.com/articles/technology/technology/features/2010/the_great_american_information_emperors/how_theodore_vail_built_the_att_monopoly.html

8. http://www.hbs.edu/faculty/Publication%20Files/07-011.pdf

9. L. Peters, 'Managing Competition in German Coal, 1893 1913', *The Journal of Economic History*, 49/2 (1989), pp. 419–33

10. H. Morikawa, *Zaibatsu: Rise and Fall of Family Enterprise Groups in Japan* (Tokyo, 1992)

11. Kolko, *The Triumph of Conservatism*

12. K. O'Rourke, 'Tariffs and Growth in the Late 19th Century', *The Economic Journal*, 110 (2000), pp. 456–83

13. http://www.worldeconomics.com/Data/MadisonHistoricalGDP/Madison%20Historica%20GDP%20Data.efp

14. http://www.marxists.org/archive/hilferding/1910/finkap/preface.htm

15. P. Michaelides and J. Milios, 'Did Hilferding Influence Schumpeter?', *History of Economics Review*, 41 (Winter 2005), pp. 98–125

16. https://www.marxists.org/archive/lenin/works/1916/oct/x01.htm

17. R. Luxemburg, *The Accumulation of Capital* (New Haven, 1951), p. 468

18. Hermann Kraut, *Berlin Cinemas*, 1973

19. http://www.marxists.org/archive/lenin/works/1916/imp-hsc/ch10.htm

20. http://www.marxists.org/archive/bukharin/works/1917/imperial/15.htm

21. K. Kautsky, 'Ultra-imperialism', *Die Neue Zeit*, September 1914, http://www.marxists.org/archive/kautsky/1914/09/ultra-imp.htm

22. M. Ried, 'A Decade of Collective Economy in Austria', *Annals of Public and Cooperative Economics*, vol. 5 (1929), p. 70

23. E. Varga, 'Die Wirtschaftlichen Problem der proletarischen Diktats', quoted in H. Strobel, *Socialisation in Theory and Practice* (London, 1922), p. 150

24. J. M. Keynes, *The Economic Consequences of the Peace* (New York, 1920), p. 1, http://www.econlib.org/library/YPDBooks/Keynes/kynsCP1.html

25. E. Varga, *The Great Crisis and its Political Consequences; Economics and Politics. 1928–1934* (London, 1935), p. 20

26. http://www.marxists.org/archive/trotsky/1938/tp/tp-text.htm
27. http://www.marxists.org/archive/bukharin/works/1928/09/x01.htm
28. http://www.internationalviewpoint.org/spip.php?article1894
29. http://larrysummers.com/wp-content/uploads/2014/06/NABE-speech-Lawrence-H.-Summers1.pdf
30. C. Perez, *Technological Revolutions and Finance Capital: The Dynamics of Bubbles and Golden Ages* (Cheltenham, 2002)
31. Calculated from Maddison data for 1950, http://www.ggdc.net/maddison/oriindex.htm

4. THE LONG, DISRUPTED WAVE

1. A. Horne, *Macmillan: The Official Biography*, vol. II (London, 1989)
2. N. Crafts and G. Toniolo, 'Postwar Growth: An Overview', in N. Crafts and G. Toniolo, *Economic Growth in Europe since 1945* (Cambridge, 1996), p. 4
3. Maddison data
4. Crafts and Toniolo, *Economic Growth in Europe*, p. 2
5. S. Pollard, *The International Economy since 1945* (London, 1997), loc 232
6. http://www.russellsage.org/sites/all/files/chartbook/Income%20and%20Earnings.pdf
7. http://www.esri.go.jp/jp/workshop/050914/050914moriguchi_saez-2.pdf
8. G. Federico, *Feeding the World: An Economic History of Agriculture 1800–2000* (Princeton, 2005), p. 59; C. Dmitri, A. Effland and N. Conklin, 'The 20th Century Transformation of US Agriculture and Farm Policy', USDA Economic Information Bulletin 3, 2005
9. C. T. Evans, 'Debate in the Soviet Union? Evgenii Varga and His Analysis of Postwar Capitalism, 1946–1950', *Essays in History*, 32 (1989), pp. 1–17
10. E. Varga, *Izmeneniia v ekonomike kapitalizm v itoge vtoroi mirovoi voiny* (Moscow, 1946)
11. http://www.marxist.com/TUT/TUT5-I.html
12. A. Crosland, *The Future of Socialism* (London, 1956)
13. P. Baran and P. Sweezy, *Monopoly Capital: An Essay on the American Social* Order (New York, 1966)
14. http://external.worldbankimflib.org/Bwf/60panel2.htm
15. H. Hazlitt, 'For World Inflation?', 24 June 1944, in H. Hazlitt, *From Bretton Woods to Inflation: A Study of Causes and Consequences* (Chicago, 1984), p. 39
16. J. A. Feinman, 'Reserve Requirements: History, Current Practice, and Potential Reform', *Federal Reserve Bulletin*, June 1993, p. 587

17. C. Reinhart and B. M. Sbrancia, 'The Liquidation of Government Debt', NBER Working Paper 16893, March 2011, p. 21, http://www.nber.org/papers/w16893

18. Ibid., p. 38

19. I. Stewart, *Organizing Scientific Research for War, An Administrative History of the Office of Scientific Research and Development* (Boston, 1948), p. 19

20. Ibid., p. 59

21. J. Gleick, *The Information: A History, a Theory, a Flood* (New York, 2011), loc 2998

22. A. Glyn et al, 'The Rise and Fall of the Golden Age', WIDER Working Paper 43, April 1988, p. 2

23. http://www.nber.org/chapters/c9101.pdf p485

24. http://irps.ucsd.edu/assets/001/500904.pdf

25. Glyn et al, 'The Rise and Fall of the Golden Age', p. 112

26. Ibid., p. 23

27. See, for example, P. M. Garber, 'The Collapse of the Bretton Woods Fixed Exchange Rate System', in M. Bordo and B. Eichengreen, *A Retrospective on the Bretton Woods System: Lessons for International Monetary Reform* (Chicago, 1993), pp. 461–94

28. M. Ichiyo, 'Class Struggle and Technological Innovation in Japan since 1945', *Notebooks for Study and Research*, 5 (1987), p. 10

29. 'The Sick Man of the Euro' *The Economist*, 3 June 1999, http://www.economist.com/node/209559

30. http://www.washingtonpost.com/blogs/worldviews/wp/2015/02/20/germanys-economy-is-the-envy-of-europe-so-why-are-record-numbers-of-people-living-in-poverty/

31. G. Mayer, 'Union Membership Trends in the United States,' Congressional Research Service, 2004

32. J. Vissier, 'Union Membership Statistics in 24 Countries', *Monthly Labor Review*, January 2006, p. 38, http://www.bls.gov/opub/mlr/2006/01/art3full.pdf

33. E. Stockhammer, 'Why Have Wage Shares Fallen? A Panel Analysis of the Determinants of Functional Income Distribution' ILO Research Paper, 2013

34. A. V. Korotaev and S. V. Tsirel, 'A Spectral Analysis of World GDP Dynamics: Kondratieff Waves, Kuznets Swings; Juglar and Kitchin Cycles in Global Economic Development and the 2008–09 Economic Crisis', *Structure and Dynamics*, 4 (1) (2010)

35. http://www.tradingeconomics.com/united-states/bank-lending-rate

36. John F. Papp et al, 'Cr, Cu, Mn, Mo, Ni, and Steel Commodity Price Influences, Version 1.1', US Geological Survey Open-File Report 2007–1257, p. 112

37. http://www.imf.org/external/pubs/ft/fandd/2011/03/picture.htm

38. http://dollardaze.org/blog/?post_id=00565

39. www.the-crises.com

40. S. Khatiwada, 'Did the Financial Sector Profit at the Expense of the Rest of the Economy? Evidence from the United States', ILO Research Paper, 2010

41. http://unctadstat.unctad.org/TableViewer/tableView.aspx

42. http://unctadstat.unctad.org/TableViewer/tableView.aspx

43. D. McWilliams, 'The Greatest Ever Economic Change', Gresham Lecture, 13 September 2012, http://www.gresham.ac.uk/lectures-and-events/the-greatest-ever-economic-change

44. See, for example, S. Amin, *Unequal Development: An Essay on the Social Formations of Peripheral Capitalism* (New York, 1976)

45. D. Milanovic, 'Global Income Inequality by the Numbers: In History and Now', Policy Research Working Paper 6259, World Bank, November 2012, p. 13

46. R. Freeman, 'The New Global Labor Market', *Focus*, vol. 26 (1) (2008), University of Wisconsin–Madison Institute for Research on Poverty, http://www.irp.wisc.edu/publications/focus/pdfs/foc261a.pdf

47. S. Kapsos and E. Bourmpoula, 'Employment and Economic Class in the Developing World', ILO Research Paper 6, June 2013

PART II

1. K. Kelly, 'New Rules for the New Economy', *Wired*, 5 September 1977, http://www.archive.wired.com/wired/archive/5.09/newrules.html

5. THE PROPHETS OF POSTCAPITALISM

1. R. Singh, 'Civil Aero Gas Turbines: Technology and Strategy', Speech, Cranfield University, 24 April 2001, p. 5

2. J. Leahy, 'Navigating the Future', Global Market Forecast 2012–2031, Airbus, 2011

3. D. Lee et al, 'Aviation and Global Climate Change in the 21st Century', *Atmospheric Aviation*, vol. 43, 2009, pp. 3520–37

4. M. Gell et al, 'The Development of Single Crystal Superalloy Turbine Blades', *Superalloys*, 1980, p. 205

5. http://www.mtu.de/en/technologies/engineering_news/others/Sieber_Aero_Engine_Roadmap_en.pdf

6. Data on the Balance Sheet, SAS Institute/CEBR, June 2013

7. P. Drucker, *Post-capitalist Society* (Oxford, 1993), p. 40
8. Ibid., p. 175
9. Ibid., p. 193
10. Y. Peng, 'Internet Use of Migrant Workers in the Pearl River Delta', in P.-L. Law (ed.), *New Connectivities in China: Virtual, Actual and Local Interactions* (Dordrecht, 2012), p. 94
11. P. Romer, 'Endogenous Technological Change', *Journal of Political Economy*, vol. 98, no. 5, pt 2 (1990), pp. S71–S102
12. Ibid. p. S72
13. Ibid., pp. S71–S102
14. http://www.billboard.com/biz/articles/news/digital and mobile/1567869/business-matters-average-itunes-account-generates-just
15. D. Warsh, *Knowledge and the Wealth of Nations: A Story of Economic Discovery* (New York, 2007)
16. http://en.wikipedia.org/wiki/Apple_A7#cite_note-AnandTech-iPhone5s-A7-2
17. http://commons.wikimedia.org/wiki/File:Bill_Gates_Letter_to_Hobbyists.jpg
18. R. Stallman, *The GNU Manifesto*, March 1985, http://www.gnu.org/gnu/manifesto.html
19. http://gs.statcounter.com
20. http://www.businessinsider.com/android-market-share-2012-11
21. K. Kelly, 'New Rules for the New Economy', *Wired*, 5 September 1977, http://www.wired.com/wired/archive/5.09/newrules.html
22. Ibid.
23. Ibid.
24. http://www.digitaltrends.com/mobile/history-of-samsungs-galaxy-phones-and-tablets/
25. http://www.emc.com/collateral/analyst-reports/idc-the-digital-universe-in-2020.pdf
26. http://www.itu.int/en/ITU-D/Statistics/Pages/stat/default.aspx
27. Kelly, http://www.wired.com/wired/archive/5009/newrules.html
28. Ibid.
29. R. Konrad, 'Trouble Ahead, Trouble Behind', cnet, 22 February 2002, http://news.cnet.com/2008-1082-843349.html
30. Y. Benkler, *The Wealth of Networks: How Social Production Transforms Markets and Freedom* (New Haven, 2006)
31. Ibid.
32. http://en.wikipedia.org/wiki/Wikipedia:Wikipedians
33. https://wikimediafoundation.org/wiki/Staff_and_contractors

34. http://en.wikipedia.org/wiki/Wikipedia, accessed 28 December 2013

35. http://www.alexa.com/topsites

36. www.monetizepros.com/blog/2013/analysis-how-wikipedia-could-make-2-8-billion-in-annual-revenue/

37. K. Arrow, 'Economic Welfare and the Allocation of Resources for Invention', in *The Rate and Direction of Inventive Activity: Economic and Social Factors*, NBER, 1962, pp. 609–26

38. *MEW* (MarxEngelsWerke), vol. 29 (London, 1987), p. 225

39. M. Nikolaus in K. Marx, *Grundrisse* (Harmondsworth, 1973), p. 9

40. K. Marx, *Grundrisse*

41. Ibid.

42. http://distantwriting.co.uk/TelegraphStations1862.html

43. S. Tillotson, 'We May All Soon Be "First-class Men": Gender and Skill in Canada's Early Twentieth Century Urban Telegraph Industry', *Labor/Le Travail*, 27 (Spring 1991), pp. 97–123

44. Marx, *Grundrisse*

45. P. Virno, 'General Intellect', in A. Zanini and U Fadini (eds.), *Lessico Postfordista* (Milan, 2001), trans. A. Bove

46. Marx, *Grundrisse*

47. N. Dyer-Witheford, *Cyber-Marx: Cycles and Circuits of Struggle in High-technology Capitalism* (Illinois, 1999)

48. Y. Moulier-Boutang, *Cognitive Capitalism* (Cambridge, 2011), p. 53

49. http://ycharts.com/indicators/average_hourly_earnings

50. http://management.fortune.cnn.com/2012/02/13/nike-digital-marketing/

51. C. Vercellone, 'From Formal Subsumption to General Intellect: Elements for a Marxist Reading of the Thesis of Cognitive Capitalism', *Historical Materialism*, 15 (2007), pp. 13–36

52. Dyer-Witheford, *Cyber-Marx*

53. J. Rifkin, *The Zero Marginal Cost Society: The Internet of Things, the Collaborative Commons, and the Eclipse of Capitalism* (New York, 2014)

54. See P. Mason, 'WTF is Eleni Haifa?', 20 December 2014, http://www.versobooks.com/blogs/1801-wtf-is-eleni-haifa-a-new-essay-by-paul-mason

6. TOWARDS THE FREE MACHINE

1. http://www.sns.gov.uk/Simd/Simd.aspx

2. http://www.econlib.org/library/Smith/smWN2.html#B.I,%20Ch.5,%20Of%20the%20Real%20and%20Nominal%20Price%20of%20Commodities

3. A. Smith, *Lectures on Jurisprudence* (Oxford, 1978), p. 351

4. For a demonstration of this, see John F. Henry, 'Adam Smith and the Theory of Value: Chapter Six Considered', *History of Economics Review*, 31 (Winter 2000)

5. http://www.econlib.org/library/Smith/smWN2.html

6. 'Towards the Free Machine', http://www.econlib.org/library/Ricardo/ricPr.html

7. D. Ricardo, *On the Principles of Political Economy and Taxation* (London, 1821), ch. 30, http://www.econlib.org/library/Ricardo/ricP7.html

8. http://avalon.law.yale.edu/19th_century/labdef.asp

9. For a complete discussion of the debates on value see I. I. Rubin, *A History of Economic Thought* (London, 1989)

10. http://www.cleanclothes.org/news/2013/11/20/clean-clothes-campaign-disappointed at new bangladesh minimum wage-level

11. Calculated using 2014 minimum wage of 5300 tk, against retail price rise of 34 tk per kg.

12. In this section I am following the outline of the theory as presented in A. Kliman, *Reclaiming Marx's 'Capital': A Refutation of the Myth of Inconsistency* (Plymouth, 2007)

13. http://www.Icddrb.org/who-we-are/gender-issues/daycare

14. K. Allen, 'The Butterfly Effect: Chinese Dorms and Bangladeshi Factory Fires', *Financial Times*, 25 April 2013, http://blogs.ft.com/ftdata/2013/04/25/the-butterfly-effect-chinese-dorms-and-bangladeshi-factory-fires/?

15. J. Robinson, *Economic Philosophy* (Cambridge, 1962)

16. A. Einstein, 'Physics and Reality', *Journal of The Franklin Institute*, vol. 221 (1936), pp. 349–82

17. OECD, 'Education at a Glance 2014: OECD Indicators', OECD, 2014, p. 14

18. L. Walras, *Elements of Pure Economics: Or the Theory of Social Wealth* (London, 1900), p. 399

19. http://library.mises.org/books/William%20Smart/An%20Introduction%20to%20the%20Theory%20of%20Value.pdf

20. Walras, *Elements of Pure Economics*, p. 6

21. W. S. Jevons, 'The Periodicity of Commercial Crises, and its Physical Explanation', in R. L. Smyth (ed.), *Essays in the Economics of Socialism and Capitalism: Selected Papers Read to Section F of the British Association for the Advancement of Science, 1886–1932* (London, 1964), pp. 125–40

22. C. Menger, *Investigations into the Method of the Social Sciences with Special Reference to Economics*, trans. F. J. Nock (New York, 1985), p. 177

23. S. Keen, *Debunking Economics: The Naked Emperor Dethroned* (London, 2011), loc 474

24. Walras, *Elements of Pure Economics*

25. http://www.ibtimes.co.uk/game-thrones-purple-wedding-becomes-most-shared-illegal-download-ever-1445057

26. J. Hagel et al, 'From Exponential Technologies to Exponential Innovation', Deloitte, 2013

27. N. Wiener, *Cybernetics or Control and Communication in the Animal and the Machine* (Cambridge MA, 1948), p. 132

28. http://www.pitt.edu/~jdnorton/lectures/Rotman_Summer_School_2013/thermo_computing_docs/Landauer_1961.pdf

29. R. Landauer, 'The Physical Nature of Information', *Physics Letters A*, 217 (1996), pp. 188–93

30. http://spectrum.ieee.org/computing/hardware/landauer-limit-demonstrated

31. http://www.marxists.org/archive/marx/works/1857/grundrisse/ch15.htm

32. V. Naranje and K. Shailendra K, 'AI Applications to Metal Stamping Die Design: A Review', *World Academy of Science, Engineering and Technology*, vol. 4, 2010

33. OECD, 'Measuring the Internet Economy: A Contribution to the Research Agenda', OECD Digital Economy Papers, 226, OECD Publishing, 2013

34. http://dx.doi.org/10.1787/5k43gjg6r8jf-en

35. http://www.bls.gov/news.release/pdf/ocwage.pdf

36. C. B. Frey and M. A. Osborne, 'The Future of Employment: How Susceptible Are Jobs to Computerisation?', Oxford Martin School Working Paper, 2013, p. 38, http://www.futuretech.ox.ac.uk/future-employment-how-susceptible-are-jobs-computerisation-oms-working-paper-dr-carl-benedikt-frey-ms

37. A. Gorz *Critique of Economic Reason* (London, 1989), p. 127

7. BEAUTIFUL TROUBLEMAKERS

1. R. Freeman, 'The Great Doubling: Labor in the New Global Economy'. Usery Lecture in Labor Policy, University of Atlanta, GA, 2005

2. T. Piketty, *Capital in the 21st Century* (Harvard, 2014)

3. http://newleftreview.org/II/21/fredric-jameson-future-city: 'It seems easier for us today to imagine the thoroughgoing deterioration of the earth and of nature than the breakdown of late capitalism'

4. http://shanghaiist.com/2010/05/26/translated_foxconns_employee_non-su.php

5. See P. Mason, 'WTF is Eleni Haifa?', 20 December 2014, http://www.versobooks.com/blogs/1801-wtf-is-eleni-haifa-a-new-essay-by-paul-mason

6. D. A. Galbi, 'Economic Change and Sex Discrimination in the Early English Cotton Factories', 1994, http://papers.ssrn.com/paper.taf?abstract_id=239564

7. A. Ure, *The Cotton Manufacture of Great Britain Systematically Investigated*, vol. II (London, 1836), p. 176

8. http://www.tandfonline.com/doi/pdf/10.1080/00236568508584785#. UeVsMBY9TCE

9. K. Marx, *Capital*, vol. I, Ch. 15 (London, 1887), p. 287

10. F. Engels, *The Condition of the Working Class in England* (London, 1987), loc 2990

11. M. Winstanley, 'The Factory Workforce', in M. Rose (ed.), *The Lancashire Cotton Industry: A History since 1700* (Lancashire, 1996), p. 130

12. W. Lazonick, *Competitive Advantage on the Shop Floor* (Harvard, 1990)

13. Engels, *The Condition of the Working Class*

14. B. Palmer, *A Culture in Conflict: Skilled Workers and Industrial Capitalism in Hamilton, Ontario, 1860–1914* (Montreal, 1979)

15. Kealey's study of the iron moulders' union in Toronto shows them setting the wage rate for each new design and imposing it across the industry. See G. Kealey, 'The Honest Working Man and Workers' Control: The Experience of Toronto Skilled workers 1860–1892', *Labor/Le Travail*, 1(1976), p. 50

16. Quoted in ibid., p. 39

17. Ibid., p. 58

18. F. W. Taylor, *The Principles of Scientific Management*, 1911, p. 18

19. Ibid.

20. Ibid.

21. G. Friedman, 'Revolutionary Unions and French Labor: The Rebels behind the Cause; or, Why Did Revolutionary Syndicalism Fail?', *French Historical Studies*, vol. 20, no. 2 (Spring, 1997)

22. http://www.llgc.org.uk/ymgyrchu/Llafur/1926/MNS.pdf

23. V. I. Lenin, *What Is to Be Done?*, 1902, http://www.marxists.org/archive/lenin/works/download/what-itd.pdf

24. V. I. Lenin, 'Imperialism and the Split in Socialism', in V. I. Lenin, *Imperialism: The Highest Stage of Capitalism* (Sydney, 1999), p. 131

25. Quoted in A. Santucci, *Antonio Gramsci* (New York, 2010), p. 156

26. W. B. Yeats, 'Easter, 1916', http://www.theatlantic.com/past/docs/unbound/poetry/soundings/easter.htm

27. http://www.spartacus.schoolnet.co.uk/TUcwc.htm

28. M. Ferro, *October 1917: A Social History of the Russian Revolution* (London, 1980), p. 151

29. C. Goodrich, *The Frontier of Control* (New York, 1920), p. 264
30. G. Orwell, 'Looking Back on the Spanish War', in G. Orwell, *A Collection of Essays* (New York, 1979), p. 201
31. http://www.economist.com/node/21550764
32. C. W. Mills, 'The Sociology of Stratification', in I. L. Horowitz (ed.), *Power Politics & People: The Collected Essays of C. Wright Mills* (Oxford, 1967), p. 309
33. D. Bell, 'The Capitalism of the Proletariat', *Encounter*, February 1958, pp. 17–23
34. http://www.marxists.org/reference/archive/marcuse/works/one-dimensional-man/one-dimensional-man.pdf p33
35. S. Wright, *Storming Heaven: Class Composition and Struggle in Italian Autonomist Marxism* (London, 2002), p. 54
36. R. Alford, 'A Suggested Index of the Association of Social Class and Voting', *Public Opinion Quarterly*, vol. 26, no. 3 (Autumn, 1962), pp. 417–25
37. E. Hobsbawm, 'The Forward March of Labour Halted', *Marxism Today* September 1978, p. 279
38. R. Alquati, *Sulla Fiat e Altri Scritti* (Milan, 1975), p. 83
39. A. Gorz, *Critique of Economic Reason* (London, 1989), p. 55
40. Ibid., p. 58
41. J. Gorman, *To Build Jerusalem: A Photographic Remembrance of British Working Class Life, 1875–1950* (London, 1980)
42. R. Hoggart, *The Uses of Literacy: Aspects of Working-Class Life* (London, 1957)
43. G. Akerlof, J. Yellen and M. Katz, 'An Analysis of Out-of-Wedlock Childbearing in the United States', *Quarterly Journal of Economics*, vol. 111, no. 2
44. C. Goldin and L. Katz, 'The Power of the Pill: Oral Contraception and Women's Career and Marriage Decisions', NBER Working Paper 7527, February 2000
45. O. Ornati, 'The Italian Economic Miracle and Organised Labor', *Social Research*, vol. 30, no. 4 (Winter, 1953), pp. 519–26
46. Ibid.
47. P. Ginsborg, *A History of Contemporary Italy: Society and Politics 1943–1988* (London, 2003), pp. 298–9
48. 'Class Struggle in Italy: 1960s to 70s', anonymous, prole.info
49. *Lotta Continua*, #18, November 1970, quoted in ibid.
50. A. Glyn et al, 'The Rise and Fall of the Golden Age', WIDER, Working Paper 43, April 1988

51. Ibid.
52. P. Myerscough, 'Short Cuts', *London Review of Books*, vol. 35, no. 1, 3 January 2013, p. 25
53. http://www.bls.gov/fls/flscomparelf/lfcompendium.pdf
54. ILO
55. C. Lapavitsas, 'Financialised Capitalism: Crisis and Financial Expropriation', RMF Paper 1, 15 February 2009
56. Ibid.
57. http://homes.chass.utoronto.ca/~wellman/publications/littleboxes/little box.PDF
58. R. Sennett, *The Culture of the New Capitalism* (New Haven, 2005)
59. R. Sennett, *The Corrosion of Character: The Personal Consequences of Work in the New Capitalism* (New York, 1998)
60. A. Negri and M. Hardt, *Declaration*, ebook, 2012, https://antonionegri-inenglish.files.wordpress.com/2012/05/93152857-hardt-negri-declaration-2012.pdf
61. Y. Peng, 'Internet Use of Migrant Workers in the Pearl River Delta', *Knowledge, Technology, and Policy*, 21, 2008, pp. 47–54

PART III

1. G. Orwell, *Nineteen Eighty-Four* (London, 1949)

8. ON TRANSITIONS

1. A. Bogdanov, *Red Star: The First Bolshevik Utopia* (Bloomington, 1984), p. 65
2. http://www.marxists.org/archive/lenin/photo/1908/007.htm
3. Quoted in J. E. Marot, 'Alexander Bogdanov, *Vpered* and the Role of the Intellectual in the Workers' Movement', *Russian Review*, vol. 49 (3) (1990), pp. 241–64
4. http://www.marxists.org/glossary/orgs/w/o.htm#workers-opposition
5. N. Krementsov, *A Martian Stranded on Earth: Alexander Bogdanov, Blood Transfusions and Proletarian Science* (Chicago, 2011)
6. R. Stites, 'Fantasy and Revolution', in Bogdanov, *Red Star*, p. 15
7. M. Ellman, 'The Role of Leadership Perceptions and of Intent in the Soviet Famine of 1931', *Europe-Asia Studies*, vol. 57 (6) (2005), pp. 823–41
8. https://www.marxists.org/reference/archive/stalin/works/1931/02/04.htm

9. M. Harrison 'The Soviet Economy in the 1920s and 1930s', *Capital & Class*, 2:2 (1978), pp. 78–94

10. G. Ofer, 'Soviet Economic Growth 1928–1985', RAND/UCLA Center for the Study of Soviet International Behavior, JRS-04 (1998)

11. H. Hunter, 'A Test of Five-Year Plan Feasibility', in J. Thornton, *Economic Analysis of the Soviet-Type System* (Cambridge 1976), p. 296

12. A. Kon, 'Political Economy Syllabus', pp. 19–20, quoted in Y. Preobrazhensky, *The New Economics* (Oxford, 1964), p. 57

13. V. Pareto, *Cours d'Economie Politique*, vol. 1 (Lausanne, 1896), p. 59. Cited in J. Bockman, *Markets in the Name of Socialism: The Left Wing Origins of Neoliberalism* (Stanford, 2011)

14. E. Barone 'The Ministry of Production in the Collectivist State', in F. Hayek (ed.), *Collectivist Economic Planning: Critical Studies on the Possibilities of Socialism* (London, 1935), p. 245

15. L. von Mises *Economic Calculation in the Socialist Commonwealth* (New York, 1990), p. 13

16. Ibid., p. 14

17. L. Robbins, *The Great Depression* (London, 1934), p. 151.

18. O. Lange, 'On the Economic Theory of Socialism', *Review of Economic Studies*, vol. 4 (1) (1936), pp. 53–71

19. Bockman, *Markets in the Name of Socialism*, loc 1040

20. Von Mises, *Economic Calculation*, p. 22

21. L. Trotsky, 'The Soviet Economy in Danger', *The Militant*, October 1932, https://www.marxists.org/archive/trotsky/1932/10/sovecon.htm

22. L. Trotsky *The Soviet Economy in Danger* (New York, 1932)

23. W. P. Cockshott and A. Cottrell, 'Economic Planning, Computers and Labor Values', Working Paper, January 1999, http://www.ecn.wfu.edu/socialism/aer.pdf

24. O. Yun, *Improvement of Soviet Economic Planning* (Moscow, 1988)

25. Cockshott and Cottrell, 'Economic Planning, Computers and Labor Values,' p. 7

26. P. Cockshott, A. Cottrell and H. Dieterich, *Transition to 21st Century Socialism in the European Union*, Lulu.com, 2010, pp. 1–20

27. A. Gorz, *Capitalism, Socialism, Ecology* (London, 1994), p. 1

28. J. M. Keynes, 'The Economic Possibilities for our Grandchildren', in J. M. Keynes, *Essays in Persuasion* (New York, 1963), pp. 358–73

29. D. Thompson, 'The Economic History of the Last 2000 Years: Part II', *The Atlantic*, 20 June 2012

30. http://www.plospathogens.org/article/info%3Adoi%2F10.1371%2Fjournal.ppat.1001134

31. D. Herlihy, *The Black Death and the Transformation of the West* (Cambridge, 1997), p. 48

32. E. L. Eisenstein, *The Printing Revolution in Early Modern Europe* (2nd edn, Cambridge, 2005)

33. http://intersci.ss.uci.edu/wiki/eBooks/BOOKS/Bacon/Novum%20 Organum%20Bacon.pdf

34. P. M. Sweezy and M. Dobb, 'The Transition from Feudalism to Capitalism', *Science & Society*, vol. 14 (2) (1950), pp. 134–67

35. P. Anderson, *Passages from Antiquity to Feudalism* (London, 1974), loc 3815

36. Preobrazhensky, *The New Economics*, p. 79

9. THE RATIONAL CASE FOR PANIC

1. http://www.cpesap.net/publications/en/

2. http://www.climatechange2013.org/images/uploads/WGI_AR5_SPM_ brochure.pdf

3. J. Ashton, 'The Book and the Bonfire: Climate Change and the Reawakening of a Lost Continent', Speech, Swiss Museum of Transport, Lucerne, 19 January 2014

4. 'World Energy Outlook 2012', IEA, http://www.iea.org/publications/ freepublications/publication/WEO2013_Executive_Summary_English.pdf

5. http://carbontracker.live.kiln.it/Unburnable-Carbon-2-Web-Version.pdf

6. http://priceofoil.org/2014/10/28/insurers-warned-climate-change-affects-viability-business-model/

7. http://www.scientificamerican.com/article/dark-money-funds-climate-change-denial-effort/

8. http://mobile.bloomberg.com/news/2014-11-02/fossil-fuel-budgets-suggested-to-curb-climate-change.html?hootPostID=1bdb3b7bbbbb61 9db600e477f2c6a152

9. http://www.economist.com/news/briefing/21587782-europes-electricity-providers-face-existential-threat-how-lose-half-trillion euros

10. http://www.iea.org/techno/etp/etp10/English.pdf

11. http://www.greenpeace.org/international/en/campaigns/climate-change/ energyrevolution/

12. Ibid.

13. 'Fifth Annual Report of the Registrar General', London, 1843

14. 'World Population Prospects: The 2012 Revision, Key Findings and Advance Tables', United Nations, 2013

15. http://www.georgemagnus.com/articles/demographics-3/
16. 'Annual Survey of Large Pension Funds and Public Reserve Pension Funds', OECD, October 2013
17. M. Mrsnik et al, 'Global Aging 2010: An Irreversible Truth', Standard & Poors, 7 October 2010
18. N. Howe and R. Jackson, 'How Ready for Pensioners?', *Finance & Development*, IMF, June 2011
19. 'World Population Prospects: The 2012 Revision'
20. http://esa.un.org/unpd/wpp/Documentation/pdf/WPP2012_%20KEY %20FINDINGS.pdf
21. B. Milanovic, 'Global Income Inequality by the Numbers: in History and Now', Policy Research Working Paper 6259, World Bank, November 2012
22. G. Mognus, Speech, IFC and Johns Hopkins Medicine International Health Conference 2013, http://www.ifc.org/wps/wcm/connect/620b56 004f081ebf99242b3eac88a2f8/George+Mognus'+Keynote+Speech+–+19 0313.pdf?MOD=AJPERES
23. D. H. Lawrence, *Lady Chatterley's Lover* (London, 1928), p. 1
24. http://www.huffingtonpost.com/2014/03/17/china-internet-censorship_n_4981389.html
25. http://www.groupibi.com/2011/10/india-targets-36-billion-global-cosmetic-surgery-market-cnbc-ibi-industry-news/

10. PROJECT ZERO

1. H. Simon. 'Organisations and Markets', *Journal of Economic Perspectives*, vol. 5 (2) (1991), pp. 25–44
2. E. Preobrazhensky, *The New Economics* (Oxford, 1964), p. 55
3. See, for example, P. Mason, 'WTF is Eleni Haifa?', 20 December 2014, http://www.versobooks.com/blogs/1801-wtf-is-eleni-haifa-a-new-essay-by-paul-mason
4. V. Kostakis and M. Bauwens, *Network Society and Future Scenarios for a Collaborative Economy* (London, 2014)
5. M. Wark, *A Hacker Manifesto* (Cambridge MA, 2004)
6. See, for example, 'Fair Society, Healthy Lives' (The Marmot Review), UCL Institute of Health Equity, February 2010, http://www.instituteof healthequity.org/projects/fair-society-healthy-lives-the-marmot-review
7. J. D. Farmer, 'Economics Needs to Treat the Economy as a Complex System', *Crisis*, December 2012

8. J. Benes and M. Kumhof, 'The Chicago Plan Revisited', IMF Working Paper 12/202, August 2012, https://www.imf.org/external/pubs/ft/wp/2012/wp12202.pdf

9. See http://www.degruyter.com/view/j/bis and http://www.basicincome.org/bien/aboutbasicincome.html

10. D. Graeber 'On the Phenomenon of Bullshit Jobs', *Strike!* Magazine, 17 August 2013

11. K. Marx, *Grundrisse*, ed. M. Nicolaus (Harmondsworth, 1973), pp. 207–750, https://www.marxists.org/archive/marx/works/1857/grundrisse/ch/4.htm

Acknowledgements

Thanks are due to my editor at Penguin, Thomas Penn, and to copy-editors Shan Vahidy and Bela Cunha. Thanks also to my agent Matthew Hamilton, Andrew Kidd before him and the team at Aitken Alexander. The following people and organizations gave me a platform to present early versions of this work, and interrogated it: Pat Kane at NESTA FutureFest; Mike Haynes at Wolverhampton University; Robert Brenner at the Centre for Social Theory and Comparative History, UCLA; Marianne Maeckelbergh and Brandon Jourdan at the *Global Uprisings!* Conference in Amsterdam, 2013; and Opera North, Leeds. Thanks specifically to Aaron Bastani, Eleanor Saitta, Quinn Norton, Molly Crabapple, Laurie Penny, Antonis Vradis and Dimitris Dalakoglou, Ewa Jasciewicz, Emma Dowling, Steve Keen, Arthur Bough and Syd Carson of Morson Group, who have contributed to my thinking about the subjects in this book. Thanks also to my editor at *Channel 4 News*, Ben De Pear, who gave me a month's unpaid leave to finish the first draft; to Channel 4 for giving me the headspace to write it; and to Malik Meer, the editor of the *Guardian*'s G2, who gave me column inches to try out some of these ideas in print. Finally thanks to my wife, Jane Bruton, without whose support, love and brilliance this book would not be possible.

Index